HAROLD GUETZKOW
Northwestern University

CHADWICK F. ALGER
Northwestern University

RICHARD A. BRODY
Stanford University

ROBERT C. NOEL
General Electric
Technical Military Planning Operation

RICHARD C. SNYDER
Northwestern University

Simulation
in International Relations:
Developments for Research and Teaching

PRENTICE-HALL, INC.
Englewood Cliffs, N.J.

PRENTICE-HALL INTERNATIONAL, INC., London
PRENTICE-HALL OF AUSTRALIA, PTY., LTD., Sydney
PRENTICE-HALL OF CANADA, LTD., Toronto
PRENTICE-HALL OF JAPAN, INC., Tokyo

© 1963 by
PRENTICE-HALL, INC.
Englewood Cliffs, N.J.

Chapter Three is reprinted courtesy of Northwestern University.

The International Relations Program conducts graduate training and
research at Northwestern; it is one of five programs within the Department of Political Science. Although the exploratory simulation of international systems described in this volume constitutes an important segment of the International Relations Program, it is designed to supplement
other research and teaching activities, which include field work in
foreign offices and international organizations, all directed toward the
development of basic theory in international relations. The senior staff
of the Program consists of Professors Chadwick F. Alger, Harold
Guetzkow, James A. Robinson, and Richard C. Snyder.

Library of Congress Catalog Card Number: 63-12019

Current printing (last digit):
11   10   9   8   7   6   5   4   3   2

PRINTED IN THE UNITED STATES OF AMERICA
C

Foreword

This book is a report on the development of a simulation of international relations undertaken by the International Relations Program of Northwestern University. The essays were assembled so that we might share our experience with others who may be interested in appraising and/or undertaking an experimental approach to the study of international political systems. The limitations of the inter-nation simulation in its present primitive state of development are recognized—and thus it is with reluctance that we publish at all. But because it is a privilege to push forward in this venture, it seems responsible to tell of our explorations in more detail than has been possible by word of mouth or by demonstration to visitors to our laboratory.

The chapters in this book tell how we use the simulation for purposes of research and teaching. The pieces attempt to be candid in explaining our difficulties, showing how the formulation of the simulation has evolved slowly, segment by segment, as logged in Appendix A. The essays indicate our perspectives, assuring each and all that no one at Northwestern holds the belief that the inter-nation simulation is more than a supplemental tool to our more traditional ways of building theory about international affairs.

In the opening chapter, Richard C. Snyder, who is co-director with me of Northwestern's International Relations Program, provides us with a helpful perspective. Chapter Two is my overview of the inter-nation simulation, reprinted without modification from the July, 1959, issue of *Behavioral Science*. This general piece is followed by three chapters that present the inter-nation simulation in considerable detail. Chapter Three reproduces the Participants' Manual; it will enable those who want to view the simulation from the "inside" to gain something of the perspective of the decision-makers. It is largely the work of Robert C. Noel, although all of us aided in its evolution. (Along these same lines, Appendix B exhibits examples of conference transcripts, the inter-nation newspapers, and other materials generated in the simulation.) Chapter Four is a descriptive account of how the simulation evolved during its early phases. It was written by Mr. Noel, who played the most important role in the simulation's initial development. Chapter Five is an attempt on my part to state the contents of the substantive theory of international relations embodied in the inter-nation simulation. It sketches, to the best of our understanding and with some degree of rigor, just exactly what has been "put into" the simulation in terms of a theory of international relations. I deeply regret that the chapter turned out to be of such great length that my original intention to justify and document our theoretical formulations in the literature of international relations proved impractical. Those interested in the use of simulation for the teaching of international relations will find Professor Chadwick F. Alger's Chapter Six most exciting. Professor Alger has been using the simulation as a laboratory exercise in his classes in international organization since 1959. His skill and sensitivity as a teacher are exhibited in the essay, as well as in the special Appendix C of teaching materials that he gathered for this volume. The final chapter, by Richard A. Brody, re-establishes our perspective by surveying how others use simulation in their study of international relations.

Colleagues find it useful to know something of the chronology of the development of the inter-nation simulation. A log of the simulations that have been operated by the International Relations Program at Northwestern is presented in Appendix A. The chapters of the book itself were written at various points in the development of the simulation. Chapter Two was composed during the early pilot stages of the project in the winter of 1958-59. Chapters Three, Four, and Five were written at a climactic point in the evolution of the simulation during the winter of 1959-60, just before exploratory work was undertaken in differentiating military capability into conventional and nuclear forms. Professor Brody wrote his review of the literature during the winter of 1960-61 in preparation for his doctoral experiment on the N-country problem, which he then conducted during the following summer. Professor Alger wrote his essay only after completing a third year of experience with the simulation as a laboratory exercise for his courses in international relations. When all the pieces were assembled, Professor Snyder wrote his "Perspectives" piece, for he felt that the book could be misunderstood if only more traditional standards were used in making an assessment. The research runs undertaken after the spring of 1960 are not reported in this volume. Their results are still in analysis.

Acknowledgments

Although initial planning of the inter-nation simulation began with Richard C. Snyder during our year together at the Center for Advanced Study in the Behavioral Sciences (1956-57), it was the encouragement of my new Northwestern colleagues, including Chadwick F. Alger, George I. Blanksten, Ann Douglas, R. Barry Farrell, and James A. Robinson, which prevented abandonment of the project during its initial year. Robert C. Noel and Denis G. Sullivan (now of the University of Illinois) served as my graduate assistants during the initial formulation of the simulation, working long and late to meet our operating deadlines; much of the contents of Chapters Three, Four, and Five developed in our work together. William C. Caspary mathematized the formulations of Chapter Five for me; Philip A. Beach prepared the content analysis of materials for Alger's Chapter Six on the use of simulation in college teaching.

When one operates a simulation, one incurs debts that cannot be repaid. My colleagues in the Departments of Psychology and Sociology suffered intolerable interferences in their experimental research programs by our intensive use of Northwestern's versatile group laboratory, designed many years before anyone thought of doing simulation in international relations. The courtesies extended by Messrs. Charles A. McClelland, Thomas W. Milburn, C. Easton Rothwell, and Wilbur Schramm during our California runs were far beyond the obligations of friendship. During the "Asilomar" run, Professor Rothwell (then Director of the Hoover Library on War, Peace, and Revolution) provided facilities and assembled ex-foreign service participants; Professor Schramm (of Stanford University) induced two of the outstanding editors on the Pacific Coast to head our "world newspapers"; Professors McClelland (of San Francisco State College) and Schramm provided operating assistants to serve as couriers and calculators. During the "China Lake" run, Dr. Milburn and his associates at the Naval Ordnance Test Station provided all of the participating, and some of the operating, personnel, so that with the help of four of Professor Wendell Bell's (UCLA) graduate students, it was possible to conduct the run as though it had taken place in our laboratory in Evanston.

Our undergraduate and graduate assistants were indispensable; I am ever grateful to Messrs. Patrick Chang, Ralph A. Gelander,

Richard A. Gephardt, Daniel Levine, and Donald Skinner. Perhaps no one turns out to be more critical in binding a venture together than our ever-present and ever-competent Program Secretary, Mrs. Elaine Pancoast. To her and to others who helped her meet our deadlines, and to Mrs. Ida Stafford, who typed the final manuscript for this volume, our enduring thanks.

Without the aid of the Carnegie Corporation of New York it is doubtful that the early pilot work would have been undertaken. Then, in the fall of 1959, the Air Force Office of Scientific Research underwrote exploratory and experimental work (Contract No. AF49(638)-742 and Grant No. AF-AFOSR 62-63) through the Behavioral Sciences Division, Office of Aerospace Research. Special funds were received from Project Michelson of the Naval Ordnance Test Station (Contract Nos. N123(60530)23299A(NMF) and N123 (60530)25875A) for the run at China Lake and for the work on the simulation of the events during the six weeks prior to the outbreak of World War I. We gratefully acknowledge not only the funds, but also the guidance and encouragement received from the men behind the funds: William A. Marvel, Charles E. Hutchinson, Herman J. Sander, G. S. Collady, and Thomas W. Milburn. Their faith in the potential value of efforts to simulate international systems constituted a challenge for all of us to do our best, even when the going got tough and the task seemed impossible.

Anonymous remain the all-important participants, who often asked just the "right" questions and made many invaluable suggestions. Equally anonymous—but even more helpful—were the scholars and policy-makers of this and past centuries who have developed the ideas upon which we based the inter-nation simulation. When a venture as broad and brash as this is undertaken, one needs the resources of all.

My profoundest debt is to Richard C. Snyder, my friend and mentor.

HAROLD GUETZKOW

International Relations Program
Department of Political Science
Northwestern University

Table of Contents*

---

* Detailed contents are outlined at the beginning of each chapter.

vii

Chapter One

Some Perspectives on the Use of Experimental Techniques in the Study of International Relations[1]

Richard C. Snyder

We hope that this volume will be only one of a series of reports by numerous scholars on what appears to be an important contemporary development in the behavioral sciences: the application to international relations of essentially experimental techniques. Subsequent chapters are concerned primarily with a particular set of simulation activities comprising one phase of the over-all research and training objectives of the Northwest-

---

[1] This chapter extends several comments on simulation in the writer's "Some Recent Trends in International Relations Theory and Research," in A. Ranney, ed., *Essays on the Behavioral Study of Politics* (Urbana: University of Illinois Press, 1962).

1

ern International Relations Program. Such activities are complementary to our field work in foreign offices and international organizations and to the development of a body of propositions, all directed toward building more adequate theory about international relations. The authors have a vested interest in related and similar undertakings by other centers and individuals, whose efforts are discussed in Chapter Seven. If continual communication, collaboration, and replication prevail among those engaged in a variety of simulation and gaming exercises, errors, fadism, and wasteful duplication may be minimized.

Dawson (1962) has discussed the variety of usages associated with "simulation" and "gaming." Although distinctions are often necessary, the terms will be used synonymously here. After outlining major trends in simulation-like experimental techniques, comparisons will be made of rigorous versus quasi-experimental uses of simulation, contrasting its use for purposes of discovery with verification. Some attention will be given to the employment of simulation in teaching and training, and the possible impact of experimental techniques on the evolution of policy-oriented simulation will be considered. The chapter will conclude with a brief attempt to set the entire endeavor within the framework of a multiple strategy for the increase of reliable, useful knowledge.

Employment of experimental techniques in the study of international relations both represents, and is partially founded on, research in a number of the social sciences, which has carried these techniques substantially beyond their previous domain of inquiry (Shubik, 1960). Because the laboratory and the computer are playing an increasingly larger role in the accumulation of knowledge about human behavior, it is desirable to put the present effort in broader perspective. Accordingly, the introductory comments that follow are directed to a more general level.

I. Major Trends in Simulation

The following typify significant trends within the larger contemporary movement to extend the application of experimental techniques:

1. *The use of human subjects under quasi-laboratory conditions to create replicas of complex organizations, systems, and social processes.*
   Examples: Bloomfield (1960); Guetzkow and Bowes (1957);

Lasswell (1960); Schelling (1961); Siegel and Fouraker (1960); Strodtbeck (1962).

2. *The use of human subjects in nonlaboratory but contrived "natural" settings for the purposes listed under (1).*
   Examples: Sherif, *et al.* (1961); Turner (1957); White and Lippitt (1960).

3. *The use of machines to experimentally simulate mental and social processes as well as social systems.*
   Examples: Coleman (1962); Orcutt, *et al.* (1961); Pool and Abelson (1961); Simon (1960, Chapter IV); Raytheon (1961).

The difficulties accompanying extension of experimental methods to the levels of analyses and units of behavior that concern most sociologists, political scientists, historians, economists, and anthropologists are obviously imposing (Chapin, 1947; Campbell, 1962). That experimental techniques have been confined largely to limited areas of individual behavior and to small groups is no accident. However, a rather rapid penetration of these techniques into hitherto unoccupied areas—business decision-making, bargaining, diplomatic and war games, man-machine systems, higher mental processes, community conflict, and so on, is now taking place. Economists and political scientists are also engaged in experimentation. Even a prominent historian, Samuel Eliot Morison, has replicated the voyage of one of Columbus' ships.

Some of the factors associated with this outburst of activity may be mentioned briefly. In a persuasive justification, Siegel and Fouraker (1960) state that, "In the specific case of bilateral monopoly, it would be extremely unlikely that appropriate naturalistic data could be collected to test the theoretical model." They add that this is not only because the phenomenon is rare but because existing data would not be rich enough to test their theory. It seems reasonable to assume that the same thing may be true of other phenomena in which data are sufficient to prove the existence of an event or actions but not abundant enough to permit theoretical interpretations.

A second factor is the need for relatively quick insights into novel problems that have no apparent counterpart in prior experience—impacts of urban redevelopment plans, or the implications of the spread of nuclear weapons among nations. In this case, the future must be projected from a very narrow base, and simulation may compensate in part for otherwise acute data deficiencies.

Third, the development of more versatile computing machines has speeded up the process of playing out various combinations of variables and strategies and of extending the number of future stages that can be embodied in calculations. Equally noteworthy is the recent use of machines to augment laboratory exercises in which human subjects engage in complex computations.

Fourth and finally, as theoretical and research aspirations have grown to include large structures and systems together with the changes that take place in them, the need for microcosms, miniature versions, and holistic models is more readily perceived by social scientists. Scholars have begun to build bridges from small group theory and research to the organizational and institutional levels (Grace, 1955; Verba, 1961). Thus small group experiments on communication nets appear to have direct relevance for the analysis of more complex groups (Mulder, 1959). It has been demonstrated that *organizations,* as distinct from *small groups,* can be simulated with a limited number of subjects in the laboratory (Guetzkow and Bowes, 1957). Bargaining experiments (Schelling, 1960) represent the identification of empirical units within larger institutional or system contexts, which are closer to being isomorphic with the contrived units. Experimentation via simulation is essentially a technique for managing, separating, and observing related segments of the seamless web of phenomenal complexity.

Is there something these extensions of experimental technique have in common? It is suggested that all are rooted in the analog foundations of science. There is "something out there" (*i.e.,* the social world) and there is "something in here" (*i.e.,* the laboratory, the machine, the researcher's mind) which bear a special relationship to each other. If one scans the various examples, the relationship is established in many ways, but some sort of usable "likeness" is a universal aim or result. To be sure, this likeness is a matter of degree, a sliding scale of more or less similarity.

In one sense, the idea of reproducing phenomena without using the original can be described as a sampling procedure. Of all the aspects or properties of something "out there" only selected ones are used. Such is the case even for "complete" replications (*e.g.,* a mock-up of a weapon that may be different in size). Thus different simulations can be conceived of as falling on a continuum of samples, the points along which represent the proportion of characteristics actually employed to the total sample space. The closer the sample comes to exhausting the total number of attributes, the more "realistic" is the particular form of the simulation.

Another shared characteristic deserves mention: the use of substitute mechanisms or surrogate functions. The reproduction of mechanisms is itself a prime objective. But economy and feasibility may compel the use of equivalent rather than identical ways of inducing certain effects. Therefore, the existence of an independent variable in real situations is separate from the representation of that variable in the experimental situation. The experimenter or simulator replaces the natural forces, random factors, and accidents assumed to operate in the real world.

Simulation techniques may be differentiated, therefore, on the basis of the nature of their forms of representation, as well as the number of items included in their "samples." The scaling-down process—the sampling of attributes and the use of surrogate processes—involves the peril of inadvertent changes in kind when the counterpart of what is "out there" is constructed "in here." Perplexing problems arise from this fact, but so do unique opportunities: for example, to observe the impact of rare events and surprise. The central problem is, of course, to keep the qualitative difference from basically distorting extrapolation.

The foregoing is a brief reminder that surface impressions of simulation activities can be very misleading; this is one case where there is much more than meets the eye. Simple laboratory operations observed by a neophyte are likely to be interpreted literally, a circumstance that obscures the complicated creation of analogs. Extension of laboratory and other experimental techniques beyond the discipline of individual psychology, and even beyond the more manageable phenomena of small group behavior, raises fundamental issues, including the problems of relevance and of the complex interrelations between the scientist and the multiple realities he attempts to describe, explain, and predict. One difficulty lies in an unequal understanding of, and experience with, these techniques among social scientists, to say nothing of laymen whose image of the laboratory centers on the invention and testing of gadgets. For many in both groups, leaps to the laboratory from international relations (and vice versa) will seem nonsensical.

Nonetheless, evidence presented in this book, as well as in the literature documented by Brody in Chapter Seven, suggests that simulation and gaming are emerging as potentially powerful exploratory modes of research, training, and teaching in international relations. The case is by no means established as yet, but a number of reasonably hard-headed scientists and practitioners are investing heavily in a rapidly growing cross-disciplinary activity.

Though there are noteworthy exceptions (*e.g.*, March, 1953-54;

Lasswell, 1960), simulation has entered political science largely via
international relations. Several reasons for this can be cited. War
gaming is an ancient practice and an evolution into exercises fea-
turing dipomacy and political strategies was to be expected. "Grand
strategy" embodying the nexus between military and nonmilitary
components has led to potentially fruitful adaptations of the large-
scale war game—particularly the effort to interrelate political and
military factors in a limited war situation (Ellis and Greene, 1960).
In addition, the familiar descriptive model of international politics
as essentially a matrix of interdependent moves by complex entities
has paved the way for attempted applications of game theory
(Deutsch, 1954; Kaplan, 1957). Moreover, since the study of international relations is an interdisciplinary enterprise, scholars possessing experimental competence and having direct interest in international phenomena can ply their trade outside the traditional
bounds of disciplinary research.

II. Discovery vs. Verification

TYPES OF EXPERIMENTATION

If we adopt a strict definition of "experiment," *i.e.*, controlled
observation, repeated trials, and systematic manipulation of crucial
variables, this basic scientific procedure—for the present at least—has
relatively little application to the study of human behavior outside
of psychology. Indeed, it is sometimes asserted that for most social
phenomena—including individual behavior—there can be no scientific analysis because the conditions of rigorous experimentation
cannot be fulfilled. On the other hand, if we allow for *degrees* of
rigor and for *quasi-experimental exploration,* the trial and error of
everyday political and social life and the semicontrolled exercises
in contrived situations may fall within our purview. Campbell (1962)
stresses the value of quasi-experiments in weeding out competing
hypotheses whose variables can be dealt with by means of the imaginative use of control groups. The logic of the statement that
natural social experiments are virtually impossible is compelling,
but it is also a fact that little effort has been made to identify and
examine self-conscious experiments by real-world actors. Trial-and-
error records are rarely kept and the accumulated experience arising
from, for example, the establishment of utopias or ideal communities
has not been systematically evaluated (Nordhoff, 1961). Somewhere
between the laboratory experiment and the natural social experiment lies the *in situ* experiment, for example, Sherif's Robbers' Cave

Experiment on cooperation and conflict in a boys' camp (1961). One may be permitted a feeling of excitement when certain propositions that emerge from this study have very close parallels in Bozeman's *Politics and Culture in International History* (1960). Bozeman's historical analysis generates the hypothesis (pp. 106-107) that when all nations (or political units) face the same uncertain environment or hazards, a common set of norms will develop (as in the case of the Rhodean law of the sea). Sherif, *et al.*, generate the hypothesis (p. 44) that when groups share common goals and are interdependent, standardized norms emerge that will regulate their relationships in common activities.

Repeatability is a key element in all controlled experimentation upon which so much of science rests. Even purists will admit that neither the experimenter nor experiments will be literally identical on successive trials. The question is how much of what kind of significant noninduced, unwanted change takes place with what consequences for the purposes of inquiry. That history does not *repeat* itself is an enduring proverb, yet if history does not in some way *imitate* itself, what sense can be made of the assumption that past experience is relevant to future occurrences? Hidden by our *a priori* assertions and by surface dissimilarities, perhaps the difference between *some* laboratory experiments and *some* actual situations is more a matter of degree than of kind. Further, it may be argued that real life events which in a proximate way meet the requisites of true experiments are nearly always one-shot affairs. The point is that the differences between real life and laboratory experimentation should not be pushed to an extreme in which insights and predictions derived from the latter could not conceivably have application in the outside world or, contrariwise, in which possibilities of fruitful similarities between less-than-completely controlled operations in the laboratory and the often less-than-random trial and error of human beings are ignored.

HEURISTIC USES OF SIMULATION

At this stage in the development of the social sciences, and especially at this stage in the development of simulation techniques for analyzing international relations, most experiments belong in the discovery phase of science-building, not in the verification phase (Snyder, 1962a). Athough in some areas of behavior genuine experiments are possible and indeed necessary, and although experimental validation is an ultimate test of hypotheses, this is not now the case in most sectors of political analysis. On the positive side, it is more sensible to start with simple and manipulable systems (or replicas of such systems) as a way of gaining intellectual control over larger, less directly observable systems, which the analyst cannot rearrange in terms of his theoretical purposes. On the negative side, it is important to avoid premature attempts at verification.

Concentration on the discovery potential or heuristic values of experimental devices like simulation or gaming frees us from the strictures of Mill's canons, which properly concern verification. This is not to equate totally unplanned, loosely conceived experiments with *uncontrolled* (as technically distinct from controlled) laboratory exercises. On the contrary, the heuristic potential of gaming will depend not just on how the "reality" problem is handled, but on the basic skills of the experimenter in contriving situations that show an explicit theory at work in the behavior of players and machines operating within bounded limits and opportunities for action and interaction.

Viewed from the vantage point of discovery, simulation as a form of experimention has several marked advantages. Quite apart from the significant freedom of the experimenter to manipulate, an obvious, yet perhaps underrated feature lies in the opportunity for direct observation. The ability to "see" a system or situation unfold is given rather infrequently to the social scientist in the everyday world. Structure—especially in large-scale social interactions—is notably invisible. In the laboratory, not only can objective properties of structure, *e.g.*, the direction, frequency, and content of communication, be counted and analyzed, but the subjective properties, *e.g.*, the perceptions, evaluations, and choices of participants in the structure, are more readily accessible. The possibility of a synthesis of objective and subjective methods was a central part of Moreno's original argument for the socio-drama. To "see" is not to discover, of course, but as Townsend (1953) argues, one is much more likely to discover by means of a first hand encounter with phenomena than by armchair speculation or deductive analysis.

Often we forget that despite our admittedly imperfect knowledge of the external world, we nonetheless entertain some fairly rigid notions about how things happen and what should happen under certain conditions. Curiously enough, the confession of surprise is relatively rare in this writer's experience and then it is tinged with a negative quality, a feeling of disappointment. But the unexpected would seem to be the essence of discovery, and the contrivance of circumstances under which surprises may occur would seem to be an aim of scientific procedures (Parkes, 1960; Selye, 1960). The systematic probings of experimental explorations ought to yield the unexpected as well as substantiate the familiar.

In addition to its values in permitting direct observation, thereby decreasing the rigidity with which social systems are perceived, simulation allows penetration of systems which seem hopelessly complex. It perhaps will permit analysis of change, specification of the interrelations of quantifiable and qualitative variables, and the exploration of linkages between levels of analysis. Consider an example of each of these potential utilizations from the field of international relations, with all its complexity, in this order:

First, both as a matter of policy and as a matter of explanation and prediction, the impact of technological developments on foreign policy and on the stability of strategic deterrence is not completely understood. No adequate definition of the problem is commonly accepted. What are the consequences of the rate and direction of growth of the science and technology of weapons and industrial productivity? What are the consequences of different rates of growth among national antagonists? What are the effects of estimated projections of technological change on current decisions and planning? As a supplement to other kinds of study, the simulation technique appears to offer an immediate and economical way of identifying more precisely a likely range of implications of basic changes in one significant set of variables (Brody, 1962).

Second, what are the interrelations of political and military factors —of hard and soft variables? More specifically, how (if at all) do weapons systems condition political choices? What is the perceived significance of certain weapons and their deployment in a certain fashion? Is an arms race a vicious circle of hardware production with its own internal logic, or is it a problem of perception, expectation, and risk-taking by political élites, or a mixture of these? Richardson's highly formal models (1960) contain built-in psychological mechanisms that are recognized by Richardson but left largely implicit (Sutton, 1961). Efforts might be made to "play out" Richardson's equations on computers; his formulations might be used to program the parameters and variables into a dynamic laboratory exercise in which implicit subjective aspects of arms races could be treated explicitly either as dependent or independent variables. Such variation under controlled conditions might illuminate a cycle of changing relationships between hardware and nonhardware factors in which rational decisions at one stage lead to irrational bases of choice at the next stage.

Third, at the nexus of unit (society, nation) characteristics and actions on the one hand, and interunit (intersocietal, international) interactions on the other, lies (we all strongly suspect) a set of crucial empirical and theoretical relationships. Most propositions concern either of these two levels of analysis. Few specify interrelationships. There is perhaps more than an interesting parallel between these two levels in inter-nation relations and the two levels present in group experiments: the objective (observer-orientated) and the subjective (actor-orientated) structures; the internal (perceived) and external (observed) structures. The interlevel problem here is no less complex, as perceptual discrepancies among group members and as hidden but embarrassing discrepancies between observer's construed structure and actors' perceived structure amply demonstrate. As already noted, however, in the experimental situation it is possible to collect data on the ways both levels are perceived by the actors, as well as on observer-actor differences in perception. Furthermore, surface parallels of another sort may be suggestive, namely, the conflict between private (individual) and collective (group) aspirations and between official and secret value systems. Kindleberger (1958) has asked: does an international system work because certain system rules are internalized by those acting for the participating units, or does it result from the conjunction of non-system or intraunit forces which shape the patterns of interaction? Hence, simulation may be an heuristic entering wedge for the development of a concept of unit-interunit relationship in international behavior.

Those who have listened to tape-recordings or read transcripts of negotiations and discussions between individuals and groups in laboratory exercises have been impressed by the often startling similarities of basic themes which appear and even the identical words employed by politically inexperienced subjects as compared to diplomatic messages or other revealed official sources. As in the case of the Bozeman-Sherif comparison mentioned earlier, the observer or experimenter has the feeling he is glimpsing fundamental mechanisms at work. Obviously this does not prove anything in and of itself, yet these induced echoes of real life have occurred frequently enough to stretch the credibility of chance as the explanatory factor. Two examples of this kind of record are found in the research reported by the Hermanns (1962) and by Ratoosh (1961).

Thus, from a technical and a substantive point of view, the heuristic values of simulation in the study of international relations seem noteworthy indeed. Suffice it to say in the present context, one is led to different implications if one regards simulation as a flexible mode of discovery and clarification rather than as a mode of rigorous test or validation.

III. Simulation for Teaching and Training

To date, simulation has been employed more extensively for training and teaching than for research and theory-building, as is indicated in the literature already available on the use of simulation for instructional purposes (*Infra*, Chapter Six; Dill, Jackson, and Sweeney, 1961; Greenlaw, *et al.*, 1962). Those who have had first-hand experience feel that simulation or gaming is certainly a helpful and perhaps a very powerful new instructional device. Granted that adding another dimension to the skills of official decision-makers is quite different from teaching international relations to undergraduates or high school students, are there nonetheless underlying features of such exercises which are fundamental to learning in general?

LEARNING THROUGH VICARIOUS DECISION-MAKING

To reread William James' Talks to Teachers (1908) delivered in 1892 is instructive because James stresses the need to make learning more activity-oriented: "*No reception without reaction, no impression without expression*" (italics his, p. 39). He goes on to say:

> Laboratory work and shop work engender a habit of observation, a knowledge of the difference between accuracy and vagueness, and an insight into nature's complexity and into the inadequacy of all abstract verbal accounts of real phenomena. . . (p. 40).

More than a half-century later James S. Coleman (1960) echoed the contention that students need an opportunity to *act* on what they are being taught, to "take the role of the other," and to participate in intergroup situations. He specifically mentions simulation and gaming (pp. 306-308), capping his analysis with the exhortation: "find ways to let adolescents *act*" (italics his, p. 309).

Despite a large number of executive training programs for government and business personnel, no one is confident that the awkward gulf between theory and practice in the training context has been bridged by case reading and lectures plus discussion (Guetzkow, Forehand and James, 1962). Can the distance of college and high school students from international reality be foreshortened by activity in a simulated counterpart to that reality? On the face of it, individual mental rehearsal of complex alternatives through the reading of cases would appear to be more limited in its scope and reliability than direct participation in a simulated group problem-solving situation in which responses and counter moves are made by other persons. Gaming—in its several varieties—offers an opportunity to play out a strategy over a period of time and to observe concrete consequences of decisions. Moreover, the importance of theory is easier to demonstrate when a system is actually in operation. The degree of transferability of experience will depend heavily on the particular domain of social behavior, on the state of research and theory, and on the sophistication with which games are designed. But the explicitness required by calculations, decisions, and actions that characterize business and political gaming is usually missing in reading a case study or listening to a lecture.

In his *The Process of Education* (1960, Ch. 6), Jerome Bruner makes the point that the provision of vicarious experience is a necessary adjunct to other modes of learning. Much student apathy concerning politics and national issues may be due to the relatively long postponement of adult roles and to the presentation of abstractions or facts that are outside the students' real life experience. On the basis of trials in a small number of colleges and high schools, reactions of students and teachers suggest that social scientists may be developing in simulation a most effective means of bringing distant policy realism within the individual's personal experience in a manner which cannot be matched by other teaching materials. The Northwestern University Department of Political Science is engaged in an experimental program which hopefully will throw additional light on this point (Robinson, 1962).

MOTIVATION IN THE SIMULATION CONTEXT

Can one duplicate the requirements of actual situations or the moral properties of momentous political decisions in simulation? Do participants ever escape the realization that "it does not really count"? What effect does the fact that the experience is vicarious have upon its values for learning? We do not have satisfactory answers to these questions, nor is it clear that the problem itself is fully understood. The critical question is whether the artificiality of the contrived exercise eliminates an indispensable counterpart of reality, namely, a full sense of responsibility—of having to live with decision consequences.

Before concluding that the surrogate motivations involved in training are a crippling defect for the use of simulation, several things should be kept in mind. First, there is abundant evidence that participants take simulation very seriously indeed and are capable of complete absorption, so much so that contacts among participants and thinking about simulation events are extended beyond the laboratory. This seems to be true both of younger students and mature executives. Perhaps even more impressive is the indication of genuine tensions in simulated inter-nation systems similar to those manifest in the world, even though nations are "manned" by amateurs. These observations may be *prima facie* evidence that motivation within the simulation may not be spurious.

Second, a connection between play-acting and hypnosis has been noted for a long time. Throwing one's self into a dramatic role apparently creates a psychic state not entirely unlike the trance, except that the former is usually self-induced. Individuals differ widely in their susceptibility to hypnosis. It does not seem far-fetched to suggest that as a methodological technique, participants in simulation exercises could be tested for susceptibility—in this case to the demands of the particular form of role assumption demanded by gaming. Getting so caught up in a contrived situation that one *does* behave in accordance with system rules or constants and in response to unfolding interactions, rather than in accordance with personal whim may be analogous to the inability of a hypnotized subject to lower his outstretched arm even when he feels he is quite free to do so. Though simulation participants are aware that they are not actually making decisions in a real foreign office, their behavior produces effects which in turn cause a "shock of recognition" of real-world likenesses.

Third, the particular form of a simulation exercise and its purpose must be kept in mind. A realistic diplomatic game played by foreign policy officials as a dress rehearsal would have the advantage of built-in protection against irresponsibility, though even here the actual positive and negative sanctions of the political arena are absent. On the other hand, a less realistic game played by less experienced players might not suffer because what is needed for the experiment to be fruitful is for the participants to take the exercise at face value and to play diligently according to the rules. There is at least some evidence that changing the size of, say, monetary rewards (within the limits of what experimenters can afford) does not alter the behavior of subjects significantly. Moreover, data reveals marked stress when war is imminent or occurs in inter-nation simulation (Driver, 1962).

Fourth, perhaps it should be considered an open question whether responsible decision-makers experience their own actions (either in anticipation or *post hoc*) in the same way it is alleged that simulated activities must be experienced in order to be useful or legitimate. There is practically no evidence on this point. At least some basis exists for assuming that officials must act in a certain way regardless of personal values, that they also become involved in a "game-for-its-own-sake," and that under yet other conditions the motives of individual statesmen may transcend the requirements of the international or national systems. It is perhaps worth raising, in this connection, the question of the extent to which certain features of national decision-making reduce felt personal responsibility for acts carrying grave consequences.

Until systematic evaluation of both research and training simulations has progressed much further, we will probably not know just how much of a handicap we are up against. The whole problem may be bound up with the nature and extent of epiphenomenal effects associated with various exercises. Subjective and objective data drawn from many runs ought to provide clues regarding the consequences of the lack of real life rewards and punishments.

These thoughts are in no sense intended to brush aside the questions posed above. A caveat has been raised against the assumption that answers are self-evident. Judgment should be suspended until a more adequate empirical basis has been established. Robinson and Snyder (1962) have underway a research comparison of the education outcomes of alternative methods of teaching, contrasting man-machine simulation with the case method and the policy problem assignment.

RELATION OF TEACHING-ORIENTED SIMULATION TO RESEARCH

There exists an unfortunate gap in communication among those primarily engaged in transmitting knowledge or skills and those working in research and theory-building. With some exceptions the following groups are isolated from each other: (a) university faculties—content specialists; (b) professional schools of education—pedagogical technique specialists; and (c) certain psychologists—learning specialists. The costly consequences of this separation of content and method, and of content and method from principles of learning, are being increasingly recognized. On the teaching and training side, the simulation movement may provide a concrete opportunity for collaboration among the three groups.

Teaching and research simulation activities ought to feed each other. In the first place, simulation techniques are "empty" in the sense that a very wide range of theories, problems, and decision-making factors can be fed into, or adapted to, the instructional process. There is no inherent reason why the most important and recent theoretical and research advances cannot be incorporated, if effective communication is maintained. Furthermore, insofar as forms of simulation embody basic theory concerning the functioning of the international system, the emergence of policy problems and crises can be captured without the disadvantages of the fleeting quality so often associated with a current events approach.

Because there are alternative ways of representing and programming the major variables and different procedures for laboratory exercises, teaching and training adaptations necessitated by different institutional loci and objectives are desirable and feasible. However, a close working relationship between teachers and experimenters must be maintained in order to preserve theoretical adequacy in the face of teaching needs. There is probably a very thin line between such adjustments and the capacity of simulation to reproduce faithfully the basic properties of foreign policy-making and state interaction. It seems particularly important for those engaged in research via simulation to gain the benefit of reactions by mature officials to the theory incorporated in gaming, as well as to the rules of play. One of the aims of simulation is to recreate central features of the conceptual environment of policy-makers. As experimental subjects or trainees, the latter are in a unique position to evaluate the choice and representation of key factors.

No one can deny that the rigidities introduced in connection with controlled experimentation inhibit certain teaching functions, but one of the most pressing reasons for interrelating teaching and research simulations is the great value of increasing the "N" of both loose and quasi-controlled exercises. Insights arising from teaching and training activities should be captured and added to the pool derived from research-oriented exercises. The discovery function of simulation will be enhanced in proportion to the number of exercises performed with some care, *if* observations are communicated by educators to research centers.

With the spread of simulation even in limited forms, replication becomes possible. Exploratory runs have progressed to the point where the multiplication of trials could yield significant data. This is particularly true in the case of more easily manipulable variables like economic factors or alliance patterns. Also, the range of variation of action and interaction patterns which can be spawned by identical initial system conditions is not yet known. Only additional controlled simulations will provide this information. Finally, if common evaluation procedures for different kinds of exercises can be applied in a proper sample of institutional settings, we should be able to develop standardized exercises based on instructional effectiveness without stifling local initiative and adaptation.

IV. Policy-Oriented and Research-Oriented Simulation

It is commonly regretted by busy, responsible policy-makers that action seems to be the enemy of thought. In addition, much has been made of the contrary pulls of theory and policy. It is not surprising that this difference in orientation should be manifest in the simulation movement. Nor is it surprising that diplomatic games using experienced subjects for realistic simulations concentrate on policy problems. Practical needs provided much of the original impetus for the extension of simulation to human organizations and systems.

Certainly there is an important difference between the use of gaming techniques to solve or illuminate a policy problem or to "play out" alternative strategies in the absence of strictures inherent in the everyday work situation on the one hand, and more controlled simulations designed to arrive at theoretical explanations of international behavior on the other. And it is also evident that many theories and propositions developed by scientists are of little immediate use to policy-makers. Without minimizing either the relevance problem or the barriers to the utilization of social science by practitioners, it can be suggested that exaggeration or distortion of these relationships should be avoided.

Much depends on the nature of a particular problem and the way in which it is formulated. Some so-called applied problems can be converted into theoretical challenges. For example, the question: "What will be the effects of such and such a level of damage from nuclear attack on a society?" can be read narrowly as implying a set of postattack logistical contingencies, or it can be read as a problem of identifying the prerequisites for continued functioning of a total system under certain conditions. The latter interpretation shifts the question from an essentially engineering perspective to one requiring a theory of how a society operates. Interestingly enough, this problem is being explored by simulation techniques (*e.g.,* Orcutt, *et al.,* 1961). While these techniques are applied research in one sense, they require the application of new and existing social theory in order to program the computer.

A similar example is the "N-country" problem, which to a great degree poses the same puzzles for the theorist and the policy-maker —at least so far as the possible political consequences of the spread of nuclear weapons is concerned. As indicated above, this too is being explored via simulation (Brody, 1963). A third example is closer to immediate military matters, namely, the simulation of how the Strategic Air Command might react to a nuclear attack (Carter, 1960). While rehearsal of existing response machinery is somewhat closer to reality, aspects of general organization and communication theory are incorporated and hence such research may include more basic elements.

Finally, the problem of unilateral initiatives in foreign policy illustrates the possible merging of the interests of the theorizer and the policy-maker. Relatively little is known about the necessary conditions for deliberate initiation of moves intended to reduce tensions or armaments by reciprocation; nor is much known about the actual functioning of tacit bargaining, which implies bids for joint strategies or tactics through acts rather than words. Unilateral actions raise feasibility questions for policy-makers while at the same time they involve psychological factors such as perception, meaning, communication, and trust. The formulations of Osgood (1960) designed to provide a basis for "graduated reciprocal tension reduction" are being subjected to experimental exploration by the Western Behavioral Sciences Institute under contract from Project Michelson.

These examples have two things in common: (1) a lack of relevant past experience which can be systematically codified and (2) the application and exploration of theories and techniques hitherto not extensively applied or explored even though the policy problems are "applied" in the usual sense. Simulation appears therefore to be useful for mixed pure and applied problems. Whether the *same* laboratory or machine exercise can serve both needs must be decided in the individual case.

Quite apart from the foregoing, simulation may be a significant method for clarifying the interrelations of knowledge and action. Boguslaw (1961) has proposed a distinction between "established" and "emergent" situations, the former being amenable to the application of previous learning situations, and the latter much less so, if at all. Most social theorizing deals with established situations, whereas policy-makers often are caught, or perceive themselves to be caught, in emergent situations characterized by unidentified parameters, unpredictable system states, and a lack of analytic solutions. Can emergent situations be brought under intellectual control by a more sophisticated methodology for analyzing recurrent situations, and can a capacity for handling emergent situations more effectively be learned by policy-makers? Tentatively, we might answer in the affirmative.

Simulation can help with respect to both questions. In the first place, simulation not only permits the repetition of parameter conditions and system states, as well as the calculated altering of combinations of these factors, but it is possible to go back to a prior situation and play out alternatives which were available to, yet not chosen by, participants. In addition, it is possible to alter the conditions of the prior emergent situation in order to discover what might have changed the decision. The fact that repeated trials could reveal a stable pattern of consequences of various alternatives might facilitate the construction of a more objective basis for the acceptance of analytic tools to replace the participants' intuitive judgments. On the training side, a technique for measuring effectiveness in handling emergent situations has been described (Boguslaw and Pelton, 1959).

V. A Multiple Strategy for Work in Simulation

Different simulation and gaming exercises may be viewed as complementary components of a multiple strategy for advancing knowledge. Rivalry for funds, attention, and acceptance is probably inevitable, given the organization of the academic community in the United States. If competition results in the spread of labor and capital among several lines of development, so much the better, because it is too early to decide where major investments ought to be made. However, a free enterprise model may be inappropriate due to the time and money required for substantial progress. It seems very unlikely that we can do everything on the desired or requisite scale.

But the most compelling reasons for stressing the complementarities in simulation are intellectual and scientific. The connections between teaching-training and research, and between policy-oriented and basic research-oriented approaches have been outlined. Various forms of simulation and gaming are not entirely substitutable for one another; each has advantages the others do not have. But there is notable complementarity. For example, the Gullahorns (1962) argue persuasively that electronic digital computers offer a more fruitful method for converting verbal formulations of theory into working models than does mathematicization. Machine simulation offers a relatively quick and inexpensive way of playing out several different strategies for desired periods of future time, but exercises using human subjects seem better adapted to the identification and manipulation of judgmental factors and variables more difficult to quantify or put in symbolic terms.

The magnitudes of time, money, and skills which simulation requires put a premium on good communication, shared evaluations, replication, and joint projects—perhaps more so than is true of other research techniques. To reiterate a point made above, simulations include a broad set of operations, from high speed computers programmed with formal models to loosely structured human interaction exercises, and many combinations of machines, man-machine, and man-man experiments.

The number of scholars involved in the simulation movement is rather small, though growing rapidly. It is still possible to develop an explicit strategy within directional guides, and to include freedom for variation. An outline for such a strategy may be conceived as follows:

1. *Specification of Alternative Simulation Techniques. Characterization in Terms of:*
   Research and training objectives best suited to each
   Stage of development
   "Data grab"—particular kinds of expected results.
2. *Specification of Central Questions Grouped Around Three Major Foci:*
   Decision-making
   Bargaining and negotiations
   Systems and system properties.
3. *Specification of Key Problems. Characterization in Terms of:*
   Research and training functions
   Degree of novelty
   Types of solutions sought
   Basic knowledge sought.
4. *Specification of Stage of Development Respecting Activities, Which Combine 1, 2, and 3:*
   Exploration—of particular simulation procedures and of
     t   key variables
   Quasi-controlled runs
   Rigorous experiments.

Any simulation strategy must include one more indispensable element: close linkage to field research, to the development of propositional inventories, and to nonexperimental theory-building (Snyder, 1962a). By implication, it is imperative that the theoretical and substantive contributions of those outside the simulation movement be sought continuously.

VI. References

Benson, O., "Simulation of International Relations and Diplomacy," in H. Borko (ed.) *Computer Applications in the Behavioral Sciences*. Englewood Cliffs, N.J.: Prentice-Hall, Inc., 1962.

Bloomfield, L. P., "Political Gaming," *United States Naval Institute Proceedings*, LXXXVI (1960), 57-64.

Boguslaw, R., "Situation Analysis and the Problem of Action," *Social Problems*, VIII (1961), 212-219.

——— and W. Pelton, "STEPS—A Management Game for Programming Supervisors," *Datamation*, November-December, 1959.

Bozeman, A., *Politics and Culture in International History*. Princeton: Princeton University Press, 1960.

Brody, R. A., "Some Systemic Effects of the Spread of Nuclear Weapons Technology: A Study Through Simulation of a Multi-Nuclear Future," *Journal of Conflict Resolution*, VII (1963), 663-753.

Bruner, J., *The Process of Education*. Cambridge: Harvard University Press, 1960.

Campbell, D. T. and J. C. Stanley, "Experimental and Quasi-Experimental Designs for Research on Teaching," in N. L. Gage (ed.) *Handbook of Research on Teaching*. Chicago: Rand McNally & Co., 1962.

Carter, L., "Exercising the Air Defense System." Santa Monica: System Development Corporation, 1960, mimeographed.

Chapin, F. S., *Experimental Designs in Sociological Research*. New York: Harper & Row, Publishers, 1947.

Coleman, J., in Patterson, F. (ed.) *The Adolescent Citizen*. New York: The Free Press of Glencoe, Inc., 1960.

———, "The Simulation of Processes in Social Controversy," in H. Guetzkow (ed.) *Simulation in Social Science*. Englewood Cliffs, N.J.: Prentice-Hall, Inc., 1962, pp. 61-69.

Dawson, R. E., "Simulation in the Social Sciences," in *ibid.*, pp. 1-15.

Deutsch, K., "Game Theory and International Politics," *The Canadian Journal of Economics and Political Science*, XX (1954), 76-83.

Dill, W., J. Jackson, and J. W. Sweeney (ed.) *Proceedings of the Conference on Business Games as Teaching Devices, April 26-28, 1961*. New Orleans: Tulane University, School of Business Administration.

Driver, M. J., *Conceptual Structure and Group Processes in an Inter-Nation Simulation. Part One: The Perception of Simulated Nations.* Princeton, N.J.: Research Bulletin RB-62-15, Educational Testing Service and Princeton University, 1962.

Ellis, J. and T. Greene, "Contextual Study: A Structural Approach to the Study of Political and Military Aspects of Limited War." Santa Monica: The RAND Corporation, P-1840, 1959.

Grace, H., "A Quantitative Case Study in Policy Science," *Journal of Social Psychology,* XLI (1955), 197-219.

Greenlaw, P. S., L. W. Herron, and R. R. Rawdon, *Business Simulation in Industrial and University Education.* Englewood Cliffs, N.J.: Prentice-Hall, Inc., 1962.

Guetzkow, H. and A. Bowes, "The Development of Organizations in a Laboratory," *Management Science,* III (1957), 380-402.

———, G. A. Forehand, and B. J. James, "An Evaluation of Educational Influence on Administrative Judgment," *Administrative Science Quarterly,* VI (1962), 483-500.

Gullahorn, J. T. and J. E. Gullahorn, "The Computer as a Tool for Theory Development," unpublished paper, 1962.

Hermann, C. F. and M. G. Hermann, "On the Possible Use of Historical Data for Validation Study of the Inter-Nation Simulation." Naval Ordnance Test Station, Contract No. N123 (60530) 25875A, China Lake, California, 1962, mimeographed.

James, W., *Talks to Teachers on Psychology: And to Students on Some of Life's Problems.* New York: Holt, Rinehart and Winston, Inc., 1908.

Kaplan, M., *System and Process in International Politics.* New York: John Wiley & Sons, Inc., 1957.

Kindleberger, C., "Scientific International Politics," *World Politics,* XI (1958), 83-88.

Lasswell, H., "Technique of Decision Seminars," *Midwest Journal of Political Science,* IV (1960), 213-236.

March, J., "Husband-Wife Interaction Over Political Issues," *Public Opinion Quarterly,* XVII (1953-54), 461-70.

Mulder, M., "Power and Satisfaction in Task-Oriented Groups," *Acta Psychologica,* XVI (1959), 178-225.

Nordhoff, C., *The Communistic Societies of the United States.* New York: Hillary Press, 1961.

Orcutt, G. H., M. Greenberger, J. Korbel, and A. Rivlin, *Microanalysis of Socioeconomic Systems: A Simulation Study.* New York: Harper & Row, Publishers, 1961.

Osgood, C. E., "Graduated Reciprocation in Tension-Reduction: A Key to Initiative in Foreign Policy." The University of Illinois, Institute of Communications Research, Urbana, December, 1960, mimeographed.

Parkes, A., "The Art of Scientific Discovery," *Midway,* III (1960), 58-75.

Pool, I. and R. Abelson, "The Simulmatics Project," *Public Opinion Quarterly,* XXV (1961), 167-183.

Ratoosh, P., "Experiments in Non-Zero Sum Games." Naval Ordnance Test Station, Contract No. N60530-5774, Management Science Research Center, University of California, Berkeley, 1961.

Raytheon Company, *First Progress Report of the Strategic Model Simulation of Wars, Weapons, and Arms Controls.* Bedford, Mass.: Preliminary Systems Design Department, Advanced Development Laboratory, 1961.

Richardson, L., *Arms and Insecurity.* Pittsburgh: Boxwood Press, 1960.

———, *Statistics of Deadly Quarrels.* Chicago: Quadrangle Books, 1960.

Robinson, J. A. and R. C. Snyder, U.S. Office of Education, Project No. 1568, 1962.

Schelling, T., *The Strategy of Conflict.* Cambridge: Harvard University Press, 1960.

Selye, H., "What Makes Basic Research Basic?" in R. Thruelsen and J. Kobler (eds.) *Adventures of the Mind.* New York: Vintage Books, 1960, pp. 145-157.

Sherif, M., *et al, Intergroup Conflict and Cooperation: The Robbers' Cave Experiment.* Norman: University of Oklahoma, Institute of Group Relations, 1961.

Shubik, M., "Bibliography on Simulation, Gaming, Artificial Intelligence and Allied Topics," *American Statistical Association Journal,* LV (1960), 736-751.

Siegel, S. and L. Fouraker, *Bargaining and Group Decision-Making: Experiments in Bilateral Monopoly.* New York: McGraw-Hill Book Co., Inc., 1960.

Simon, H., *Models of Man: Social and Rational.* New York: John Wiley & Sons, Inc., 1957.

———, *The New Science of Management Decisions.* New York: Harper & Row, Publishers, 1960.

Snyder, R. C., "Experimental Techniques and Political Analysis: Some Reflections in the Context of Concern Over Behavioral Approaches," in J. C. Charlesworth (ed.) *The Limits of Behavioralism in Political Science,* a symposium sponsored by The American Academy of Political and Social Science, October, 1962, pp. 94-123.

———, "Some Recent Trends in International Relations Theory and Research," in A. Ranney (ed.) *Essays on the Behavioral Study of Politics.* Urbana: University of Illinois Press, 1962, pp. 103-171.

Strodtbeck, F. L., "Social Process, the Law, and Jury Functioning," in W. T. Evan (ed.) *Law and Sociology: Exploratory Essays.* New York: The Free Press of Glencoe, Inc., 1962.

Sutton, O., review of Lewis F. Richardson's *Arms and Insecurity* and *Statistics of Deadly Quarrels,* in *Scientific American,* CCIV (1961), 193-200.

Townsend, J., *Introduction to Experimental Method for Psychology and the Social Sciences.* New York: McGraw-Hill Book Co., Inc., 1953.

Turner, M., *The Child Within the Group: An Experiment in Self-Government*. Stanford: Stanford University Press, 1957.

Verba, S., *Small Groups and Political Behavior: A Study of Leadership*. Princeton: Princeton University Press, 1961.

White, R. and R. Lippit, *Autocracy and Democracy: An Experimental Inquiry*. New York: Harper & Row, Publishers, 1960.

Chapter Two

A Use of Simulation in the Study of Inter-Nation Relations

Harold Guetzkow

Events, as recorded in all their variety in historical and contemporary documents, are the usual basis for the development of theory about relations among nations. These international events our theory must explain, and these events we eventually hope to predict. Such theory-building—consisting of the development of adequate concepts and the relations of these concepts to each other in propositions—must encompass the

welter of facts from life situations. Our theories of international relations—be they implicit or explicit—are the stuff from which we compose our policies and write our newspapers and textbooks. This essay describes an initial effort to utilize simulation techniques as complementary means both for the development of theory and for instructional purposes.[1]

Simulation is an operating representation of central features of reality. Simulations may take the form of war games, of pilot chemical plants, of ship-and-harbor scale models, of computer-inventory systems. There are a multitude of such representations (Malcolm, 1958). Will a social simulation of inter-nation relations prove to be of value as a heuristic device for theory development in international relations research? May inter-nation simulation be arranged to allow live participants to play component units for training purposes? Three exploratory runs of an inter-nation simulation in the laboratory of the Program of Graduate Training and Research in International Relations at Northwestern University in 1957-58 suggest that simulation technique may be useful for purposes of both research and training.

I. Background for Simulation

The efforts in simulation at Northwestern were stimulated by two streams of intellectual endeavor, one represented in the war game and the other deriving from the social psychological group experiment.

The war game has been in existence for many centuries. During the nineteenth century it flowered in the "rigid" game, in which complicated problems were played by military decision-makers with outcomes determined by elaborate rule books. During the latter

---

[1] Early plans for the simulation were thought through during my stay at the Center for Advanced Study in the Behavioral Sciences. The three exploratory runs reported in this paper were supported in 1957-58 by funds from the Carnegie Corporation of New York. My colleagues and students at Northwestern made many suggestions during the seminars devoted to the formulation of these runs. Professors Richard C. Snyder, George I. Blanksten, and R. Barry Farrell personally participated in the early trial run. Mr. Denis A. Sullivan shared some of the preliminary results from his inventory of propositions in international relations, which further helped guide my selection of key variables. But above all, full credit must go to Mr. Robert C. Noel for developing the mechanics of the simulation in a most creative way, never allowing theoretical objectives to be swamped by practical necessities.

part of the nineteenth century, the "free" game was reinstated, in which the game "director," a battle-experienced military officer, determined the outcomes of plays on the basis of his judgment. Participants in World Wars I and II employed the war game as a training device—and in World War II, the device was used extensively as a quasi-research tool, for prediction of the outcome of military efforts, such as the Battle of Midway and the invasion of the Ukraine. After World War II the development of the war game continued, returning to more rigid forms with the cumbersome rule book being replaced by the lightning-swift programmed computer. From the point of view of the student of international relations, the flowering of a RAND Corporation effort—the military-political game, COLD WAR, as developed by its Division of Mathematics and the POLITICAL EXERCISE, as initiated by Goldhamer and developed in its Division of Social Science (Goldsen, 1956)—is most useful.[2]

The immediate impetus for explorations in simulation came from the author's work in the social psychology of groups. Since the 1930s, experimental psychologists and sociologists have developed face-to-face groups in laboratories to test theories of group interaction (Cartwright and Zander, 1953; Hare, Borgatta, and Bales, 1955). This work with contrived face-to-face groups has been elaborated in the laboratory study of organizations with component parts at both the Graduate School of Industrial Administration at Carnegie Institute of Technology (Guetzkow and Bowes, 1957) and at Case Institute of Technology. An inter-nation simulation may be thought of as another step in the construction of social systems, the contriving of an interorganizational system.

But the deeper source for this work is found in the developments in decision-making, as exemplified in the work of Simon and Snyder. Simon and his colleagues developed their interests in decision-making from the perspective of public and, later, private administration (Simon, Smithburg, and Thompson, 1950; March and Simon, with Guetzkow, 1958). Snyder and his colleagues developed their ideas from the perspective of decision-making in foreign politics (Snyder, Bruck, and Sapin, 1962; Snyder, 1958).

---

[2] We are most grateful to RAND personnel for the many courtesies extended during our visits to Santa Monica and Washington. Drs. John Kennedy, Robert Chapman, Olaf Helmer, Lloyd Shapley, and Milton Weiner shared their experience in developing the COLD WAR game; Drs. Hans Speier and Joseph Goldsen allowed us many hours for discussion of their POLITICAL EXERCISE.

II. Description of the Inter-Nation Simulation

Contrived face-to-face groups, even when they are created in the experimenter's laboratory, are more replications of reality than they are simulations. The component units—that is, the persons participating in the experiment—necessarily respond to their social environment as human beings even though the environment may be artificially simplified. In the war game, however, there is more role-playing, in which the actors need to imagine many features of the military situation and respond to each other's moves in terms of these self-imposed role conceptions. Usually there is time compression, so that, for example, a month's warfare may be enacted within a day. The mechanical and civil engineer often builds his simulation by reducing his phenomena in scale. The operations research analyst represents the flow of traffic in symbolic form, so that he may use digits in a computer as simulation of a distribution of vehicles. In making such an analogue, there often is simplification, as when traffic is allowed only to turn left or right, even though in reality vehicles can make U-turns. All these devices have been used in developing the inter-nation simulation. We have attempted to represent social units—nations, in this case—in their interrelations with each other. We have simplified and reduced the number of variables involved. We have used both analogies and replication in contriving the parts. *Our simulation is an operating representation in reduced and/or simplified form of relations among social units by means of symbolic and/or replicate component parts.*

When one builds literary and mathematical models, one makes choices as to which features of a system are to be represented (Guetzkow, 1958a). When building social simulations, such choices also must be made. One is forced to specify units and interrelations which often may be left abstract and general in verbal models. The concreteness to be embodied in this description of the inter-nation simulation must not be taken seriously. As the work proceeds, revisions necessarily will make the representation more adequate. Eventually, variations will be introduced in order to check effects of different forms of the simulation. The choice of variables and the representation of their interlocking is highly tentative.

FIVE NATIONS AND THEIR TWO DECISION-MAKERS

In the three initial, exploratory runs described in this paper, five "nations" were operated simultaneously. During the first run,

the nations were manned by one, or two, or three decision-makers. Those three units operated by one participant tended to be outward oriented, with less attention given to internal considerations. The nation which was operated by three decision-makers became quite bogged down in its internal processes, so that it had little time left for inter-state interactions. The unit manned by two decision-makers seemed balanced in its orientations. In the second and third runs, each nation was manned by two participants, senior and graduate students concentrating in political science.

In each unit, then, an "internal decision-maker" (IDM) made the nation's final decisions with regard to over-all policies of the nation as they related to both external and internal considerations. Another participant served as "external decision-maker" (EDM), conducting the relations of his unit with other nations. The EDM reported to the IDM and might have been replaced by the latter. Yet, some IDMs used their EDMs as collaborators in their decisions. The two positions attempt to represent decision-making as it encompasses the nation as a whole, especially as the government relates to its resources and society, and as the nation relates to an external environment, consisting of other nations.

OFFICE-HOLDING

Considerable effort was made to embed the external decisions in the internal environment. The decision-makers were under pressure to maintain themselves in office. Office-holding depended upon the extent to which the expectations of the nation's validators (e.g., citizens, élites, juntas, and other forces which maintain decision-makers in office) were met. The probability of being maintained in office depended upon calculations made by the researchers as to how well both external and internal goals were being achieved by the nation in question. At the end of three periods of decision-making, the retention or loss of office was ascertained in each nation on the basis of random determinations (with the probability set as the average of the probabilities obtained for each period). By averaging probabilities, the decision-makers were able to take long-range points of view in making decisions which might decrease their momentary chances for office-holding. Such a situation typically occurs in electoral processes in which there is delayed response to official actions. However, when the probability of office-holding decreased to specified critical levels, an immediate determination was calculated, even though the routine determina-

tion was still some periods off. Such consequences simulated revolutions and coups d'état.

NATION-GOALS

In the experiment each nation attempted to accomplish its goals, which then served as a basis for its decisions. In two of the runs, the goals were formulated by the decision-makers themselves; in the third simulation, goals were assigned to the IDMs by the researchers. Goals included objectives such as security, domination, cooperation, and internal growth.

RESOURCE DECISIONS

Each nation periodically received basic resources which it could allocate to its internal functioning or utilize in external affairs, either as aid or as strategic strength. Its internal use of these resources could be distributed to its validators for immediate gratification or for building up of basic resources during the coming periods. These decisions were recorded on a decision form by the IDMs, so that they might serve as one of the bases for computation of the probability of office-holding.

INTERACTION AMONG NATIONS

Once each nation had its preliminary goals and had learned how to make its decisions with regard to its resources, the simulation was put into operation. Besides bilateral interaction, the EDMs arranged for conferences of some or all of the nations, with and without their IDMs. The EDMs made treaties, giving aid with or without restrictions. The strategic strength of the nation was used for various purposes, including intimidation of other nations. It was possible for one nation to declare war upon another, alone or with allies. Some nations endeavored to build permanent forms of international cooperation. As the interaction developed, the nations were allowed to reformulate their goals.

In the first exploratory run, there were direct communications among the EDMs in bilateral contacts and at conferences. However, to insure perspective on the total scene by the decision-makers, it was useful to create a communication system beyond the one established by the EDMs. During the second and third runs, an external communications system was devised by the researchers in which events were reported to all nations, so that there was more understanding by the decision-makers of what was happening within the interaction system. In this "world newspaper," reports were made by the researchers on the office losses as they occurred, how aid was extended, and how treaties and alliances were developed. In addition, the EDMs were permitted to publish communiqués and announcements for propaganda purposes.

LABORATORY MECHANICS

The group laboratory of Northwestern's Departments of Psychology and Sociology was used for the experiment, as pictured in Figure 2-1. Although all the participants were physically proximate,

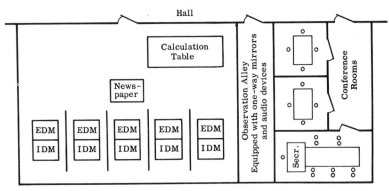

Participants' Tables
EDM and IDM separated by barrier.
Tables separated by floor screens.

FIGURE 2-1. Group Laboratory, Northwestern University.

only written communications were permitted, to allow the researchers to obtain a complete record of the transactions. Within a nation, the IDM and EDM passed messages back and forth by sliding them through the barrier separating the two halves of the table at which they were seated. Nonparticipating messengers carried the internation messages from one EDM to another. Carbons of all messages were given to the researcher-reporter, so that reports for the newspaper could be prepared from those not marked "RESTRICTED." The nations were shielded from each other by screens (not shown in Picture 1 for photographic reasons).

PICTURE 1. Two-member teams of four competing nations at work, with Dr. Guetzkow and Mr. Noel observing.

PICTURE 2. Dr. Guetzkow conferring with the external decision-maker of a nation.

The conferences were conducted at round tables, with various methods of recording. In small conferences, the decision-makers simply passed a sheet of paper back and forth, with all reading the last reply before the next response was begun. In larger conferences, a blackboard in view of all was used for the interchanges. A record was made of the messages immediately, so that each EDM might have a copy of the conference transcript.

An hour was allowed for each period of the simulation. Half-way through the period, the IDMs completed the decision forms, so that the researchers might use them in calculating the probabilities of office-holding. The consequences of their decisions were returned to the decision-makers at the beginning of the following period.

In calculating the outcomes, the researchers used a combination of rigid rules and subjective judgments. For example, the strength of states was mechanically determined from their strategic strength allocations, as combined through their alliances. On the other hand, subjective judgments were made by the simulation director as to how well the nation was achieving its evolving goals. These various measures were then combined into a single validator satisfaction measure, in terms of which office-holding was determined mathematically.

Courtesy Evanston Photographic Service.

PICTURE 3. An inter-nation round table conference.

No attempt is made in this description to give all the details of the simulation in its full concreteness. Only when the design of the simulation settles into more permanent form will it be useful to report with such elaboration. It is hoped that the above description enables the reader to picture the operations. Once we begin using the simulation for particular training or research purposes, it will be necessary, of course, to specify the details. The three runs, each lasting from three to four hours, indicate there is some hope of simulating inter-nation relations in the laboratory.

III. Simulation as Model Building

It is believed that inter-nation simulation will be of heuristic value in clarifying our theories of international relations. Although it is but one of alternative ways of building models about the operation of social systems, its operating character demands a greater clarity in formulation than is often necessitated in literary and mathematical formulations.

To construct an operable representation, one must specify variables with some precision and then interlock the variables with some exactitude. So that the participants and researchers can operate the model at a scale reduced from that of the original being simulated, a limited number of key variables must be selected. One attempts to represent a whole class of variables, such as the economic, by a more limited set of prototypic ones. To provide feedback from the decisions to the decision-makers, one simply must specify the interlocking which exists among the variables—otherwise there will be no interrelation.

As in models which present verbal structures isomorphic to the phenomena being studied, one often has characteristics hidden within the interstices of the model. Because we are using human beings as decision-makers, they bring both their personal characteristics into the model and their own implicit theories of the way in which nations should behave. Eventually it will be necessary to appraise these personal styles of decision-making and organizational presuppositions, so that their influence on the evolving inter-nation interaction may be studied. In one of our exploratory runs, the presence of a decision-maker with a particularly strong interest in dominating other nations was as determinate as the presence, in another run, of a decision-maker who wanted to implement morality standards through development of an international organization.

Perhaps the heuristic values of simulation may be increased by underspecifying parts of the model. To date our strategy has been to build a well structured base for the decisions made within each nation, but to leave the structuring of inter-nation relations ambiguous. Then the interaction generated in the simulation may evolve characteristics of an inter-nation system which are quite independent of the conscious expectations of both the participants and the researchers. It was interesting to note in one run how the demands of the simulated operation forced the development of a clearer division of labor between IDM and EDM than either wanted. Will the development of the inter-nation system force suprastate organizations, above and beyond the nation themselves, when we allow the simulation to continue for ten to fifteen hours instead of cutting it short at three or four?

It would be feasible to put the calculation of the decision consequences on computers, as is done in the business game of the American Management Association (Ricciardi and Craft, 1957). Should the translation of the decisions into office-holding probabilities be made more complicated, it may be necessary to do this. Oliver Benson has developed an all-computer simulation called "A Simple Diplomatic Game" (1958). Using an IBM 650 Stored Program Computer, Benson is developing a generalized game involving four preparatory sets of input data: national power, interest in other states, the propensity of each of nine powers to act, and geographic location. Nine action decisions may then be fed into the machine, which is programmed to compute a set of consequences, as well as counter-actions. Our simulation differs from both the AMA Business Game and Benson's Diplomatic Game in that our development allows the participants to create consequences as they derive from their intergroup interaction, quite free of programs in the computer.

One of the puzzles encountered in using simulation involving human decision-makers is the extent to which the representation shades into the phenomenon itself. In experimental work with small groups, the social psychologist actually produces face-to-face relations. One would expect in such laboratory replication of the phenomena a surer prediction to the world of nature than when one depends upon the formal isomorphism employed in a simulation. Yet, by using human components—by contriving nations as units which actually interact—to what extent has this simulation become an exemplification of the phenomena themselves? No matter, for when models developed in simulation predict important features of real inter-nation systems, the distinction becomes of little consequence.

Perhaps most exciting is the potential which simulation models hold for exploration of contemporary verbal theories about international relations. It is feasible to simulate such characteristics as variation in size of nation, representing small and great powers in the same interaction system. It is possible to so structure the simulation as to have nations with rapid growth and slow growth in interaction with each other. We have an impressive literature which can provide hypotheses for examination within the inter-nation simulation.

For instance, we might study the proposition by Haas and Whiting that although "the majority of alliances are concluded for purposes of self-preservation, the dynamics of international relations often transform them into pacts of self-extension for at least one of the parties" (1956, p. 162). By examining the messages of the EDMs, we may understand the arguments used in persuading other nations to join alliances. Then, once established, we can check the extent to which the alliance now is used for self-extension. Consider Kennan's hypothesis, that international "conflicts are to be effectively isolated and composed" the more accurate the perception of the given power relationships surrounding the conflict (1954, p. 36). By asking our decision-makers to record their perceptions of power among the units, we can check whether accuracy in such perceptions does lead to more adequate conflict management in the simulation. Because of the costly nature of simulation, it will be wise to explore a number of related hypotheses simultaneously. For example, while one is working Kennan's hypothesis, it would be feasible, by varying the number of nations, to check Kaplan's notion that "mistakes or failure in information can be tolerated more easily if the number of actors is greater" (1957, p. 34).

Gradually tighter bodies of verbal theory are being developed. One might use simulation for exploring these verbal constructions. For example, the theory of political integration created by Van Wagenen and Deutsch and their colleagues at the Center for Research on World Political Institutions might be mirrored in simulation. Would their prediction of a pluralistic security-community among the nations be realized when conditions of mutual responsiveness to each other's needs are simulated? (Deutsch, *et al.*, 1957, p. 66). Or explore Guetzkow's hypothesis that "the more adequately the members of a group envision the techniques of intergroup collaboration as means to their ends, the greater the tendency to move toward collaboration" (1957, p. 54). It would seem feasible to explore Kaplan's constructs of state systems, such as the hierarchical system, even though no exemplification of this phase exists at present in nature. Benson has utilized Quincy Wright's "propensity-to-act" notions in his all-computer simulation.

Once we settle upon a particular design for the inter-nation simulation, it will be feasible to represent the assembly of existent nations. First, one would need to characterize each of these nations on the present variables which are incorporated into the simulation. Using these characterizations as initial conditions, the simulation might be operated, generating consequences—that is, predictions of the evolution of the present international system.

It would seem, however, undesirable—in the present stage of underdevelopment of simulation—to attempt to have our participants role-play particular countries, such as Spain and Indonesia. Would not such encouragement toward role-playing tend to secure reactions in terms of the presuppositions each participant has as to the nature of a particular country's reactions in a foreign policy situation? Then, as was done in the RAND exercise, we would be embodying our participants' theories of how nations are supposed to react rather than exploring reactions produced by the interaction itself.

IV. Use of Simulation for Training

An inter-nation simulation may prove useful for training purposes in a number of situations (Guetzkow, 1958b). It may be used as exercise material in the training of policy-makers, and it may complement texts and lectures in the teaching of international relations to undergraduate and graduate students.

As the war game has been judged of practical value in providing decision-maker experience to military executives, so the manning of an inter-nation simulation may be helpful in the training of foreign policy makers. The business decision-game, developed by the American Management Association, is found useful for certain levels of management training, especially as it allows specialized executives to gain over-all perspectives.[3] It was just in this respect that the

RAND political exercise was thought to have been most fruitful. Goldsen reports,

> The game puts a premium on the mobilization and reordering of preexisting knowledge in relation to a special focus, a focus on political action, policy thinking . . . and the analytic assessments of the consequences of alternative courses of action. Seeing new

---

[3] We are grateful for the many courtesies of Mr. Virgil Kraft in allowing us full access to their simulation without cost.

inter-connections of earlier insights . . . seems to have been considerably fostered by the game . . . (1956, p. 36).

The inter-nation simulation, used in conjunction with substantive training in foreign policy, could provide quasi-practical experiences in the exercise of policy judgment. By making explicit that which is often implicit, the simulation would encourage the use of more sophisticated decision-making procedures. Because the simulation could be arranged to provide a constant bombardment of decision-events, practice in decision-making under continuous pressure might be obtained from its use by policy officers preparing for heavy interaction situations. Perhaps the inter-nation simulation can be developed as an adjunct to the case materials being used in the career development programs for foreign service officers in our Foreign Service Institute.

Undergraduate senior students were involved along with graduate students in the three initial exploratory runs reported herein. Seniors with an international relations course background seemed to profit from the experience more than those without. They felt they were actually making use of their knowledge, as they came face-to-face with the quasi-realities of foreign policy decisions. This opportunity to behave as responsible decision-makers increased their enthusiasms for further understanding of the nature of international politics. They felt they were plumbing the depth and extent of their knowledge. One of the students reported, "The simulation really brought me down to earth. I finally faced the complexities of international relations. All nations wanted their own ways and it's hard to accomplish what you want." The simulation might be integrated as a series of laboratory exercises in international relations. As Alger suggests for an international organization course, the simulation might be designed to demonstrate progressive stages of international structure, going from bilateral relations to international conferences, to intermittent councils, to continuous-session international bodies with and without secretariats (Alger).

The graduate students found their experiences in the simulation rewarding in many of the same ways as the undergraduates. But in addition, they were most intrigued with its potential as a research tool for building explicit theory.

V. References

Alger, C. F., personal communication.

Benson, O., "A Simple Diplomatic Game," in J. N. Rosenau (ed.) *International Politics and Foreign Policy*. New York: Free Press of Glencoe, Inc., 1961, pp. 504-511.

Cartwright, D. D. and A. Zander (eds.), *Group Dynamics: Research and Theory.* New York: Harper & Row, Publishers, 1953.

Deutsch, K. W., S. A. Burrell, R. A. Kann, M. Lee, Jr., M. Lichterman, R. E. Lindgren, F. L. Loewenheim, and R. W. Van Wagenen, *Political Community and the North Atlantic Area: International Organization in the Light of Historical Experience.* Princeton: Princeton University Press, 1957.

Goldsen, J. M., *The Political Exercise, an Assessment of the Fourth Round.* Washington, D.C., The RAND Corporation, D-3640-RC, May 30, 1956, mimeographed.

Guetzkow, H., "Building Models About Small Groups," in R. Young (ed.) *Approaches to the Study of Politics.* Evanston, Ill.: Northwestern University, 1958, pp. 265-281.

————, "Training for Policy-Making Roles Through Organizational Simulation," *Proceedings, 14th Annual Conference, American Society of Training Directors,* May, 1958, pp. 76-79.

————, "Isolation and Collaboration: A Partial Theory of Inter–National Relations," *Journal of Conflict Resolution,* I (1957), 48-68.

————, and Anne E. Bowes, "The Development of Organizations in a Laboratory," *Management Science,* III (1957), 380-402.

Haas, E. B. and A. S. Whiting, *Dynamics of International Relations.* New York: McGraw-Hill Book Co., Inc., 1956.

Hare, E. A. P., E. F. Borgatta, and R. F. Bales (eds.), *Small Groups: Studies in Social Interaction.* New York: Alfred A. Knopf, 1955.

Kaplan, M. A., *System and Process in International Politics.* New York: John Wiley & Sons, Inc., 1957.

Kennan, G. F., *Realities of American Foreign Policy.* Princeton: Princeton University Press, 1954.

Malcolm, D. G. (ed.), *Report of System Simulation Symposium.* New York: American Institute of Industrial Engineers (and co-sponsored by the Institute of Management Sciences and Operations Research Society of America), 1958.

March, J. G. and H. A. Simon with H. Guetzkow, *Organizations.* New York: John Wiley & Sons, Inc., 1958.

Ricciardi, F. M. and C. J. Craft, *Top Management Decision-Simulation: The AMA Approach.* New York: American Management Association, 1957.

Simon, H. A., D. W. Smithburg, and V. A. Thompson, *Public Administration.* New York: Alfred A. Knopf, 1950.

Snyder, R. C., "A Decision-Making Approach to the Study of Political Phenomena," in R. Young (ed.) *Approaches to the Study of Politics.* Evanston, Ill.: Northwestern University Press, 1958, pp. 3-38.

————, H. W. Bruck, and B. Sapin (eds.), *Foreign Policy Decision-Making.* New York: The Free Press of Glencoe, Inc., 1962.

Session of the
Permanent Representatives
to the International
Organization.

Courtesy Michael McGuire.

Courtesy Ernie George.

Summit Meeting of Heads of State.

39

Courtesy Herb Comess.

Country Offices.

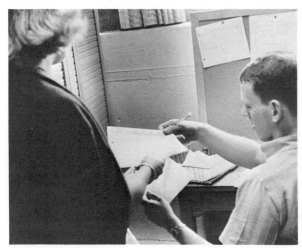

Courtesy Herb Comess.

Erga's External Decision-
Maker Dispatching Message
via Courier.

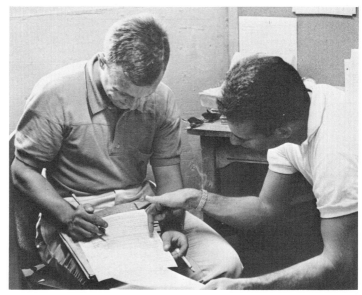

Courtesy Herb Comess.

Bilateral Conference Among External Decision-Makers of Allies.

Courtesy Michael McGuire.

Foreign Ministers' Conference of "A-E-Z" Bloc.

Staff of World Newspaper.

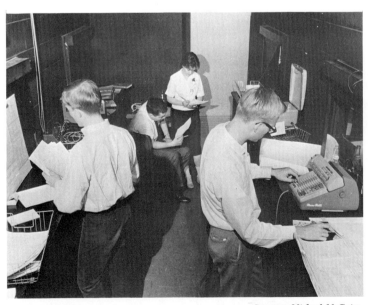

The "Computer": The Calculations Room.

Chapter Three

Inter-Nation Simulation
Participants' Manual

Robert C. Noel

I. An Overview of Inter-Nation Simulation

In representing an inter-nation system, this simulation uti-
lizes five "nation" units, each consisting of three or more participants—a "central decision-maker" holding office, one or two
"external decision-makers," and an "aspiring decision-maker,"
who is out of office. The development of relations among these
nations derives from the characteristics of the nations, and from
the rules and procedures governing the interactions among the

nations. The laboratory environment also influences the relations among nations.

The impact of the particular participants involved in the simulation probably is great, and stems from the personal characteristics of the individuals themselves, including such factors as their problem-solving styles and their motivations. Further, the participants bring to the simulation value-orientations, growing out of differences in social and cultural background. The individuals who serve as decision-makers also come with expectations as to how nations do and should interrelate. All these ingredients play an important part in determining the way in which the simulation is developed by its participants.

The internal organization of the nation is determined in large measure by the participants. The central decision-maker represents the chief of state and performs the executive function of government. He maintains his position by satisfying those who validate his office-holding. The external decision-makers represent the foreign relations structure of the nation and perform the corresponding function. They are dependent upon the central decision-maker for continuance in office. These decision-makers within a nation communicate directly with each other. The apportionment of responsibilities among the decision-makers is optional. The aspiring decision-maker(s) represent leaders of competing élites in the nation who seek to gain office.

The more highly programmed part of the simulation is the set of relations among the intranational factors specified in this manual. It was noted that each nation contains a set of decision-makers. They maintain themselves in office by virtue of their ability to satisfy intranational groups who validate their office-holding. Satisfactions are derived by these "validators" from two sources, each intended to represent a cluster of factors operating in the political, economic and social life of the nation. Given the basic capability of his simulated nation, the central decision-maker periodically makes short-term allocations to: (1) the validators' consumption of goods and services; and/or (2) his nation's force capability, both of which yield satisfactions for the validating groups. It is also possible for the central decision-maker to plan for the long term by allocating his nation's basic resources to the generation of more basic capability, which in turn may be used for future allocations. The opposing aspirant decision-maker appeals to the same validators in the hope of getting into office.

Increases in validator satisfaction generally result in increases in the probability of holding office for the central decision-maker. However, in some nations the decision-makers must be very sensitive to deprivations imposed upon their validators—in other nations decision-makers have wide latitude in the conduct of their nation's internal affairs. In all cases, however, the central decision-maker may lose office to an aspiring decision-maker who promises better to satisfy the validators' wants. This can happen either through orderly procedures or through disorderly political processes, such as revolution.

But the nations do not exist in isolation. They are allowed to communicate with each other through their external decision-makers. Direct, bilateral communications among the nations are complemented by multilateral conferences. Supplementing these communications, there is a communication system external to the decision-makers themselves, a "world newspaper." The press issues statistical reports, and publishes news items from its analysis of inter-nation communications and developments, as well as from intelligence sources. This information aids the decision-makers in understanding the current status of the always changing inter-nation system.

The interrelations among the nations may develop in many ways. Some of the nations may trade their resources, either in "raw" form as basic capability, or in converted form as force capability and consumption "units." Some decision-makers may make grants of aid to other nations within the system. It may be that alliances will develop, based upon inter-nation treaties. It is possible for the nations to establish international organizations. Should conflict develop within the system, nations may even go to war against each other.

Although the over-all consequences of many of the decisions the participants make in this simulation are generally predictable, at times the system will behave in seemingly unusual ways. In part, this characteristic is due to certain probabilistic techniques used in computing the consequences of decisions. In part, it will result from innovations introduced by the decision-makers in the system.

In these ways, then, an endeavor has been made to construct a simulation which will represent important features of the processes involved in international relations. The decision-makers work within a conceptual environment similar to the decision-environment confronted by members of governments.

TIME

As an aid to understanding what follows in this manual, a brief note may be inserted here about the time dimension in the inter-nation simulation. Time is greatly compressed. As a result the participant will find himself short on time throughout most of the exercise. The basic unit of time is the "period." It is seventy-five minutes in length. At the beginning of each period the decision-makers are given copies of the Decision Form (Figure 3, pp. 66-67)* for their nation. It contains the results for the nation of the previous period's decisions. Of course, in the first period these data will have come from the researcher, but they will provide historical background on each nation as an aid to the decision-makers in the beginning period. The Decision Form also contains blanks for entering the decisions made in the current period. The central decision-maker is responsible for completing this section of the Decision Form within thirty minutes from the time he receives it at the beginning of the period. It will then be collected. The period ends in another forty-five minutes. At the end of the period a new Decision Form is distributed, marking the beginning of the next period. During the forty-five-minute interval, when the Decision Form is being processed, the decision-makers are free to work out domestic problems and conduct international relations. This interval may be used fruitfully by the decision-makers to develop communications and negotiations, and to enter into agreements which may influence decisions to be recorded on subsequent Decision Forms.

II. The National Political System

THE DECISION-MAKERS

Each of the nations in the simulation has two or three decision-makers; a central decision-maker who holds office (CDM), two external decision-makers (EDM_x and EDM_y), and an aspiring central decision-maker who seeks to gain office (CDM_a).

Central Decision-Maker (CDM)

The central decision-maker possesses final authority in all decisions within the limits set by the risk of losing office. He should have in his focus all matters of state policy, domestic and international. At his own discretion the central decision-maker may discharge one or both of his external decision-makers.

---

* Other forms used in the inter-nation simulation are also displayed at the end of this chapter.

External Decision-Makers (EDM$_x$ and EDM$_y$)

External decision-makers are responsible directly to the central decision-maker. The external decision-makers should have primarily in view the international affairs of their nation. They conduct all regular negotiations with other nations. The division of labor with regard to the making of foreign policy is determined by the central decision-maker.

Aspiring Central Decision-Maker (CDM$_a$)

The aspiring central decision-maker is a member of the nation, but not a member of the government. He seeks to become central decision-maker by appealing to those who validate office-holding. These appeals take the form of a set of policy decisions similar to those made by the office-holding CDM. They say, in effect, "Here is what I would do if I were in office." In addition, he writes a periodic foreign policy paper. If his policies are sufficiently more attractive than the present central decision-maker's, he may replace the latter in office.

THE VALIDATORS

In addition to its decision-makers, each nation has its validators. The validators exist, however, only conceptually. Their function in the national political system is represented by certain decision consequences computed by the researcher.

The validators are conceived as those individuals and groups of individuals in the political system who occupy positions of power outside the immediate purview of top level governmental decision-making power. The validators have wants and goals which are more or less satisfied by the outcomes of governmental decisions. Because they occupy positions of power in the system, they are able to make their satisfactions and/or dissatisfactions felt by the central decision-maker (CDM). If they are satisfied, they will support his tenure in office. If they are not satisfied, on the other hand, they will support the efforts of an aspiring decision maker (CDM$_a$) to acquire office.

Validator Satisfaction

Two kinds of wants are possessed by the validators of a nation: consumption standard wants and national security wants. Their intensity varies from nation to nation and time to time. Each is a source of varying amounts of satisfaction or dissatisfaction, depending upon the degree to which it is gratified or not. Thus, over-all validator satisfaction consists of two components. They are called: (1) validator satisfaction with regard to consumption satisfaction (Decision Form, line 1); and (2) validator satisfaction with regard to national security (Decision Form, line 2). Each component is measured on an eleven-point scale.

TABLE 3-1 | VALIDATOR SATISFACTION SCALE

10   maximum satisfaction

9⎫
8⎬ high satisfaction
7⎭

6   moderately high satisfaction

5   indifference

4   moderately low satisfaction (moderate dissatisfaction)
___ [revolution threshold, p. 51 ff.]

3⎫
2⎬ low satisfaction (high dissatisfaction)
1⎭

0   minimum satisfaction (maximum dissatisfaction)

THE RELATION OF DECISION-MAKERS TO VALIDATORS

Decision Latitude

The ability of the validators to translate their satisfactions and/or dissatisfactions into effective support for or opposition to the CDM varies, however, from nation to nation and from time to time. In the simulation this effectiveness of validator support or opposition is expressed as "decision latitude," for the freedom of action of the CDM is the other side of the same coin. The concept of decision latitude is fundamental in the national political system. It expresses the sensitivity of the relation of decision-makers to validators. On the one hand, a central decision-maker in a system with a great amount of decision latitude may operate with relative impunity, regardless of the dissatisfaction of his validators; his likelihood of retaining office is not responsive to the level of over-all satisfaction among his validators. On the other hand, a central decision-maker whose system offers little decision latitude must ponder seriously the dissatisfaction of his validators; his likelihood of retaining office is very responsive to the level of over-all satisfaction among his validators. Decision latitude is measured on a ten-point scale.

TABLE 3-2 | DECISION LATITUDE SCALE

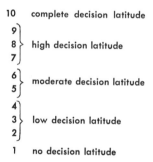

10	complete decision latitude
9 8 7	high decision latitude
6 5	moderate decision latitude
4 3 2	low decision latitude
1	no decision latitude

Changing Decision Latitude

There are two ways in which decision latitude (DL) may change. First, changes can be made in any period by the validators. The validators may become more effective, or less effective, as a result of actions taken independently of the decision-makers. These changes are noted on the Decision Form (line 42) received by the central decision maker at the beginning of a period.

Second, although the central decision-maker ordinarily must accept the changes initiated by the validator, he also can oppose the desires of his validators. The CDM can increase DL even though the validators intended that DL should stay the same or decrease. Similarly, he can prevent the validator from decreasing the DL, though not raising it himself. But there are costs involved in securing these pressured changes. The validators become dissatisfied when their decision-makers oppose their political preferences. The resulting disturbance in the national political system exacts a cost in terms of the "basic capability" of the nation. The force capability of the nation is reduced. All these costs become greater as the discrepancy between the CDM and validator positions becomes greater and as decision latitude itself approaches very high levels.

Decision Latitude and the Transference of Power

A basic feature of the national political system is the close relationship between decision latitude and provisions for the transference of political power. Assuming no change in the apparatus of internal control in a nation, the greater the decision latitude, the
greater the risk of disorderly transference of power within the nation, and vice versa. Worded differently, the greater the freedom of
action of the decision-makers, whether vested in them voluntarily or
forcibly, the greater the latent revolutionary potential among the
validators. These factors are treated in greater detail in the next section and in the section on "The Use of Force Capability—Internal
Controls" (p. 56).

THE TRANSFERENCE OF POLITICAL POWER

During each period in the simulation the central decision-maker
is informed by the researcher as to the probability of his retaining
office as contrasted with the probability of the aspiring decision-
maker (CDM_a) gaining office. The probability of office-holding depends upon: (1) the over-all level of validator satisfaction; and (2)
decision latitude, which, as will be recalled, indicates the effectiveness of validator support for or opposition to the CDM. The probability of office-holding is measured on an eleven-point scale. The
numbers may be considered as the chances in ten that office will be
retained by the CDM or gained by CDM_a.

TABLE 3-3 | SCALE FOR PROBABILITY OF OFFICE-HOLDING

10	certainty of office-holding
9⎫ 8⎬	high probability of office-holding
7⎭	
6	moderately high probability of office-holding
5	even probability of holding or losing office
4	moderately low probability of office-holding
3⎫ 2⎬	low probability of office-holding
1⎭	
0	certainty of losing office

The Orderly Transference of Power

To simulate the customary, orderly change of personnel in positions of power in a nation, there is a regular determination of office-holding every two periods. A probabilistic decision is made by the researcher on the basis of the average likelihood of office-holding for the CDM and CDM$_a$ over the two periods. Consequently, a low likelihood of office-holding in one of the two periods may be offset by the CDM with a high likelihood in the other period.

Should this determination be against the central decision-maker, he is replaced in office by an aspiring decision-maker. External decision-makers may or may not be kept on, at the discretion of the new CDM. Should the determination be in favor of the central decision-maker, he continues in office until another determination is made.

The Disorderly Transference of Power

Irregular, disorderly changes of personnel in positions of power in a nation are simulated in the following manner:

The risk of revolution is encountered by all nations when over-all validator satisfaction drops to or below a threshold of three units (See Table 3-1, p. 48). This risk is measured on an eleven-point scale (numbers 0-10). It varies from nation to nation and from time to time depending upon: (1) current decision latitude in the nation, as has been seen; and (2) the probability of successful revolution. The greater the decision latitude and the greater the probability of successful revolution, the greater the risk of having a revolution when over-all validator satisfaction drops below the revolution threshold. Thus, any CDM action that causes validator satisfaction to drop to the revolution threshold may trigger a revolution, depending upon the level of decision latitude at the time and the probability of a revolution being successful. A pressured increase in decision latitude is potentially one such action. Others will be discussed presently.

The revolution process is as follows: if, at the end of *any* period, over-all satisfaction drops under the revolution threshold, an *immediate* probabilistic decision is made by the researcher *to determine whether or not revolution occurs*. This decision is made on the basis of the risk of revolution in the nation at that time.

If revolution does not occur, the CDM retains his office and the orderly process for the transference of power prevails (even if validator satisfaction approaches zero).

If revolution does occur, a second probabilistic decision is made by the researcher *to determine its outcome.* The probability of successful revolution (the probability of CDM office *loss* via revolution) depends upon the degree of internal control (see p. 56) that the central decision-maker exercises over the validators in the nation. This probability is used by the researcher to decide the outcome of the revolution.

If the revolution is put down, the central decision-maker retains office. If the revolution is successful, he loses office to an opposing CDM_a.

Whether a revolution is put down or is successful, it still exacts a toll on the nation. The costs of revolution are expressed as about 20 per cent of the nation's basic capability units. In addition, there are strategic costs amounting to the total number of strategic capability units devoted to internal control in the period of revolution. Offsetting these costs to some extent is a reward—an increase of *two* units in over-all validator satisfaction. This occurs, in the case of a revolution which is put down, as a result of the regime having silenced hostile elements among the validators. In the case of a successful revolution, it occurs as a result of the validators having put a man to their liking in power. However, in both cases this period of respite is only temporary; over-all validator satisfaction decreases again by one unit in each of the two subsequent periods marking a return to normalcy.

In all other respects the internal workings of a nation function as usual after a revolution.

III. The National Economic System

The national economies in the simulation provide for the allocation of resources to the production of three different kinds of goods and services. Full economic decision-making power lies with the central decision-maker, since there is nothing analogous to a private economic sector.

BASIC CAPABILITY

All kinds of basic resources, physical and human, are subsumed under the concept of "basic capability." The size of a nation's basic capability accumulation reflects the nation's over-all, fundamental ability to produce all other goods and services. Consequently, it provides a measure of national wealth. Economic growth and/or stagnation are seen in its trends through time.

Decisions are made each period by the central decision-maker as to the kinds of production to which his nation's basic capability accumulation will be allocated. Each nation is given an initial amount of basic capability units (BC's) at the beginning of the simulation (BC_{beg}; Decision Form, line 9). These are available for allocation during the first period. Additions to the nation's BC accumulation (economic growth) may be achieved by: (1) devoting some portion of the initial amount to the generation of new BC's (BC_{bc} decision; Decision Form, line 10); or (2) the receipt of BC's from other nations in trade or aid. None of these newly acquired BC's is available for allocation in turn until the period following the acquisition. The same procedure is followed at the beginning of each simulation period.

In making decisions regarding the acquisition of new basic capability, the CDM should be mindful of the fact that the amount of BC's possessed by his nation at the beginning of any period will be reduced by the researcher at the end of the period by from 2 to 10 per cent, reflecting depreciation and obsolescence. To this depreciated amount will be added the *net* increment in BC's in that period (*i.e.*, new BC's remaining in the nation after all trade and aid). This sum is the nation's accumulated BC's at the end of the period—the same amount that will be available for allocation at the beginning of the next period.

Basic Capability and Validator Satisfaction

Validator satisfaction *is not* directly related to the amount of BC's a nation possesses. Its relationship is indirect through growth in the nation's ability to generate other goods *which are* directly related to validator satisfaction.

CONSUMPTION SATISFACTIONS

A portion of a nation's basic capability may be devoted to the production of goods and services to support the population. These items are termed "consumption satisfaction" units (CS's) in the simulation. They may be thought of as representing all goods and services which contribute to the standard of living of the population, particularly the validators.

During each period the CDM *must* allow a specified minimum number of CS's to remain in the nation for consumption. This is called the minimum consumption standard (CS_{min}; Decision Form, line 30). The CDM may obtain these by allocating a portion of his basic capability to the generation of CS's (BC_{cs} decision; Decision Form, line 20), or by receipt of CS's from other nations in trade or aid. There is no accumulation of CS units from period to period, as is the case with BC's. All of the CS's remaining in the nation after generation, trade, and aid are consumed in the same period (CS_{end}; Decision Form, line 29).

Consumption Satisfaction and Validator Satisfaction

Validator satisfaction with regard to consumption (VS_{cs}; Decision Form, line 1) is calculated by the researcher after the Decision Forms are collected for each period. It is determined by the ratio of the number of CS's actually left in the nation (CS_{end}) to the minimum consumption standard (CS_{min}).

The relationship between validator satisfaction with regard to consumption satisfaction and the above ratio may vary among the several nations and at different times. This represents variation in the intensity of validator wants. Generally, the greater the number of CS's actually remaining in the nation compared to the minimum consumption standard, the greater the validator satisfaction. This relationship is not the same for all nations; the validators in nations having significantly greater capacity for generating CS's are less sensitive to given changes in the number of CS's received than are the validators in nations with little capacity to produce CS's.

FORCE CAPABILITY

A portion of a nation's basic capability may be devoted to the production of military goods and services. These are termed "force capability" units (FC's) in the simulation. They may be thought of as representing all goods and services which contribute to the military capability of the nation. Since force capability is a factor of major political importance to the nation, not merely an economic item, it is treated in detail below.

GENERATION RATES

As the term implies, "generation rate" refers to the number of units of goods and services that can be generated with one basic capability unit. Only basic capability has the power of generation. In the national economic system there are three different generation rates: (1) the new *BC* generation rate (Decision Form, line 11); (2) the *CS* generation rate (Decision Form, line 21); and (3) the *FC* generation rate (Decision Form, line 32).

These rates vary from nation to nation, according to the stage of economic development of the nation as reflected by the *BC* accumulation. Differential generation rates provide incentive for international trade and specialization, according to the principle of comparative advantage.

IV. Force Capability

Each nation is given a current accumulated number of force capability units at the beginning of the simulation (FC_{beg}; Decision Form, line 8). To this amount the CDM may make additions by devoting some portion of his initial basic capability to the generation of *FC*'s (BC_{fc} decision; Decision Form, line 31), or by the receipt of *FC*'s from other nations in trade or aid. The same procedure is followed at the beginning of each period. In making decisions regarding the acquisition of new strategic capability, the CDM should be mindful of the fact that the number of *FC*'s possessed by his nation at the beginning of any period is reduced by the experimenter at the period's end from 20 to 40 per cent, reflecting depreciation, obsolescence and operating costs. To this depreciated amount will be added the net increment in *FC*'s (*i.e.*, new *FC*'s remaining with the state after all trade and aid). This sum is the nation's accumulated *FC*'s at the end of the period—the same amount with which the nation begins the following period (FC_{beg}; Decision Form, line 8).

FORCE CAPABILITY AND VALIDATOR SATISFACTION

Validator satisfaction with regard to national security (VS_{ns}; Decision Form, line 2) is calculated by the experimenter after the Decision Forms are collected each period. It is determined by a ratio measure representing the strength of a nation and its allies in relation to the strongest nation (or group of nations) not allied with it. This strength measure includes both force capability and basic capability, the latter being regarded as potential force capability.

The relationship between validator satisfaction with regard to national security and the relative strategic position of the nation is positive. Generally, the greater the relative strategic position of a nation, the greater the validator satisfaction with regard to national security—but *only to a point.* Beyond that point, when a nation together with its allies is approximately three times stronger than its strongest nonally (or allied group of nonallies), this component of validator satisfaction ceases to increase with increases in relative strategic position; it has been maximized. At the other extreme, when a nation's relative strategic position becomes very unfavorable, the nation, in effect, is no longer considered in the world military competition; the validators become indifferent to the nation's force capability in world affairs. This latter state of affairs is indicated on the Decision Form (line 2) by no entry in the VS_{ns} space; then over-all validator satisfaction is calculated from one rather than two components.

THE USE OF FORCE CAPABILITY—INTERNAL CONTROLS

There are two uses to which force capability may be put: war and internal controls in the nation. The former is discussed at length in a later section. The latter will be discussed here.

In the discussion of the disorderly transference of power (pp. 51 ff.) it was indicated that *the risk of having a revolution*, once validator satisfaction drops below the revolution threshold, depends in part upon *the probability of successful revolution*, and in part on *decision latitude*. It was also indicated there that the *probability of successful* revolution, should revolution occur, depends upon the degree of internal control the CDM exercises over the validators in the nation. It is these relationships that point up an important function of internal controls in the national political system. Without the application of internal controls revolutionary potential builds in the political system as decision latitude increases. And, should a revolution be triggered, the absence of internal controls increases the probability of it successfully deposing the CDM. Consequently, internal controls constitute an important political tool for the CDM.

These controls may be applied by a CDM decision *each* period. He may allocate a portion of the nation's force capability accumulation to internal controls (FC_{ic} decision; Decision Form, line 41). The greater the size of the allocation, the less the revolutionary potential in the political system, up to a point—control is maximized when 30 per cent of total FC's is applied. And, of course, control is at a minimum (revolutionary potential at a maximum) when no FC's are applied.

Whatever portion of FC's is allocated to internal controls in this way, it remains a part of the nation's total FC's. At the beginning of each period its depreciated value is included in the new total FC accumulation. If there is revolution in the nation, however, these

FC's are consumed (cf. p. 52). Any *FC*'s applied to internal controls are *not* considered in the periodic assessment of the nation's relative international strategic position. Thus, they do not contribute to validator satisfaction with regard to national security.

Another way in which force capability is used for internal controls has been indicated earlier in the discussion of "changing decision latitude" (cf. pp. 49 ff.). It was seen that, in cases where the CDM conflicts with the validators by increasing his decision latitude or maintaining it at a constant level, he may, nevertheless, forcibly implement his change by using force capability against them. Force capability used in this way does not enter into the calculation of the probability of successful revolution described above. A fixed amount of *FC*'s are automatically assessed at the end of a period in which the CDM forces a change in decision latitude. These *FC*'s are consumed in the process of bringing about the change. Consequently, they also do not enter into the calculation of the nation's world strategic position and validator satisfaction with regard to national security.

V. The International Politico-Economic System

The international politico-economic system contains few integrated, well-structured features. All kinds of international interaction are permissible in the simulation. The points which follow merely specify rules and consequences of certain kinds of interaction.

TRADE AND AID

It has been seen that, as a result of inter-nation differences in the generation rates for new *BC*'s, *CS*'s, and *FC*'s, international economic specialization and trade may be advantageous for the nations. This is so because the principle of comparative advantage has been incorporated in the simulation. All trading is by barter, since there is no monetary unit. And, since there is nothing analogous to a private sector of the national economies, trade restrictions (in the usual sense of tariffs, exchange controls, quotas, etc.) are precluded from the international economy.

To consummate a trade or aid transaction, the representatives of the two nations fill out in duplicate and endorse an "Official Exchange Record." This may be done in conference or by passing the "Exchange Record" via the regular methods of communication. Each representative should end up with one copy of the completed "Exchange Record" to be attached to his nation's Decision Form in the period when the transaction takes place. Of course, appropriate entries also must be made by the CDM in the spaces provided on the Decision Form. As noted earlier, *BC*'s received in trade are not available for allocation until the period following the consummation of the transaction. *CS*'s and *FC*'s received or given in trade are added (or subtracted) to those remaining at home, the sum being related to validator satisfaction at the end of the period in which the transaction is consummated.

INTERNATIONAL AGREEMENTS

Any and all other kinds of international agreements may be made by the decision-makers at their will, including the establishment of international organizations. Each, however, must be formally consummated by the representatives of the parties. They do this by drafting and endorsing the agreement and registering it with the researcher. Forms are provided for this purpose. It may be done in conference or by passing the registration form via the regular methods of communication. Enough copies should be made to provide one for the experimenter and one for the file of each representative. The experimenter's copy should be given to him *immediately* upon consummation of the agreement. Alliances involving force commitment are treated in the same manner. However, the size of the *FC* commitment must be indicated on the document for the nation to receive the validator satisfaction benefits of the alliance. When a nation enters into a strategic alliance with another, it automatically enters into strategic alliance with all the allies of the other nation.

WAR

War is one possible kind of interaction among nations. There are no restrictions as to when war may occur. When war does occur, the belligerent nation(s) receive(s) an automatic two-unit increase in over-all validator satisfaction for the period in which the war breaks out. However, this "rallying to the cause" among the validators is not lasting. In each of the two subsequent periods validator satisfaction decreases by one unit. The rules and consequences of war in the simulation are as follows:

The Declaration of War

A nation may declare war on another at any time. A formal declaration is sent to the "target nation" by way of the regular methods of communication, the only difference being that a "red flag" should be attached to all three copies of the declaration message. On a separate form the nation making the declaration, the "attacking nation," indicates the amount of force capability that it is committing to the war. It may be all or any part of the nation's total FC's which are not currently in use for internal controls. This information is restricted.

If any of the attacking nation's allies go to war simultaneously, each must make a formal declaration and force capability commitment in the same manner.

The nation against which war has been declared, the "target nation," has fifteen minutes within which it must respond to the declaration. This allows time for consultation with its allies. It may respond with or without its allies in any way it sees fit. If the response is a return declaration of war, the procedure is the same as for the attacking side—i.e., a formal declaration and commitment of force capability is made. *If no action is taken by the target nation the outcome of the war is determined solely by the attacking nation(s).*

The Conduct of War

After the target side makes commitments to the conflict (if it does), the researcher announces publicly the probability of victory for each side. When this announcement is made, another fifteen-minute period is allowed for communication, this time between the two sides to the conflict. This communication may be conducted by way of any of the regular methods. At the end of this period of time the situation is assessed. Three, and only three, states of affairs are possible.

1. The two sides may have negotiated a peace settlement.
2. The two sides may have agreed to call for a decision on the outcome of the war on the basis of the probabilities of victory or defeat announced earlier by the experimenter. This simulates a "decisive battle," and, being such, *both sides must agree to it.*
3. If agreement cannot be reached on numbers 1 or 2, both sides will be called upon for new commitments of force capability to a continuing war. These new commitments are mandatory: fifteen minutes is allowed for the respective sides to consult and decide upon the size of the new

commitments. Then, the procedure described in this paragraph is repeated—and so on until either number 1 or
number 2 is the outcome of the negotiations.

At the end of each set of negotiations between belligerents, all of
the force capability commitments made at the beginning of that
round of fighting by both sides are considered as consumed by the
war—they are irretrievably lost, regardless of the ultimate outcome
of the war. The same is true for a quantity of basic capability units
(BC's) equal to one half the number of FC's committed.

The Outcome of War

In addition to the economic and military costs of a war just
mentioned, there are other consequences. In case 1 the additional
consequences depend upon the peace settlement negotiated. All
regular procedures of the simulation remain the same. Case 3 pro-
longs the war and postpones the additional consequences. In case
2—a call for a "decisive battle"—the nation losing the battle is considered to have surrendered unconditionally. That nation then is
occupied by the victor.

Occupation is simulated in the following way. The decision-
makers of the occupied nations are forced into "exile." They may
continue to communicate among themselves and with other nations
as usual, and they may work to organize support for a liberation
movement. However, they remain "stateless persons" until they are
able to liberate their country or until they are invited by the conqueror to return to office. The Decision Form of the occupied nation
is given, along with full power of decision, to the CDM of the victorious nation. He operates in the occupied nation with maximum
decision latitude, 10, and can only be dislodged from power by a
successful war of liberation or a successful revolution; there are no
regular office-holding determinations. Revolution, that is, attempts
to overthrow the conqueror, may still happen in the usual way (cf
pp. 51 ff.). In fact, they are highly probable. Each period of occupation may trigger one, because the presence of unwanted "foreigners"
in the country creates dissatisfaction—amounting to one-unit decrease per period in over-all validator satisfaction—among the ever-
present validators, thus driving VS_m toward the revolution threshold.
Also, the occupying CDM operates with such high decision latitude
as to inflate the probability of having a revolution. However, he may
reduce the risk of revolution and, at the same time, assure one little

chance of success by applying *his own* FC's to internal controls within the occupied nation (cf. pp. 56 ff.). Any FC's belonging to the conquered nation cannot be relied upon for occupation use. However, all those FC's still in existence in the nation, and all FC's that the winning CDM can generate in the nation during the occupation may be taken as war reparations. The same is true of 25 per cent of the BC's still in existence, and all BC's that can be generated during the occupation. CS's may also be taken as reparations, but at least the minimum number of CS's described above (p. 53) must be left in the nation. More may be left, depending upon how far above zero the occupying CDM wants validator satisfaction with regard to consumption standards to be. No validator satisfaction with regard to national security is calculated for the occupied nation.

If the occupation is ended by liberation, the liberators may establish the new government in the country. If the occupying power is dislodged by successful revolution, the researcher establishes the new government.

Barring a successful liberation or revolution, the length of the occupation is determined by the occupier. He may withdraw his forces at any time, or he may continue the occupation indefinitely. Should he withdraw, he may establish a new government to his liking. He may negotiate with the deposed CDM or with the aspiring CDM to do so; or he may request (the researcher) that other "nationals" of the occupied nation be established as decision-makers. The terms of the treaty of settlement are to be determined by the parties concerned. The decision latitude of the new government will be determined by the researcher, and the nation will return to the normal operations described in this manual.

VI. Communication and Information

COMMUNICATION

Communication procedure in the simulation is designed to give the researcher an accurate, chronological record of all information available to the decision-makers.

Form

All regular communication in the simulation is by written message. Standard message forms in triplicate are provided for this purpose. The messages may or may not be marked "restricted" at the discretion of the sender. Routing instructions for the carbon copies are printed on the message forms. All messages are signed and timed by both sender and recipient.

Channels

The central decision-maker normally communicates directly only with *his* external decision-makers, the *World Times,* and the researcher. The external decision-makers normally communicate directly only with each other, the central decision-maker, external decision-makers of other states, the *World Times,* and the researcher. *Aspiring decision-makers may not communicate with anyone.*

Message Handling

In order to expedite message handling, two short-cut procedures are followed. First, an external decision-maker may pass an *incoming message* from another state on to his central decision-maker. The central decision-maker signs and times the message as having been read by him and files it. Should the CDM wish to comment about the message and return it to the EDM from whom it came, he may do so. In this instance the EDM files the message. Second, *outgoing messages* written by an external decision-maker may be shown to the central decision-maker for inspection before they are sent. The central decision-maker signs and times these messages too, signifying acknowledgement, and returns them to the external decision-maker for sending. However, should the CDM instruct the EDM not to send a message in this case, that is noted on the message form before it is returned to the EDM. The EDM then files all three copies.

Message relaying is handled by the external decision-maker, who may also relay messages between external decision-makers of other nations who may have severed diplomatic relations.

All other regular communications—clarifications, explanations, negotiations, etc.—are written on *separate message forms* and sent through regular channels.

Conferences

The decision-makers of a nation may hold oral conferences among themselves. In addition, oral *international* conferences may be called. The latter may be bilateral or multilateral. During international conferences the normal channels of communication described above may still be used for private communications, but decision-makers at the table, be they central or external, may now communicate directly with each other by way of written messages. All oral conferences, intranational and international, are recorded. However, the only conference transcripts available to the decision-makers are their own notes, copies of agreements, and press coverage.

Message Filing

Each decision-maker keeps a file of all information he receives or originates. In this file, interlaced together *in chronological order* are: (1) all messages received; (2) a carbon of each message sent; (3) international conference notes; (4) a copy of each formal international agreement; and (5) copies of the press publications.

INFORMATION

There are three sources of current information available to the decision-makers: (1) the Decision Form; (2) inter- and intra-state communication; and (3) the *World Times*, a newspaper published by the researcher.

The *World Times* publishes the *Statistical Report*, a record of the results of decisions taken in the various nations. The *Statistical Report* includes the following items for each nation in the simulation.

1. Basic capability at which period ended (BC_{end})
2. Force capability at which period ended (FC_{end})
3. Validator satisfaction re. consumption satisfaction (VS_{cs})
4. Validator satisfaction re. national security (VS_{ns})
5. Over-all validator satisfaction (VS_m)
6. Likelihood of office-holding for CDM
7. Likelihood of office-holding for CDM_a
8. Decision latitude (DL)
9. Risk of revolution (Only when $VS_m < 3$)

Also published from time to time by the *World Times* is the *World Trade Guide,* an aid to decision-makers with regard to the advantages of trade.

At frequent intervals the *World Times* also publishes its regular issues. These contain information about world events obtained from the analysis of unrestricted communications and intelligence information, press releases from decision-makers and international conferences, resolutions, propaganda, inter-state agreements, etc.

From time to time the *World Times* publishes, in addition, analyses and commentaries on world events written by some of the world's leading authorities.

REGISTRATION OF INTERNATIONAL AGREEMENT

☐ Restricted

Between:

Nation_____ Endorsed by_____ at_____
                                    (Decision-Maker)   (time)

Nation_____ Endorsed by_____ at_____
                                    (Decision-Maker)   (time)

Nation_____ Endorsed by_____ at_____
                                    (Decision-Maker)   (time)

Nation_____ Endorsed by_____ at_____
                                    (Decision-Maker)   (time)

Nation_____ Endorsed by_____ at_____
                                    (Decision-Maker)   (time)

Describe agreement here:

Does this agreement embody force capability commitment? Yes_____ No_____

Indicate details of agreement: How many FC's?

FIGURE 3-1. One copy for each party and one for the experimenter. The experimenter's copy is to be given to him *immediately* after all endorsements are made.

WAR

(To be completed by CDM of a nation immediately after it has declared war upon another nation(s).) "RESTRICTED" information.

Nation making declaration:_____

Nation(s) against which declaration is made:_____

FC's committed to war by this nation:_____FC's

    Signed by_____ at_____
          (CDM-?)   (time)
(Space below this line to be filled in by researcher.)

BC's committed to war:_____BC's   (BC's = 1/2 FC's)

Probability of victory of side consisting of nation(s)_____is_____.

Probability of victory of side consisting of nation(s)_____is_____.

_____Negotiated Peace:
                                  1/2 of FC's committed:_____FC's
      War costs to this nation:
                                  1/2 of BC's committed:_____BC's

      Decisive Battle:

          Winning nation(s)_____

          Losing nation(s)_____
                                  all of FC's committed:_____FC's
      War costs to this nation:
                                  all of BC's committed:_____BC's

    War continues for another round:
                                  all of FC's committed:_____FC's
      War costs to this nation:
                                  all of BC's committed:_____BC's

Round_____of war ended at_____.
  (number)   (time)

FIGURE 3-2.

FIGURE 3-3.

DECISION FORM

Nation_____

Period_____

OFFICE DETERMINATION:	Orderly change	Disorderly change	Office retained	Office lost
				↑Check Column

RESULTS OF PREVIOUS PERIOD'S DECISIONS

1. Validator satisfaction re consumption satisfaction (VS_{cs}). . .
2. Validator satisfaction re national security (VS_{ns}) . . .
3. Over-all validator satisfaction (VS_m). . . .
4. Likelihood of office-holding for CDM. . . .
5. Likelihood of office-holding for CDM[a]. . .
6. Decision latitude for present period (DL). . .
7. Risk of revolution from previous period (reported when $VS_m \rightarrow 3$). . .
8. Force capability accumulated as of beginning of period (FC_{beg}). . . _____ FC's
9. Basic capability available for allocation in present period (BC_{beg}). . .

BASIC CAPABILITY

*10. BC's allocated to generation of new BC's (BC_{bc}) _____ BC's
11. BC generation rate: new BC's per 1 BC
12. Newly generated BC's (product lines 10 x 11). . . .(+) _____ BC's

*13. Import trade in BC's (From: _____)
*14. Export trade in BC's (To: _____)
15. Net trade in BC's (sum lines 13 + 14; note + or -). . .( ) _____ BC's

*16. Import aid in BC's (From: _____)
*17. Export aid in BC's (To: _____)
18. Net aid in BC's (sum lines 16 + 17; note + or -). . .( ) _____ BC's

19. Net increase or decrease in BC's (sum lines 12 + 15 + 18; note + or -) ( ) _____ BC's

CONSUMPTION SATISFACTION

*20. BC's allocated to generation of CS's (BC_{cs}) _____ BC's
21. CS generation rate: CS's per 1 BC
22. Newly generated CS's (product lines 20 x 21). . . .(+) _____ CS's

(Repeat)

*23. Import trade in CS's (From: _____ CS's

*24. Export trade in CS's (To: _____ CS's

25. Net trade in CS's (sum lines 23 + 24; note + or -). . . . . . .( ) _____ CS's

*26. Import aid in CS's (From: _____ CS's

*27. Export aid in CS's (To: _____ CS's

28. Net aid in CS's (sum lines 26 + 27; note + or -). . . . . . .( ) _____ CS's

29. CS's remaining in nation (CSend) (sum lines 22 + 25 + 28). . . . . (+) _____ CS's

30. (CSmin) CS's that must remain in nation (Compare with line 29). . . . . . . [_____] CS's

FORCE CAPABILITY

*31. BC's allocated to generation of FC's (BCfc) _____ BC's _____ (Repeat) BC's

32. FC generation rate: FC's per 1 BC

33. Newly generated FC's (product lines 31 x 32). . . . .(+) _____ FC's

*34. Import trade in FC's (From: _____ FC's

*35. Export trade in FC's (To: _____ FC's

36. Net trade in FC's (sum lines 34 + 35; note + or -). . . . . . .( ) _____ FC's

*37. Import aid in FC's (From: _____ FC's

*38. Export aid in FC's (To: _____ FC's

39. Net aid in FC's (sum lines 37 + 38; note + or -). . . . . . .( ) _____ FC's

40. Net increase or decrease in FC's (sum lines 33 + 36 + 39; note + or -) ( ) _____ FC's

*41. Portion of FCbeg (line 8) applied to internal controls this period
     (Express as percentage and as absolute quantity—30% max.) [_____ %] _____ FC's

DECISION LATITUDE

42. Validator initiated changes in decision latitude for next period _____

*43. CDM initiated changes in decision latitude for next period (max - ± unit) _____

* Possible decisions.

† Check that the sum of the three entries on single lines in the check column (lines 10 + 20 +31)
  equals the item on the double line (line 9) at top.

Completed by _____ at _____ . _____
              (Decision-Maker)   (time)

OFFICIAL EXCHANGE RECORD

(Use a separate form for each transaction.)

_____BC's from_____ to_____
(quantity)   (nation)   (nation)

_____CS's. from_____ to_____
(quantity)   (nation)   (nation)

_____FC's from_____ to_____
(quantity)   (nation)   (nation)

Indicate one:

    Trade ☐

    or Aid ☐

              Grant ☐ or loan ☐   If loan, give terms of loan:

    or Repara-☐
      tions

Endorsed by_____at_____
      (Decision-Maker)   (time)

Endorsed by_____at_____
      (Decision-Maker)   (time)

FIGURE 3-4. One copy for each party—to be attached to Decision Form of each nation.

AMERICAN BUSINESS FORMS, INC., — CHICAGO, ILL.

159-3	TO:	FROM:
	TIME SENT:	

MESSAGE:

READ BY   AT TIME: READ BY   AT TIME:

SEND THIS COPY TO ADDRESSEE

GIVE THIS COPY TO EXPERIMENTER

KEEP THIS COPY FOR YOUR FILE

FIGURE 3-5.

Chapter Four

Evolution of the Inter-Nation
Simulation

Robert C. Noel

The early pilot runs of the inter-nation simulation have been sketched but briefly in Chapter Two. Our present goal is to document how we evolved the basic structure of the inter-nation simulation. This chapter describes and discusses three subsequent runs of the simulation conducted for exploratory purposes during 1958 and 1959, giving special attention to improvements made in response to deficiencies revealed by its use. In order to avoid too abstract a treatment, the more analytic parts of this essay are interspersed with concrete descriptions of events as they occurred in the three runs.

Had more detailed, but simultaneously more comprehensive, theories of international relations existed at the time of the initial development of the inter-nation simulation, one such might have been chosen as a foundation for the construction of the simulation. Even then, however, one would have been hard put to choose among competing conceptualizations. Because of our belief that the simulation is essentially an attempt at theory-building for use in research and teaching, it seemed useful to proceed in the early phases of the work in a more intuitive, exploratory way. Our international relations staff group was steeped in the literature of the discipline. One of us was developing an inventory of propositions from important textbooks on the subject (Sullivan, 1962). It was in this milieu that the underlying characteristics of the simulation took form.

Although the work reported below is part of an effort to bring rigor and systematization to international relations, it is prescientific in nature. Recognizing the inadequacy of the pilot runs undertaken during the 1957-58 academic year, we undertook additional runs to fill gaps in our experience with the simulation. We revised our simulation procedures, adding and eliminating features as our feeling for the nature of the exercise grew. We made close observations of our runs while they were in progress; we interviewed participants after the runs were completed.

In the sections below, an attempt is made to convey the flavor of this period of trial and error. Conclusions reached on the basis of past experience are presented along with speculation about useful revisions which then might be undertaken in subsequent runs. Interspersed will be found concrete descriptions of the three exploratory runs themselves.

I. Appraisal of Pilot Runs and Proposed Revisions

The principal conclusion reached as a result of the early pilot runs of the inter-nation simulation undertaken during 1957-58 was that the "miniature world" of the simulation was not so dissimilar to the "real world" as to discourage further efforts. There were important respects, however, in which the simulation was not found comparable.

DEVELOPMENT OF IDEOLOGICAL OVERTONES

Several of the participants argued convincingly that the early intra-nation system model was too heavily weighted with economic considerations—that it focused the decision-maker's attention on the allocation of resources and foreign trade to the exclusion of aspects of national political systems, which are usually considered relevant in international relations. Of particular importance was the contention that the model contained no specific ways through which ideological factors were explicitly programmed. Two steps were taken in an effort to remedy this shortcoming in anticipation of another run of the simulation.

First of all, an implicit feature of the model was made explicit. The relationship between the validators in the domestic polity and the governmental decision-makers had been expressed by a simple linear function, deriving a probability of office-holding for the central decision-maker's regime from an index of over-all validator satisfaction with the results of some of the decisions taken by that regime. Such a linear function, or equation, would be in the form: $y = ax + b$, where the variable y is interpreted as the probability of office-holding, where the variable x is taken as an index of over-all validator satisfaction, and where the constants a and b tell how the straight line connecting office-holding (on the vertical axis) is to be graphed in its relationship to validator satisfaction (on the horizontal axis). Such a graph is given in Figure 5-1c (page 112).

Given our interpretations of the two variables (y as probability of office-holding and x as validator satisfaction), what theoretical interpretation can be made of the two constants (a and b) in this linear equation? Taken in this context, are they in fact fixed constants as we had been assuming?

The a constant gives the slope, or the angle, of the line relating y with x. It may be thought of as reflecting the responsiveness of the office-holders to over-all validator satisfaction. Perhaps, then, this slope was not to be held constant, either through time for any one nation or across nations. Its explicit variation would enable us to characterize the simulated nations on an important dimension. A nation with a large slope (*i.e.*, when the regime's probability of office-holding is represented as sharply responsive to validator satisfaction) could be thought of as typifying aspects of a "direct democracy." Change in the mood of the validators would bring with it a marked change in the stability of the regime. On the other hand, a small slope would seem to describe aspects of an "entrenched autocracy." Change in the satisfaction of the élites would induce little change in the regime's stability.

Interpretation is not complete until the intercept, or b, parameter is taken into account. The b constant gives the point at which the line relating y with x crosses or intercepts the vertical axis, when the relationship between the two variables is graphed as described above. When the over-all validator satisfaction is zero, the probability of office-holding once again may vary from low to high probabilities, depending upon the relative sensitivity of the regime to its validators.

The intercept, then, was inversely related to the slope to create ten possible ways in which office-holding was related to over-all validator satisfaction. Scaled from 1 to 10, these slope-intercept combinations were called "decision latitude." They are displayed in Figure 5-1c (p. 112).[1] As viewed by the decision-maker, the differences between the lines are seen as differences in the freedom of action he enjoys in making his decisions. At the beginning of a run, the nations might be assigned widely varying decision latitudes. The decision-makers would be permitted to change their nations' decision latitudes under specified conditions.

As a second means of building ideological factors, a new source of validator satisfaction was introduced into the next run. The proclivity that "people prefer other people to be like themselves" was attributed to the validators. It was posited that the greater the similarity of other nations' decision latitude values to that of the nation in question, the greater the validator satisfaction in the latter nation. It was felt that the introduction of this factor would stimulate the decision-makers to attempt to get other nations to adopt decision latitude values similar to their own—to change the nature of their political systems. Thus, two programmed techniques were evolved whereby international relations in the simulated world might accommodate ideological overtones.

DEFINITION OF NATIONAL INTERESTS

Another dissatisfaction noted in the pilot work concerned "setting the world into motion." In role-played games, as Brody notes in Chapter Seven, the simulation usually takes off from contemporary events. In such a highly structured situation, complete with scenario, the participants seldom feel at a loss as to how to begin. In our

---

[1] The exact form of the equation used in a number of runs during and after 1958 is given in Equation 1 of Chapter Five (p. 111).

more abstract game, an initial feeling of ambiguity as to goals was encountered at times in the pilot runs. In an effort to counter this tendency, we first tried the technique of providing national goals which decision-makers must seek and, then, the technique of validating directly the national goals conceived by the decision-makers themselves. Both devices, however, tended to limit innovation and to predetermine international behavior more than seemed fruitful. Our focus was and is to observe such things as the formulation of national interests as they flow from varying definitions of the situation. Consequently, it was decided that the next run of the simulation should be started differently.

Rather than to direct the choice of national goals, the simulator simply provided each decision-maker with a fabricated history of past decisions and a record of political and economic consequences of those decisions in his nation. In this way the participant was provided with an advanced idea of the limits within which he had to work to solve the internal problems that had been programmed into his nation. To avoid shaping the international outcomes, no information was provided, however, concerning past relations among the nations. From their national profiles alone the decision-makers hopefully would develop and choose alternative goals and actions, all of which might be instrumental, to the achievement of long tenure in office. Verisimilitude was developed in this way. As in the simulation, national interests seem continuously the object of ambiguity, as well as controversy, among the statesmen of the world.

NUMBER OF DECISION-MAKERS COMPRISING THE NATION

Of the three different sizes of decision-making units used earlier (one-man, two-man, and three-man), a two-man unit was most appropriate, given the existing level of richness and complexity of the system. There were a central decision-maker (a chief of state) and an external decision-maker (a foreign minister). More than two persons might find too little activity to sustain interest. Fewer than two might eliminate the possibility of developing intraorganizational phenomena, such as a division of labor, coordination, and the delegation of authority, which had lent realism in earlier runs.

MODIFICATION OF INTERNATIONAL RULES AND PROCEDURES

Turning to the international rules and procedures, two facets of earlier experience warranted attention. One concerned procedures for international communications. It had been the practice to allow only written communication in order to keep the interaction pace within bounds and to obtain, simultaneously, a complete record of the interactions. It soon became apparent, however, that in so doing we had eliminated an important incentive for convening international conferences—the opportunity to expedite communication by getting together and talking face-to-face. Face-to-face conferences conducted entirely in writing offered few advantages over non-face-to-face written communication conducted among the various foreign offices. In an effort to remedy this shortcoming, conference procedures were amended to allow impromptu, oral communication concerning matters of procedure and clarification; but written communication was continued for matters of substance.

EXPLICIT ROUTINES FOR WAR

The other modification of international rules and procedures related to provisions for the conduct of war. For the sake of simplicity in the early pilot runs, the participants were told simply that war was available to them as a policy alternative, but it would not be programmed. Instead, the simulation director would merely use his subjective judgment in deciding the outcome. In none of the pilot runs did the decision-makers seriously consider going to war. One participant reported that war was precluded as an alternative by the vagueness of the provisions for its consequences. It was decided that the next run should incorporate more explicit provisions for war. The resulting revisions substituted a stochastic decision for the simulation director's judgment as to the outcome of war. The probability of victory was to be derived from a comparison of the strategic strength of opposing sides. War destruction was introduced, being expressed as reductions of the belligerents' basic and force capabilities. Thus, although the dependence of the war routines on the caprice of the simulation director had been removed, reducing the tendency of the participants to interact directly with him, uncertainty about the outcome of war remained, reflecting the state of affairs as it exists in the world of reality.

These revisions encompassed the central shortcomings brought to light by the pilot explorations. Minor adjustments also were made in details to insure smoother operation of the mechanics of the simulation. Let us turn, now, to an examination of the revised simulation as it operated during the subsequent run, made during the summer of 1958. The chronology is presented in some detail so that the reader may obtain insight into what constitutes the contents of the inter-nation simulation. The detail will serve as a base to allow comparison with subsequent runs, so the reader may judge how the evolution of the simulation occurred.

II. The Simulation in Operation: Summer, 1958

DESCRIPTION OF INITIAL CONDITIONS

After the foregoing revisions were made in the basic structure of the simulation, an extensive run was undertaken during the summer of 1958, the longest one yet conducted. A first session in the morning was used for initiating the subjects into the complicated procedures, with a practice run in the afternoon. Three subsequent days were devoted to eighteen hours of operation, with intermissions of a week between each session. The participants were requested to avoid discussing the simulation in their contacts outside the laboratory, inasmuch as involvement in the simulation creates needs for communication among the participants. Our subjects were recruited from among junior, senior, and graduate students in the social sciences who were attending the summer session of Northwestern University. They were paid a nominal honorarium for the four days' work, in addition to being provided with box lunches during the short noon break.

Although the underlying structure of the simulation was prescribed before any run could be started, it now was necessary to assign particular numbers to the variables characterizing each nation. These initial values of the nation's capabilities, rates of productivity, and decision latitude constituted the concrete characterization of the programmed parts of the system. They represented the results of the various decisions supposedly made in the nation's "past," and in this way constituted an embodiment of each nation's history.

In order to represent something of the variations existing among nations of the real world, initial values were assigned as presented in Tables 1 and 2. The "generation" rates, which reflect the underlying resources and productivity of each nation, were fixed throughout the operation of the simulation. As the system developed, each nation's basic and force capabilities could increase or decrease. The "starting" decision latitudes were arbitrarily given as 9, 7, 5, 3, and 2 for nations G, K, M, P, and S, respectively.[2]

The differences among the nations with respect to their starting

---

[2] During these exploratory runs, letters were used to designate the nations; later artificial names were bestowed (cf. footnote 3, page 94).

capabilities were relatively small in magnitude; there were no giants in the system. On the other hand, the differences in the productivity, or "generation," rates were considerable. Yet, even the richest nation was a long way from being capable of producing quantities of consumer goods sufficient to satiate its validators' desire for a high standard of living with less than its total basic capability. All the decision-makers, especially those of the poorer nations, would be

TABLE 4-1 | COMPARISON OF CAPABILITIES AT BEGINNING AND END OF 1958 SUMMER RUN

NATION	BASIC CAPABILITY		FORCE CAPABILITY	
	Initial Values	End Values*	Initial Values	End Values*
G	10,000	11,100	500	300
K	12,000	19,900	1200	1500
M	14,000	12,600	1400	500
P	16,000	22,000	2400	3500
S	18,000	20,500	2700	3500

* The end values, representing changes in capability at the end of the run, are discussed at the end of chronology, p. 83 below.

TABLE 4-2 | PRODUCTIVITY RATES

NATION	BASIC CAPABILITY UNITS GENERATED PER BC UNIT ALLOCATED	FORCE CAPABILITY UNITS PER BC BC UNIT ALLOCATED	CONSUMER GOODS UNITS GENERATED PER BC UNIT ALLOCATED
G	0.75	0.50	1.00
K	1.00	1.50	1.50
M	1.00	0.50	1.00
P	1.00	2.00	1.50
S	1.00	2.00	1.00

The figures read as follows: Units of X produced each period by each unit of Basic Capability (BC) allocated by the nation's decision-makers for such purposes. Thus Nation P's decision-makers can produce 100 extra Basic Capabilities (i.e., 1.00 × 100), 200 Force Capabilities (i.e., 2.00 × 100), and 150 units of Consumer Goods (i.e., 1.50 × 100) for each 100 units of Basic Capability devoted to such utilization.

under some pressure from their validators to increase consumption levels in the short-run and basic capability accumulations in the long-run. However, the decision-makers were free instead to opt for the diminution of these economically based political pressures by resorting to political rather than economic actions. The validators' desires might be more or less ignored if the decision-makers proved able to attain and/or preserve a high decision latitude. At the beginning of the run, there was much variation in decision latitude among the nations.

The national profiles at the beginning of the run may be summarized as follows: Nation G was underdeveloped and had a past history of internal revolution. At the time of the new regime's accession to power, however, its decision latitude was quite high. Nations K and M, although also underdeveloped, had managed to preserve political stability in the recent past in the face of their economic problems—this in spite of fairly moderate decision latitude in M. Nations P and S, although neither rich nor fully developed, were the wealthiest and strongest nations in the world. They each enjoyed a favorable productivity rate for force capability. The new government about to take over in P was the first such change in some time, whereas S had a history of more frequent, but normal, transitions in its office holders. Unless changed, the political structure in both P and S was such that the office tenure of the decision-makers would be quite dependent upon their ability to satisfy their validators. As noted earlier, no information was provided the new decision-makers about the international history of their contrived world.

CASE CHRONOLOGY

The following description of the extensive run made during the summer of 1958 is presented in the form of a chronology so that, in one instance, the reader may gain more of the feel of how a simulation unfolds. Other runs to be described later in this essay, involving foreign students and professionals, will not be treated in as much detail.

The following narrative is based on data collected by direct observation, through questionnaires administered during the run, perusal of communication records, and personal interviews with the participants after conclusion of the final runs. A description of the simulation as it evolved may be centered initially around the activities of Nation G, which through its two internationally-minded decision-makers, exerted an influence disproportionate to its size. The central decision-maker was an energetic and forceful individual with a clear sense of purpose, who made every effort to build the nation's economy to a point at which it could support a high standard of living. At the same time he attempted to raise current consumption levels. Taking cognizance of G's inability to build and support a sizable strategic force, he sought to secure the nation's integrity through the formation of mutual security agreements.

To achieve these goals the central decision-maker of G initially tried a bilateral approach. Early in the run he requested aid from the other nations. P and S, being the wealthiest, were singled out to receive particularly urgent appeals. These efforts met with little success. The decision-makers of P felt that nothing should be done to help the regime in G because of its high, autocratic decision latitude. Proud of their low decision latitude, P's decision-makers flatly refused G's request. Preoccupied with internal concerns, the decision-makers of Nation S failed even to answer G's appeals. At best, G's bilateral approaches to the solution of her economic problems produced meager results. A small but advantageous trade with Nation K, which itself sought economic aid, was the net outcome.

Motivated by the urgency of his nation's needs, G's central decision-maker soon changed tactics. Though continuing his nation's efforts to conclude bilateral arrangements, he changed to a multilateral strategy in the economic sphere. At his initiative an international summit meeting was convened, ostensibly to discuss world problems in general, but actually to hear G's proposals for the establishment of an international bank for economic development. The initial session of the conference was attended by all heads of state, accompanied by their external decision-makers.

After some discussion, the conference unanimously approved the principle that an international bank should be established. Nations G, K, and M were in favor of the idea, while S did not seem concerned either way. P's support was cleverly, but conditionally, enlisted: G had timed a decrease in decision latitude to coincide with the beginning of the conference. In return for her support for the bank, P insisted that the scope of the conference be broadened to include the discussion of universal disarmament. The conference turned over to the external decision-makers the task of working out the details of the bank agreement. Preliminary discussions on disarmament were to be held after the completion of this task.

Encouraged by his success in the international conference, the central decision-maker of G concentrated his attention on the attainment of his other main objective—assuring the security of his nation. Recalling G's earlier successful trade transactions with K, he invited the central decision-maker of that nation to meet with him for bilateral talks.

Nation K, too, had an energetic pair of decision-makers. They had set goals of economic growth and international trade for their nation, with a minimum of emphasis on force capability commensurate with national security. At the time of the invitation to confer with

G, they were enjoying considerable success in the accomplishment of these goals. Through the intelligent use of scarce resources and advantageous international trading, K had already moved from a fourth to a third position, with 15,500 basic capabilities, surpassing Nation M and leaving G far behind. K had held its armament level fairly constant. Unknown to the central decision-maker of G, however, was the fact that the forceful manner in which G had been conducting its international relations had aroused the suspicions of both decision-makers in K.

With this background, the talks between the central decision-makers of G and K commenced. If not completely satisfactory from G's standpoint, the conversations were productive of some results. G had sought a pact under which each nation would undertake to guarantee the other's security against any attack. The central decision-maker of K, however, would not go so far. Perhaps out of fear that G had international ambitions that would involve K in international conflict, K offered formally only to guarantee G against attack from K in return for a similar guarantee from G. G attached a trade agreement as a rider, and the bilateral nonaggression pact was signed.

Meanwhile, at the conference of all foreign ministers, a set of provisions had been drafted for the establishment of an international bank for economic development. The negotiations had been long and difficult. K had reservations about certain aspects of the draft, but would go along if assured a voice in the bank's operation. Nation M, which had supported the principle of *a* bank, found itself in solitary opposition to *the* bank, as it finally was designed by the conference. The external decision-maker of M correctly predicted that the draft would be rejected upon his submission of it to the home government. In the note of rejection, the central decision-maker of M explained:

> We hope our non-participation in the bank will not be taken as intransigence on our part. We have not joined because economically it is not in our interest. We would be placing more in the bank than we could draw out, considering the interest we would have to pay. At our present *BC* level, our contributions for three periods would be 768 *BC*'s, a very large portion of our resources. We hope we will not be condemned for pursuing our own interests.

The other four nations ratified the agreement, however, and the International Bank came into existence.

No sooner had the Bank been established than its machinery was put to test. The central decision-maker of G assigned his external decision-maker the task of obtaining a loan of basic capabilities. Action was long delayed by the tardiness with which initial contributions to the Bank were made. In addition, the Board members had to divide their attention between the Board and their duties at other conferences and at home, as the external decision-makers of their respective nations.

While G's external decision-maker was handling the negotiation of the loan, its program for economic development showed small signs of progress. G's central decision-maker continued his efforts to conclude mutual security arrangements. Encouraged by P's support of the Bank, he now approached the central decision-maker of P.

Like G and K, P's decision-makers also were active on the international scene. Their activity was grounded in full accord on national goals. P was to be the leading example of a stable, prosperous, self-avowed democracy. In this account it was succeeding fairly well. Nation P had risen to a par with Nation S in basic capability accumulation during the early part of the run. Soon after the first signs of economic progress the regime initiated a policy at home of encouraging greater validator influence on governmental action, a policy which continued until decision latitude hit its minimum, a level reached also only by S among the nations of the world. In an effort to discourage autocratic tendencies abroad, it was the intention of P's decision-makers to give aid only to those regimes having democratic structures similar to its own. Efforts also were to be made to achieve universal, complete disarmament.

Interestingly enough, in spite of her decision-makers' intentions and in spite of the fact that S was the only other democracy in the world, P found herself in an arms race with S early in the run. This inadvertently had been touched off by a series of miscalculations on the part of P's central decision-maker in allocating resources to the production of force capability. He had intended only to offset depreciation, holding the accumulation constant; but since his estimates of depreciation were so high, it resulted in P pulling ahead of S in force capability. S responded with an increase. P responded similarly, and so on. The situation was confounded by the difficulty of establishing adequate communications with S, although assurances were exchanged. In an effort to halt this situation before it grew to serious proportions, P had placed disarmament on the agenda of the international conference.

Early in the run both decision-makers in P harbored considerable resentment and distrust for Nation M. This was repeatedly expressed in their contacts with other nations. These feelings had no basis in known issues. Concomitant propaganda against M was heightened as a result of M's refusal to join the International Bank, after which event Nations G and S shared P's feelings. Only K displayed much trust in M, either before or after the Bank episode.

In the context of these situations the central decision-makers of G and P began negotiation concerning G's desire for a mutual security pact. In spite of P's earlier opposition to G, P stood to receive some small direct benefit by having G allied with it in the event that its arms race with S should get out of hand. This was no strong bargaining point for G because of its small military force. Moreover, P could demand that G decrease decision latitude. But G in turn could hold out the promise of support for P's efforts to achieve permanent disarmament, since this would be to its advantage as well, and G, of course, would benefit from any economic aid that P might give. Both were suspicious of Nation M. Both nations agreed to come to each other's defense in the event of outside aggression. In addition, they promised to engage in certain international trade transactions.

By this time G finally had received its loan from the International Bank, though it turned out to be but 750 *BC's*. A new conference was under way to consider disarmament proposals. The conference had elected the central decision-maker of S as chairman. In a session attended by all central and external decision-makers, P and G explained their newly formed pact as being purely defensive in nature. They expressed a willingness to join the other nations in immediate steps toward total disarmament. The conference, however, was able to achieve only a first step in that direction, agreeing to arms limitation. Although M once again was critical of the conference's action, it concurred to avoid being further stigmatized as opposed to the principle of disarmament.

The terms of the arms limitation agreement were as follows:

> No more than 10 per cent of a nation's basic capability accumulation may be allocated to the production of force capability each period.
> In case of violation, the following will happen:
> 1. A world conference will be called immediately.
> 2. All other nations agree to exercise economic sanctions and trade restrictions against states which do not comply with the agreement.
> The *World Times* will report the allocation of basic capability to the production of force capability in each nation.

M's criticism of this treaty was that its terms, if met, could allay

the mutual fears only of nations that were relatively equal in armaments when the plan was instituted and that would remain relatively equal in basic capability accumulation. Such was the case
with P and S. As a consequence of the adoption of the plan, P and S
allowed portions of their force capabilities to become obsolete and
to depreciate away, thus alleviating some of the tensions over the
armaments race. Nonetheless, they were still wealthy and strong
relative to M. What bothered M was that the arms limitation agreement perpetuated the superior strategic position of the larger nations as long as they enjoyed an economic superiority. In light of
M's declining, rather than increasing wealth, this very well might
be a long time.

M's point was well taken. But it was not until the others moved
from the immediate conference situation that they took cognizance
of it. G, the first to do so, was still struggling to get its economic
development program in a position of sustained growth. It had a
nonaggression pact with K and a mutual defense agreement with P,
but Nation S continued as a potential threat, being economically
and strategically much stronger than G, and thus favored by the
pact. Given realization of the point made by M, it was not surprising
to find G's central decision-maker broaching the topic of mutual
security with the central decision-maker of S.

A look at the national goals pursued by S adds to the irony of the
armaments race sparked by P's miscalculation. Both decision-makers
in S sought universal disarmament, as did the decision-makers of P.
But they also felt that S should maintain its strength to protect its
democracy until a viable disarmament agreement could be reached.
Thus, in the absence of adequate communication between the two
nations, the central decision-maker of S felt he had no choice but to
increase force capability to keep pace with P. It was not until the
adoption of the arms limitation agreement that progress was made
by S and P in the clarification of intentions, with a resultant simultaneous decrease in force capability. But the problem was not
solved. For, even after this expression of good will, and even under
the terms of the agreement, there were signs of disturbance caused
by the normal fluctuation of force capability accumulations from
depreciation and obsolescence.

With this stage for his meeting with S, G's central decision-maker
found his task easy. The idea of being linked with P through a
mutual security pact with G held considerable appeal for the central decision-maker of S. Such an arrangement would serve to deter
P, just in case it actually did have designs on S. And the combina-

tion of S, G, and P would give cause for thought to any potential aggressor against S. In addition, the good offices of G, who by now enjoyed friendly and intimate relations with P, could be used to pave the way for direct bilateral negotiations with P on the question of total disarmament, S's ultimate goal. A mutual security pact was thus signed between G and S.

This event was not without impact on Nation M. In part because of its nonparticipation in the International Bank and criticism of the arms limitation agreement, and in part because of P's agitation against it, M had been subjected to increasing criticism and treated with distrust and isolation by G, S, and P. K alone continued its trust in M. M viewed with alarm the G-S pact, with its indirect involvement of P.

At home M was in serious trouble. Its basic capability accumulation had undergone a continuous decline, and an already small strategic capability accumulation had become even smaller. Its government had consumed the major portion of its decision-making effort in internal quarrels, trying to agree on a proper national course. The external decision-maker was particularly distrustful of P and placed major emphasis on the need for adequate defense preparations. The central decision-maker, somewhat isolated from international politics by the fragmentary communication of his external decision-maker, did not share this fear of P. His principal concern was in building a sound economic basis for a high standard of living by taking advantage of potentially favorable terms of trade. But the signing of the G-S pact, linking P, G, and S, brought an end to this lack of governmental coordination. M's two decision-makers became united on the urgently felt need to take steps to secure their nation's security from external threat.

There was only Nation K left for M to approach. Both decision-makers in M had high regard for K. For, as indicated before, only K had not been critical of M's stand on the Bank and disarmament issues. On the other side, K had always looked upon M as being trustworthy, and respected M's independent course of action. In addition, K had long been suspicious of P and G—P for its ideological stand (K by now had the highest decision latitude in the world) and G for its aggressive pursuit of economic assistance earlier. The linking of G, P, and S in a web of security pacts was, therefore, taken as cause for concern in K, too. Thus, as this run of the simulation came to its close, K and M signed a mutual security pact.

The "world" now looked considerably different from the way it did when it began. There were the interlocking mutual defense arrangements—G with P, G with S, M with K, and finally a non-aggression pact between K and G. Though of questionable effectiveness, there was an armaments limitations agreement. An international economic institution had been established. The ordering of nations in terms of basic wealth and strength had changed considerably, as shown in the values characterizing the nations at the end of the run in Table 4-1 (p. 76).

CONCLUSIONS AND FURTHER REVISIONS

What were the results of our efforts to improve upon the earlier version of the inter-nation simulation? What further revisions were now needed?

Changes in Ideological Programs

As Guetzkow has stressed in his description of the inter-nation simulation (Chapter Five, especially pp. 133 ff.), the unprogrammed interactions among the nations yielded ideological overtones. How well did our attempts, as described above (pp. 71-72), to reinforce such ideological developments by supplying a programmed base in decision latitude work out? The first device of supplying manipulable ranges of decision latitude (Figure 5-1c, p. 112) for each nation seemed fairly satisfactory.

However, our second device, which programmed ideological struggles between the nations by relating each nation's validator satisfaction to the extent to which other nations had similar decision latitudes, was considerably less than effective. S had been conscious of its low decision latitude, its "democracy." Some of the actions of G and K reflected awareness of their high decision latitude values. But only P responded directly to the opportunity to increase validator satisfaction by persuading others to adopt a similar decision latitude.

At this point it was decided that the small contribution of similarity in decision latitude to the political aspect of the system did not warrant the complications involved in its retention. Persisting in our endeavor to create programmed ways of emphasizing political factors in the simulation, a modified source of validator satisfaction was created for use in the next round to replace the mechanism just abandoned. Perhaps a more formal rating of the national esteem of each nation by all the others might prove useful in simulating aspects of the prestige race for world leadership, which seems to exist in the affairs of nations. It was planned that each nation would rate the others at the end of each period in response to the question, "Score each nation on the scale provided in terms of the amount of esteem you have for it." Then the combined ratings of the decision-makers, both central and external, would be fed into the computation of each nation's validator satisfaction. The underlying notion was to provide a way in which the validators of a nation might influence their own decision-makers because of considerations of national prestige, that is, because of the esteem which their nation was given by others.

We decided also to clarify further the political significance of decision latitude in the Participants Manual for future runs, the hope being that a better understanding of its meaning would in itself provide a sufficient basis for enriched, but unprogrammed, ideological developments among the nations.

Delineation of National Interests

With regard to the problem of generating goals from the initial situation, we were encouraged by the results revealed in the 1958 summer run. It will be remembered that an important early change in our procedures was developed by allowing the participants to create their own goals from their interpretations of their nation's initial historical conditions, as they interacted with the other nations. By providing the participants with enough time to study their nation's characteristics, they soon had formulated goals for their countries in which they felt quite involved. No further changes in the subsequent runs seemed warranted with respect to the problem of the definition of national interests.

Number and Organization of Decision-Makers

A variety of organizational developments occurred among the five decisional units. The efficient division of work and coordination between G's decision-makers, for example, stood in striking contrast to the difficulties experienced by S and by M in functioning as a coordinated unit. Whereas the two-man unit seemed adequately to reflect real-world organizational characteristics, it did not meet new needs generated by the inter-nation system itself. We had not anticipated the personnel needs coming with establishment of an inter-nation institution. The additional work load placed by the International Bank upon its Board members (the external decision-makers) tended to bog down their operations elsewhere. Richer units in the system, by virtue of their superior economic position, were bombarded by communications from the smaller nations. A national unit of larger size seemed in order. It was decided that the next run should operate with three-man decisional groups, the third man being a second external decision-maker. It was decided also that his role would be described as being similar to the first external decision-maker, the problem of coordination and division of labor being left to the decision-makers themselves.

Further Rearrangement of International Rules and Procedures

Our efforts to distinguish more clearly between normal, written communication and the procedure at face-to-face international conferences were not completely successful in the summer run of 1958. It will be recalled that the procedure for conference interactions was to use impromptu oral communication on matters of procedure and formal manuscript reading with regard to matters of substance. The task of enforcing this distinction fell to the simulator. But, as appeared with hindsight, he found himself being drawn into interactions with the participants in defense of his decision. Since it is important to avoid such unsystematic influences, it was felt necessary to change the conference procedure in the middle of the run. The new rule adopted allowed extemporaneous oral communication on all matters. To provide a record, the conferences were recorded on dictation machines.

Elaboration of Routines for War

The final point of concern from these early explorations was our procedure for the conduct of war. It will be recalled that our approach was essentially to make explicit the rules applying to the conduct of war. There were no wars in the 1958 summer run. We wondered whether the rules contained a built-in bias against war: there simply was little advantage in going to war, because war involved such high costs to both loser and winner that any potential material gain would almost certainly be too small to offset the sure losses. Reconsidering, we developed a new set of procedures for the simulation of war which allowed for immediate gains, especially if the intensity and scope of the conflict were limited. Details of the new procedures regulating the development and aftermath of war are presented in the Participants' Manual (Chapter Three). War was conceived as a series of engagements, between which negotiation was possible. Winners were allowed reparation rights and the option of occupation.

Credibility of Office Loss

In addition to providing more experience with the problems of earlier runs, the 1958 summer exercise also revealed new difficulties. In the chronology presented above, no reference was made to changes in office during the run. In fact, none occurred. But this was only because there were no extra participants available with whom deposed decision-makers could be replaced. The central decision-makers of both Nation G and Nation M supposedly lost office. The transitions in both cases would have been orderly, there having been no instance of a revolution. In postsimulation interviews the participants revealed that the threat of losing office provided little motivation for action since the participants knew no replacements were available. Because of the central position in the intra-national system model of the threat of losing office as sketched by Guetzkow (Chapter Five, p. 118), it was felt essential that extra decision-makers should be on hand in the next run to replace physically those who might lose office.

Redevelopment of Revolution Mechanism

The absence of revolution during the 1958 summer run stimulated reconsideration of the procedures involved in revolutions. First, it seemed the revolution threshold had been set too low; instead, a higher level was chosen for subsequent runs, thereby increasing the attention which needed to be paid to revolutionary propensities. In addition, the constant probability of office maintenance during revolution seemed entirely unrealistic. It was decided to elaborate the revolutionary process through a two-step procedure. First, once the revolutionary threshold had been reached, the actual occurrence of a revolution was to be made dependent upon the level of decision latitude and the extent to which force capability was being applied within the nation for purposes of internal control. Second, should an insurrection actually occur, the probability of the current decision-makers retaining their office was to be made a stochastic rather than a constant process. But no matter what the outcome of the revolution, the impact of the upheaval was postulated to destroy certain of the nation's basic capabilities and temporarily to increase the over-all validators' satisfaction. An overthrow of government often produces sufficient civil turmoil to interfere with the nation's productivity. But when an unsuccessful government is thrown out of office, validators often have expectations—at least for a while—that perhaps things will improve.

Choice of Participants

Broadly speaking, there was similarity among the goals pursued and the means used by the five nations in the system. Yet the situations in which the decision-makers found themselves were quite different, and the possible variety of alternative approaches was large indeed. It seems not unreasonable to suggest, then, that the likenesses in goals and solutions were a product of the fact that all of the participants were American college students. In this sense we were not simulating what many consider to be an important aspect of international political life—cultural and ethnic differences.

In addition to cultural and ethnic homogeneity, our college student participants, of course, lacked experience in the conduct of foreign affairs. Decision-makers in foreign offices, in embassies throughout the world, and in international bodies bring to their task many expectations as to how the relations among nations should be conducted. These preconceptions often result in self-fulfillment. It may be advantageous to use naive subjects, from the point of view of the development of original solutions, because they are bound by less rigid concepts of how an international system operates. And in probing operating characteristics of the inter-nation simulation, it would be well also to explore its operation with men of experience in public and foreign affairs.

To gain insight into the potential impact of cultural and ethnic heterogeneity and the consequences of experience in international decision-making, plans were drawn for the participation of foreign students and mature professionals in the next two runs of the simulation. Additional revisions of aspects of the basic structure of the simulation, already indicated above, were incorporated in these runs.

III. The Simulation in Operation: January, 1959

With revisions made, the inter-nation simulation was readied again for operation in January, 1959. Two runs were conducted. The first took place at Northwestern University with foreign students as participants for one entire day. The second run took the simulation to Asilomar, California, where two days of operation were scheduled, involving active and former foreign service officers. The remaining positions in the roster of decision-makers needed for the simulation were filled by political scientists who specialize in international affairs. These professionals were all United States nationals.

Instead of presenting a chronological reconstruction, as was done for the preceding exercise, our discussion of each of these runs will focus on general points of concern.

THE FOREIGN STUDENT RUN OF THE SIMULATION

In this run of the simulation there were three active decision-makers in each nation, plus an alternate wherever possible. The line-up of decision-makers was as follows: Nation G was staffed by three American graduate students. Two of them were currently on leave from their positions as officers in the United States Foreign Service, while a third had served with that organization for several years before beginning his academic career. A fourth American political science graduate student acted as a stand-by, an aspiring decision-maker for G. For Nation K we were fortunate in being able to recruit four Chilean graduate students in economics from the University of Chicago. The decision-makers of Nation M were all graduate students from West Africa—three from Nigeria and one from Liberia. Nation P was more heterogeneous. One decision-maker was an Australian graduate student, another an undergraduate from Spain, and the third a German undergraduate. Finally, Nation S consisted of two Japanese graduate students and one American; we were unable to recruit another Asian for the run. There were no aspirants for P or S.

The three aspirants observed the activities of their respective nations, so as to maintain their own interests and develop some familiarity with the situation into which they might be asked to step.

This run was marked by difficulties from the very beginning. Many of the foreign students could afford little time away from their school work and jobs, so the run could be scheduled to last but one full day, preceded the night before by a briefing session. Even at that, two persons missed the initial briefing. Coupled with this was the language problem. The manual and the oral briefing were both in English, and we found that not all of the foreign students had full command of ordinary English, not to mention facility in acquiring the technical vocabulary of the simulation. As a consequence, the run was slow in getting started. In the hope that discussion among the members of the decisional units might aid understanding, the rule against oral communication within the nation was relaxed. Despite the difficulties, the simulation finally did get under way, and, by the end of the day, its operations were complex and intriguing.

We were able to tap by questionnaire something of the richness and variety of the run. One question sought to find what goals the participants were seeking at that time. In their own words, here are the answers the participants gave:

Nation G: American decision-makers; started with a decision latitude of 5, basic capability of 15,000, and force capability of 1,000.

CDM: Attempt to reach trade agreements with S and P.

EDM_x: Establishment of mutually advantageous trade relations with other countries.

EDM_y: Obtain aid from P in BC's or CS's and then to reconvert these into FC's.

Nation K: Chilean decision-makers; started with a decision latitude of 6, basic capability of 37,000, and force capability of 3,100.

CDM: Trade in order to get BC's and achieve our goals:
1. Improve living standards.
2. Prepare for attacks from abroad.
3. Achieve a democratic government.
4. Use our relative advantages in international trade.

EDM_x: Declaration of war with P against S in order to stop their increase and benefit ourselves from their resources.

EDM_y: Maintain BC's and FC's in the right proportion in relation to internal and external troubles.

Nation M: West African decision-makers; started with a decision latitude of 4, basic capability of 57,000, and force capability of 2,100.

CDM: An economic trade deal.

EDM_x: Plan for economic cooperation between P, K, and M.

EDM_y: Negotiate trade agreements.

Nation P: European decision-makers; started with a decision latitude of 7, basic capability of 78,000, and force capability of 7,900.

CDM: Prevention of own EDM's and Nations M and K from
declaring war against S.

EDM$_x$: To avoid an aggressive pact system around S against
us; therefore form a pact with K and M. Neutral-
ization of G by aid.

EDM$_y$: Revolution against own CDM and war against S.

Nation S: Asian decision-makers; started with a decision latitude
of 3, basic capability of 103,000, and force capability
of 1,900.

CDM: Strict neutrality (non-military alignment).

EDM$_x$: A trade with P. We offer 5,000 *BC*'s and expect *CS*'s
from P.

EDM$_y$: The general avoidance of war through being very
strong and neutral.

The flexibility of the simulation's framework is illustrated in a
fascinating conspiracy developed by the German and Spaniard who
occupied the two external decision-making offices in Nation P, as
they endeavored to implement aggressive intentions against Nation
S. As is indicated in the statement of goals presented above, Nation
S was peaceful. S's decision-makers were too bogged down internally to have presented any threat to anyone. Their actions were
entirely consistent with their goal of strict neutrality and their military build-up was understandable, considering the very low relative level of their *FC*'s at the beginning of the run. At the time of
these events, S still was far weaker than P. Yet S was perceived as a
threat by P, K, and M. S also was apparently perceived as a juicy
plum waiting to be plucked, for she was rich, weak, and from a
"world's-eye view," impotent. Immediate war against her by P, alone
or with K and M, was avoided only because the Australian who
served as central decision-maker of P refused on both moral and
rational grounds (P also was wealthy) to allow it; it was he who had
to sign the declaration according to the rules of the game.

A conspiracy against the central decision-maker of P then was
organized by his own external decision-makers. The rules of the
game made no explicit provision for the accession of external decision-makers to power via coups d'état; they provided only for

transfer of power to aspiring decision-makers. So these two external
decision-makers cleverly worked within the rules to accomplish their
end. By feeding their central decision-maker misleading information
and poor policy advice, they hoped to have him thrown out of office
via the regular methods—either by revolution or orderly office change.
Knowing there was no alternate person on hand for P, they reasoned
that one of them necessarily would be put in as the replacement
for the central decision-maker.

In this revolutionary conspiracy the German and Spaniard enlisted outside support. They had little trouble in lining up the Chile-
ans in Nation K, where there was an interest in the acquisition of
more resources, even if such had to be taken as war booty. Among
the Africans in M they found sympathetic ears, although not unanimously so. Against the protestations of one external decision-maker
(an Efik), M's central decision-maker and subordinate (both Yorubas)
agreed: (1) to aid the external decision-makers of P in their dirty
work; and (2) to then join P in war against S. Thus, P, K, and M
were ready to dismember S. G's activity was an inconsequential element in the plan. For, although operated by a competent group of
decision-makers who enjoyed good relations with S, she was too
small to pose any threat to the plan's success. G might simply be
"neutralized" by the conditional offer of much needed economic aid.

There is little doubt that this masterful intrigue would ultimately
have succeeded had a contravening event not occurred. Before the
P-K-M coalition had time to get their plan under way, there was a
political change in M. The reluctance of the new central decision-
maker (a Vai from Liberia) to go along with one external decision-
maker (the Yoruba from Nigeria who supported the idea) slowed
the implementation process long enough for time to run out on
the simulation.

Had *a priori* assessment been made of the participants' conceptions of how international systems operate, would it have been
possible to have predicted which decision-makers might respond in
aggressive ways? Although such was not feasible because of the
limited time access we had to our subjects, it was possible to explore
this idea for nation M. We asked Dr. Robert A. LeVine, an anthro-
pologist, to put in writing—before the run began—some general predictions based upon his knowledge of the backgrounds of our
African participants.

First, LeVine was asked to make observations about the three
tribes to which our four decision-makers from Africa belonged.
Then, LeVine was asked to develop hypotheses and derive from

such hypotheses more concrete predictions as to how the four participants would behave in the course of the upcoming simulation.

These observations were made before the runs involving the four African students actually took place. Note also that Dr. LeVine's comments were written in 1959, before Nigerian independence was achieved. The central decision-maker of M and his cohort external decision-maker were both of the Yoruba tribe of Western Nigeria. Before the run began, LeVine explained that:

> The Yoruba are a large tribe, the dominant group in Western Nigeria, with ancient traditions of monarchy and urbanism, the monarchies being "city-states." The Yoruba are a politically powerful group and have the most Western education of any people in Nigeria. Educated Yorubas try to identify themselves with Nigerian nationalism as a whole rather than with tribalism or internecine hostility. Their main hostility is directed against the British with whom they have had so much contact, because as a member of a dominant cultural group they stand to gain a great deal from independence.

The external decision-maker who opposed the idea of M joining the conspiracy was an Efik of Eastern Nigeria. The Efik, LeVine already had told us:

> . . . are a small but important group living among egalitarian societies in the eastern region, and they are more concerned with intertribal hostility than with anticolonialism as such. They fear that independence will bring them domination by the more numerous tribes.

The new central decision-maker in M, a Vai tribesman from Liberia, shared important background characteristics with the Efik student, as LeVine had previously described:

> The Vai are virtually ruled by a secret society whose two chiefs have supernatural powers and divine connections. In values, their political system is less authoritarian than a Nigerian monarchy. However, Liberia is dominated by the Americo-Liberian element, descendants of freed slaves who discriminate against tribal groups such as the Vai on grounds of color, language, culture, and sophistication. All political power is Americo-Liberian.

With this background material, LeVine advanced the following hypotheses and related predictions about the simulation, before the run was undertaken:

> *Hypothesis I:* Individuals belonging to a politically dominant cultural group within their own nation will be more favorable to a nationalistic, isolative, independent, and even warlike foreign policy than those belonging to a group which feels itself weak and op-

pressed. The latter group will be more desirous of inter-nation collaboration.

Prediction: The Yoruba participants will stress as decision-making goals the power, prestige, and independence of their nation and its standing among others. The Efik and Vai participants will stress the support of outside groups; they will express attitudes of wanting to be helped by other nations.

Hypothesis II: Individuals belonging to a group which has been successful in warfare (the Yoruba) will favor war as an inter-nation device for achieving goals.

Prediction: The Yoruba participants will tend to favor war as a means of achieving their goals.

The congruence of LeVine's comments made before the simulation was conducted with the foreign students with the actual results is astonishing. As was noted immediately above, during the run with foreign students, the two Yorubas wished their Nation M to join in the coalition to dismember S, thus being "more favorable to a . . . warlike foreign policy." The Efik and Vai, on the other hand, were not aggressive; rather they were "more desirous of inter-nation collaboration."

THE USE OF PROFESSIONAL PARTICIPANTS:
THE ASILOMAR RUN

Before discussing the successes and failures of the revised procedures in the foreign student run, let us look at the second run conducted in January, 1959, in which the ex-foreign service officers and academic professionals in international relations participated. It made use of the same simulation framework, although initial characteristics assigned to nations[3] were different in the Asilomar run, as given in Table 4-3.

TABLE 4-3 | CHARACTERISTICS OF NATIONS AT BEGINNING OF ASILOMAR RUN

NATION	BASIC CAPABILITY	FORCE CAPABILITY	DECISION LATITUDE
Algo	15,000 BC's	925 SC's	5
Erga	20,000 BC's	1350 SC's	6
Ingo	30,000 BC's	1500 SC's	3
Omne	45,000 BC's	6800 SC's	7
Utro	50,000 BC's	4800 SC's	2

[3] To facilitate designation of the nations, alphabetic symbols used to this point in the development of the simulation were changed to more easily remembered names, as follows: G to Algo, K to Erga, M to Ingo, P to Omne, and S to Utro.

There were three active decision-makers and one alternate for each nation. The simulation ran one full day and evening and during the morning of a second day.

At the urging of the professionals, the rule against nonconference oral communication within the national units was suspended. In addition, the analogous rule pertaining to inter-nation communication, although not suspended, was recognized more in the breach than in the observance. The interaction pace was extremely rapid at both levels. This simulation tended to be a "run-away world," eliciting full utilization of the sophistication and innovativeness possessed by our well-qualified participants.

The first few periods of the run were marked by a development not heretofore witnessed. As usual, the smaller nations concentrated on problems of economic development and on raising standards of living. The striking thing from the outset was a complete absence of tensions between the two large powers, nations Omne and Utro. In peaceful collaboration they effectively dominated the world scene. The regimes in both of the great powers believed that the only rational course for them was that of peace and cooperation. Apparently none of the suspicions and fears that the mere juxtaposition of large powers generated in the foreign student run were felt by these decision-makers. The large difference between the decision latitude values of Omne and Utro made little difference.

In the midst of this calm, in some of the small nations there was rising dissatisfaction with their lots. Toward the end of the daytime periods there was evidence of a movement to end the rapprochement between Omne and Utro. To what extent this stemmed from an amalgam of the desire to enliven the game or from the possibility of deriving benefits which might result from the bipolarization of the world is not known. The movement centered on Erga; Ingo became her collaborator. Algo maintained only a peripheral relationship to this duo. The end of the day found Omne and Utro closer than ever. Bipolarization had developed, but it was a bipolarization of the two large powers against two, possibly three, small nations.

The programming of chance events, such as technological breakthroughs and natural catastrophes, had been considered at various times in the past. It was decided that the present exploratory run was an appropriate time to explore these factors. Thus, a technological breakthrough on nuclear weapons was introduced during the evening session of the first day's running. Erga was made the recipient. The feat was accomplished by giving her a gift from nature of 25,000 force capability units and increasing her force capability productivity rate from 1.5 to 10.0 *FC*'s for each basic capability unit allocated to their production.

The impact was extreme, to say the least. In a flurry of interactions, the division of the world into two camps, which had been only a tendency, became an accomplished fact. Omne had by now become self-identified as a benevolent "theocratic dictatorship." She was the leader of the "Om-Ut" bloc. Both she and Utro were upset. Erga and Ingo were pleased. By this time Erga had been characterized by many of the participants, including some of her own decision-makers, as a "dictatorship of the left." Through the skillful use of propaganda, she had managed to assume a world role disproportionate to her size. Given a foundation in power to support her actions, she began in earnest to oppose the dominance of Omne and Utro. As the evening session drew to a close, the atmosphere was tense with the expectation of war.

What transpired between 10:00 P.M. that night and the reopening of the simulation at 9:15 A.M. the following day is a matter of "historical controversy." All that is known is that in the morning war was declared. In what was defended as preventive war, Omne and Utro moved against Erga, Ingo, and Algo with a combined force of over 75,000 *FC*'s.

The first effect of the war was the capitulation of Algo. Always rather aloof and something of a mystery, she had refused to take up arms in her own defense. As a result she was immediately occupied by Omne and Utro. Unable to acquire accurate information on the potential magnitude of the offense planned by Omne and Utro, Erga and Ingo met the attack with only 19,000 *FC*'s, although more force was available. In a decisive battle the superior force of Omne and Utro prevailed. The "In-Ert" bloc, as it had come to be called, was brought to its knees. Ingo and Erga were occupied for the one period limit.

No sooner had the occupation of Algo, Ingo, and Erga ended than the world was shaken by another blow. Omne had come out of the war in the stronger position of the two big powers. Fearing that such an opportunity would never again present itself, Omne took what she termed "the regrettable decision" to strike with her remaining strategic force against Utro and the rest of the world. There was a rallying among her astonished victims and as their battle against high odds raged, the simulation came to its close.

Much of the ideological acerbation which eventually developed in this run was stimulated by the activity of the press. Two world newspapers had been established, each staffed by an imaginative group of professional journalists. At the beginning the two newspapers attempted to serve as neutral reporters of events. But as patterns of interaction developed, passionate headlines and characteristic editorials appeared. Each paper departed from its earlier neutral course, one toward the "little three" nations and the other toward the "big two." In a not insignificant way the world press reinforced the tendencies toward bipolarization, as they were developing. In fact, so much a part of the interaction did the press become, that the victorious Omne-Utro coalition was compelled to impose strict censorship in its presses during the period of occupation—to the point of closing down altogether the paper which sided with the defeated coalition of Erga and Ingo. But the "voice of the freedom loving peoples of the world" was not to be silenced. From somewhere, unknown at the time even to the director of the simulation, an underground newspaper was circulated calling upon the vanquished to "rise up and cast out the barbarous and criminal invaders."

FURTHER CONCLUSIONS

In light of the experiences in the winter of 1959, it seemed some closure was being obtained in the evolution of a simulation of international relations. Yet, other problems remained unsolved. Particular conclusions we drew from the experience obtained in the two runs described immediately above are as follows:

The Decision-Making Bureaucracies

In both of the January runs three decision-makers were used in each nation. The nations were set up this way to provide sufficient manpower to staff an international organization, should one be established. No organization was established in the foreign student run, perhaps because of its brief duration. But, there seemed to be no lack of things for the additional decision-maker to do, perhaps because the foreign students experienced problems in understanding their complicated instructions.

This was not the case, however, in the Asilomar run. In spite of the fact that an International Bank was set up in that run, plus the fact that there were innumerable international conferences, both formal and informal, some of the external decision-makers complained of having little to do. The central decision-makers, given complete freedom to communicate orally between nations, became in effect their own chief external decision-makers. Had the rules against nonconference oral communication within and between nations been enforced, this breakdown of role differentiation may not have developed. It was suggested by one central decision-maker that the intra-nation model might need to be further elaborated in order to place more internal political pressures upon the central decision-maker.

Bureaucratic phenomena seem to have been simulated in abundance. The development of organizational subgoals and consequent intraorganizational conflict within Nations P and M in the foreign student run is one case in point. One internal decision-maker in the Asilomar run later recalled some of his principal problems as being: (a) to persuade his subordinates with regard to his goals for the nation; (b) to keep a subordinate who could not be persuaded in places where he could not do any damage; and (c) to determine for both subordinates which external events were to be heeded and which ignored.

Routines for Communication

The problem of communication procedures tends to be less bothersome when oral interaction is allowed during conferences, while written messages are used for bilateral relations. Judging from the eagerness of participants to call conferences in both of the January runs, the oral procedures are seen by the participants as having significant advantages over normal written communication. In fact, we since have had to limit the number and length of conferences that can be held each simulation period. Tendencies toward excessive interaction obtained particularly at Asilomar have been discouraged in subsequent runs by reinstatement of rules providing for written communication.

Impact of Office Loss

Another problem of earlier runs was the absence of a credible threat of losing office. This threat was made realistic by the presence of aspiring central decision-makers, ready to take over when the occupant lost office. In both runs there were instances of orderly office loss. But rather than functioning as a stimulus for the formulation of national goals, the problem of retaining office appears to have been viewed by the decision-makers largely as instrumental. Objectives developing in the course of interaction between the international situation and individual aspirations of the decision-makers seem to have been the ones pursued by most participants.

Revolution Procedures

The new revolution mechanism added after the summer run in 1958 proved to be a fruitful elaboration. For some decision-makers the use of force capability for internal control served as a means of releasing them from concern with the satisfaction of their validating élites. But at the same time this placed new demands upon their resources and attention. An unanticipated consequence was the appearance in the press at Asilomar of implied and direct criticism of those who employed such methods. Some decision-makers were against the use of force as a matter of principle. But since governments which were insensitive to the desires of their validators would have a high probability of revolution unless they applied force capability for internal controls, those decision-makers who were reluctant to do so were pressured to achieve and/or maintain a low decision latitude. This revision appears to have added political and ideological realism to the simulation.

The Programming of National Prestige

As for the new source of validator satisfaction—national prestige—the results in both the foreign student and Asilomar runs were unsatisfactory. In spite of the fact that the press released publicly the esteem ratings given each nation by each other nation, the decision-makers more often than not used their ratings as political weapons, even reporting fictitious ratings. This device was an integral part of the conspiracy against the central decision-maker of Nation P in the foreign student run. Retribution through false ratings also was obtained by Omne and Erga in the Asilomar run. Consequently, this variable has been dropped altogether.

Although our attempt to program the impact of national prestige failed, it is important to note that such did not eliminate the unprogrammed operation of esteem in the international relations among the decision-makers. In fact, the professionals, some of whom were acquainted with each other before coming to Asilomar, performed well partly because of their desire to demonstrate to each other the excellence of their diplomatic skills. Well-executed international moves were the source of considerable esteem among our players during their mealtime conversations.

Realities and Unrealities of War

It seems evident from the experience with foreign participants that the revised provisions for the conduct of war did open the possibility of material gain from warfare. Nations P, K, and M clearly acted to obtain such gain. Although at Asilomar such material attention did not seem to be the key motivating factor, war now was a viable alternative. In this run war was seen in the first instance as a preventive measure, and in the second instance as a course of "last resort" in the accomplishment of political and ideological goals.

In both runs, however, the idea of going to war seemed to have varied in its moral implications. For some the decision to go to war was not viewed with a sense of its gravity in humanistic terms. Could the press be called upon to value-load the idea of preserving the "lives" of our "paper people"? It would be useful to have more understanding of the extent to which the presence of moral factors is necessary in the simulation of international relations.

World Culture vs. Game Culture

Significant aspects of the two January runs of the simulation revolved around the notion of culture. The coincidence of LeVine's cultural predictions with the play-out of the simulation by the Africans in the foreign student run cannot be taken too seriously, even though the Europeans, too, exemplified in their ruthlessness the "kernel of truth" hypothesis argued by some psychologists with respect to national stereotypes. The simulation may have demonstrated merely the operation of unique individual characteristics rather than cultural traits modal for national groupings. Perhaps the most relevant insight obtained from the foreign student runs with respect to the interaction of members of different cultures is the capability of the simulation to embody nations manned by persons of different cultures.

One of the participants in the Asilomar run made a most interesting distinction between "game culture" and "real culture," as both are embodied in participant predispositions. Distinction may be useful as a framework within which to tackle the thorny problems of "nationalism," "history," and "tradition." Real culture comes into the simulation with the participants as background from their socializations. It is manifested in their personalities, values, and ideologies; it is the product of their life experiences. Game culture, on the other hand, is the set of predispositions which develop out of the shared experiences of the simulation itself. Thus, game culture takes time to appear. It is likely, then, that it was real culture that we saw in the foreign student run of the simulation, for the run operated for less than one full day. In the early stages of the Asilomar run, the real culture of mature American intellectuals and professionals was made manifest, as in the extreme rationality of nations Omne and Utro, for example. But the Asilomar run continued almost three times longer than did that of the foreign students; it developed its own history and traditions, and one could see evolve a game culture replete with shared meanings and special symbols. Within this game culture subcultures emerged. The insertion of nuclear power served as a catalyst for reactions that were already underway. The press was a key medium for the creation of meanings and symbols, contributing greatly to the development of the richness of the game culture.

This line of observation indicates that runs of the simulation should be sufficiently long to allow game history and traditions—game culture—to develop, say thirty hours at a minimum. The process seems to be aided by spacing the sessions some days apart, allowing time for reflection between sessions. The role of a national press could be developed as an instrument of "acculturation."

IV. The Prescientific Character of the Evolution of the Simulation

This essay attempts to share concerns about many problems which were encountered in the evolution of the inter-nation simulation. It illustrates the way in which the exploratory runs of the simulation provided prescientific hunches as to how the simulation might be modified. It is misleading through focusing upon only the central problems encountered in the prescientific phase of the development of the simulation. It is misleading, perhaps, in neglecting to recount more of the alternative interpretations that were considered as we proceeded from decision to decision. But at least it is forthright in displaying the important role occupied by intuition and hunch in the formation of the simulation. The researchers had saturated themselves in the literature of international relations. They conducted three pilot runs, as mentioned in Chapter Two, and the three exploratory runs described in more detail in this chapter. The *ad hoc* nature of the evolution of the simulation through these six preliminaries is an empiricism of the rawest kind, typical of prescientific activity.

Upon the completion of the preliminary runs and our study of our results, it seemed that the structure of the simulation now was perhaps adequate for use in the teaching of international relations, as well as for systematic utilization in experimental research. For these reasons the laboratory manual was completed, as exhibited in Chapter Three. In addition, the theoretical structure of the simulation was somewhat rigorously codified, as will be seen in the following chapter.

Chapter Five

Structured Programs and Their Relation to Free Activity Within the Inter-Nation Simulation

Harold Guetzkow

Snyder has located the simulation of relations among nations within the broader context of work in international relations. Brody has analyzed the variety of games, exercises, and simulations that have been developed within international relations itself. Guetzkow has provided an over-all description of an inter-nation simulation that has been developed at Northwestern University. Noel gives details as to how this particular

103

simulation was evolved to meet theoretical needs. In this chapter, it may be helpful to attempt a somewhat rigorous summarization of the assumptions involved in the development of the programs used within the inter-nation simulation. These structured postulates then may be examined as they relate to the emergence of the free activities of the decision-makers operating within the framework of the programmed assumptions. The following analysis presents a summarization of the theoretical model developed in the simulation during 1958 and 1959.

I. Guideposts in the Construction of an Inter-Nation Model

The relations among nations are embodied in the simulation by the postulation of programs of operation with respect to the internal functioning of the several nations constituting the over-all inter-nation system. Using these programs, the decision-makers of each nation then freely develop relations between their states as they deem appropriate, given their unfolding circumstances. It is possible to vary the assumptions made within the programs, as Noel has demonstrated. Such changes in operating postulates should result in variations in the unprogrammed activities, which emerge as the nations relate to each other within the developing over-all system.

The simulation is grounded in explicit specification of a basic set of variables and programmed relations among them. But because of the use of human beings as decision-makers in the system, a variety of additional factors—and relations among them—are implicitly incorporated in the representation. Together, these two kinds of factors and their relationships produce an operating environment for the decision-makers which is designed to be isomorphic to the environment in which foreign policy decision-makers operate within the system of nations of the world.

During the course of our early work on the simulation, an option was available to attempt to program the entire model. Instead, programs were postulated only for limited intranational activities, such as office-holding and revolution. An advantage that we hoped to gain in the use of human participants rather than computing machines as decision-makers was the former's potential ability to outthink the simulators themselves. Later it may seem fruitful to program more of the behavior of the system than has been done in the representations to be described below. But perhaps the development of a completely programmed inter-nation simulation must wait until the men behind the computers have developed further the self-programming capability of their machines.

In constructing the simulation, whole sets of variables in the complex of national and international life are represented by simplified, generic factors, supposedly the prototypes of more elaborate realities. For example, the gamut of groups and processes through which decision-makers gain and maintain political office within a nation is represented in the simulation by the relation of the decision-making participants to their validators. This one programmed relationship, which will be described in detail below, provides a condensed version of a gamut of real-life activities, similar to the way in which probability distributions are used by simulators to represent elaborate, underlying mechanisms that are too complicated to detail. Yet these prototypic variables, be they of determinant or stochastic form, constitute the core of the simulation. One important part of the task of this chapter, therefore, is to delineate these core variables. No attempt, however, will be made at this time to enumerate the implicit variables—those of personality and of organization expectation—which are carried into the simulation by the persons participating as decision-makers. Disclosure of such factors awaits experimental work with the simulation.

Once the core variables have been posited, interrelations among them are then programmed through assumptions that assert what happens when the magnitude of one of the variables is changed. For example, when the probability of office-holding reduces to certain levels, validator support is considered as questionable in a program which determines whether or not the decision-makers continue to hold office. These calculations for determination of office-holding are assumptions postulated to simulate processes involved in the "orderly and disorderly transference of political power," as will be displayed below. Another important part of the task of this chapter is to state the assumptions embodied within the programs of the inter-nation simulation. The prescribed programs actually used in making the calculations in the inter-nation simulation are presented after each "Programmed Assumption."

The core variables and their programmed assumptions constitute the foundations of the simulation. The activities emerging from these postulated conditions, generated as the participants react to their simulated environments, consist of such things as arms races, trade systems, and international organizations. But because this unfolding is not prescribed, it is possible to formulate hypotheses (as contrasted with the programmed assumptions) about these developments. A description of their operation depends upon our insight in isolating the important variables which undergird these unprogrammed developments and in hypothesizing the interrelations which exist between them and the core variables. This chapter will provide examples of how the core variables and their programmed interrelations generate free variables, which in turn may be hypothesized as being linked to the foundational structure of the simulation.

Although an effort will be made to enumerate all the core variables and all their programmed interrelations, no such coverage can be attempted at this stage in our understanding of the inter-nation simulation for the free activities. Hence, the chapter will have an imbalance, with the free variables and associated hypotheses being described in a fragmentary manner. At some later time, it may be possible to present a more complete analysis of the inter-nation simulation in both its programmed and its unprogrammed features. The reader will decide whether it is fruitful at this time, despite the incompleteness, to describe the way in which the programmed characteristics of the simulation—in conjunction with the personal characteristics and organizational expectations of the decision-makers—create the free activities of the inter-nation simulation.

The programs displayed in the following text are given usually with parameters in alphabetic form, indicating that the particular values used in the runs to date might be changed, depending upon the magnitude of the relations one wishes to assert as holding among the nations. It is possible, of course, to vary also the form of the program itself, by simply adding or subtracting or by substituting new variables, and by changing the relationships asserted within an equation.

II. Decision-Makers and Their Nations

Actions within the inter-nation simulation originate through individuals and groups. The human beings participating in the simulation represent the decision-makers within national political systems. A group of two or three to five or six decision-makers, along with their resources and capabilities, operate as the nation. Some or all of these nations, in turn, may combine to form supragroups, such as regional and universal organizations.

Core Unit: Decision-Makers. Humans who develop and choose among alternative policies and actions at the nation or inter-nation levels.

Core Unit: Nations. Groups of validated decision-makers, operating within a political-military-economic system, who are capable of amalgamation and splintering.

Free Unit: Supraunits. Supranational groups of nations, developing and operating various structures, with capabilities derived from national units.

The simulation thus consists of components at three levels—individuals (decision-makers), groups (nations), and supragroups (alliances, international organizations). Some of the following assumptions and hypotheses are concerned with relations within the level of the phenomena being considered; others relate components at one level to those at another level.

ORGANIZATIONAL RELATIONS AMONG DECISION-MAKERS

One individual initially is designated central decision-maker. He is responsible for over-all national policy, both domestic and international. With him are associated other decision-makers, who constitute the nation's government. The central decision-maker possesses final authority in all decisions, within the limits set by the risk of losing his office and the constraints imposed by his associates. The exercise of final authority by the central decision-maker simulates the fact that there is usually a recognized head of state or someone exercising ultimate political power.

Core Variable: Authority. The command of each central decision-maker is honored by the simulation director, even though the decisions of the associated national decision-makers be at variance in some way with the former's directives.

Free Variable: Delegation of Authority. The central decision-maker may delegate various amounts of authority within particular domains to his associated decision-makers, either informally or formally.

The mechanical reconciliation of conflicts among the decision-makers of a nation by the simulation director attempts to simulate the exercise of actual power within a political system, which by definition resides within the "central" decision-maker. There is freedom within the delegation of authority for its abuse, if the central decision-maker does not institute adequate controls. A central decision-maker may lose partial control of his decisions until his authority is re-established by his personal control of the nation's decision forms or by confrontation of disobedient associates so that they are reversed or even disqualified from participation in the exercise by the simulation director. In a run with foreign students, the "European" nation was divided internally, one of the external decision-makers secretly having joined forces with the decision-makers in the "South American" state. Advantage was taken of delegated authority to sabotage the effectiveness of the central decision-maker's activities before the perfidy was discovered and accreditation revoked by the latter.

Free Variable: Division of Labor Among Decision-Makers. It is possible for the central decision-maker to use his authority to organize his associates so that each performs different tasks within the nation.

Some participants may become internal decision-makers, specializing in economic or military matters. Others may serve as external decision-makers, focusing upon the international affairs of their nation, regularly conducting negotiations with other nations, and/or operating the international organizations. The lack of prescribed structure among the decision-makers, except for the allocation of prime authority to the central decision-makers, allows freedom for the participants in the evolution of their decision-making roles.

Note how the two free variables are related to the core variable, in this instance, authority. The participants are given definite instructions that the central decision-maker holds the ultimate power within his nation "by definition." But the utilization which is made of this "programmed" authority by the decision-makers depends upon such unprogrammed features of the simulation as their own personality characteristics and developments within their situation. "Delegation" and "Division of Labor" are but two of an array of free variables which can be discovered within the operation of the simulation.

It may be that a division of labor gradually develops within the nation, in response to the relations of a country to other nations within the system. In one run, for example, an external decision-maker in Erga[1] became concerned with the economic aspects of his state's relations to two other nations. His counterpart focused his attention upon security affairs, working closely with the central decision-maker concerned with force. In another run of the simulation, the central decision-maker in Omne restricted the role of his external ministers to representing and reporting, allowing them little scope for policy development. In yet another run, the central decision-maker or prime minister turned over almost all internal

---

[1] It has been our practice in the simulation to designate the nations by fictitious names or by single letters.

functions to a trusted associate so that his full attention could be devoted to foreign affairs.

Unprogrammed Hypothesis. Insufficient delegation of authority within a nation produces inter-nation crises because of lag in the decision-making activities of the nation.

Unprogrammed Hypothesis. The number of decisions demanded of a nation by both internal and external relations is greater than the capability of one decision-maker.

The core variable of authority permits the central decision-maker of any nation to amalgamate his nation with others by agreeing to have his decisions subject to a supranational unit. The core variable of authority also allows for a situation in which the central decision-maker relinquishes control to an antagonistic power. The processes of amalgamation and occupation will be discussed in more detail at a later point in this exposition.

Should the researcher/teacher want to explore the implications of a more complex decision-making organization, the simulation can be so adapted. For example, by restricting direct communications among the national decision-makers to occasional internal conferences interspersed with longer periods of indirect, written communication, significant characteristics of hierarchical organizations can be simulated. Even in the present representation of foreign office operation, the need for coordination among the decision-makers is apparent, especially when they are "abroad" for prolonged periods in international conferences or organizations. Misunderstandings among the decision-makers result from differences in perspective on a particular international problem.

The manner of organization of internal activities also may have external consequences. Specialization among the decision-makers creates coordination problems for other nations. In one run, the senior external decision-maker of Utro specialized in the development of a grand alliance system, which competed with alliances among smaller nations. But the smaller nations had not designated particular decision-makers as opposite numbers to Utro's diplomat, who had great trouble developing a series of bilateral negotiations. Or, to take another example, the management of internal authority within each state creates consequences for the external affairs of all other states. Communications between states have bogged down noticeably in runs characterized by insufficient delegation of authority by the central decision-makers. During one of the 1958-59 runs, dangerous risks were incurred by Utro because of its slowness in responding to urgent pleas from its allies in a time of crisis.

OFFICE-HOLDING

By definition the exercise of power in political decision-making situations within a nation depends upon formal or informal office-holding, be it *de facto* or *de jure*. Office-holding is a mainspring of the inter-nation simulation. Although no attempt has been made thus far to represent accession to office, an endeavor is made to simulate vital characteristics of the process of remaining in office.

Core Variable: Office-Holding (pOH). The *de jure* right, as recognized by the simulation director, to make the decisions of the nation with respect to both internal and external affairs.

The retention of office by the central decision-makers depends upon their ability to elicit validation of their office-holding in competition with countermoves by aspiring decision-makers. For purposes of the simulation, this validation process consists in gaining and retaining the support of élites and interest groups within their nation, along with sufficient compliance among all its inhabitants to secure implementation of political decisions. Validation is made operational by a set of mathematical relations between the consequences of the decisions made within nations and the chances of remaining in office.

The validators within such a process may be conceived as individuals and groups in the nation's political system who occupy positions of influence outside the formal governmental structure. Through their situations of power, they influence the chances for office retention by the decision-makers in the nation. In a democracy, the validators might be voters and interest groups. In an autocracy, the validators might be some oligarchic élite or military junta. In all governmental systems, however, it seems there must be some minimal compliance by the people as a whole, even if it is only passive acceptance rooted in apathy.

Core Variable: Validator Satisfaction (VS_m). The acceptability of the central decision-maker's program to those with power to authenticate his office-holding.

The demands of the validators are postulated to arise from two sources: (1) the nation must satisfy the basic needs of its peoples— and in our "satisfaction with regard to consumption" (VS_{cs}) variable, an attempt was made to encompass the whole gamut of living needs of the validators, from bare necessities for the peasant and workman to luxuries for the guardians of the palace or members of the cabinet; (2) the nation also must satisfy the needs of its people with regard to their feelings of national security (VS_{ns}). In later parts of this chapter, details of these validating components will be described. For the moment, over-all validation of office-holding may be viewed as a function of the extent to which these prototypic needs are satisfied. The emphasis given various needs may vary over time within a nation, just as they may vary from nation to nation.

Programmed Assumption No. 1: Relation of Validator Satisfaction to Office-Holding. The probability of continuing in office depends upon the extent to which the decision-makers of the nation satisfy their validators.

This assumption is programmed as follows:

$$pOH = a(b - DL)VS_m + c(DL - d) \tag{1}$$

where pOH is the probability of continuing office-holding, and VS_m is mean over-all validator satisfaction. When DL or decision latitude is thought of as a constant,[2] Equation 1 is linear, that is, of the form $pOH = $ a constant times VS_m plus another constant. The constants were chosen so as to allow use of simpler calculation routines, given the arbitrary scale values assigned to VS_m and DL, as follows:

$$a = .01; \ b = 11; \ c = .1; \ \text{and} \ d = 1.$$

The relation between the validating process and office-holding is presented in Figure 5-1. Validation is conceptualized as a duo-stage process by which decisions regarding consumption standards and force capability are translated into partial measures of validator satisfaction (Figures 5-1a and 5-1b). These measures are then combined into a single index (VS_m), which in turn determines the probability of holding office (pOH) (Figure 5-1c). Undoubtedly the programs represented in these graphs are but approximations of the complex functions which may hold in the national societies of the world.

In operating the simulation, graphs are not given to the participants, although the general form of the functions is revealed. In making explanations, each component is described on an eleven-point scale. The two components of validator satisfaction are averaged into a single index on an identical eleven-point scale.

---

[2] Definition of decision latitude as a variable is made on p. 115.

FIGURE 5-1. The Validation of Office-Holding.

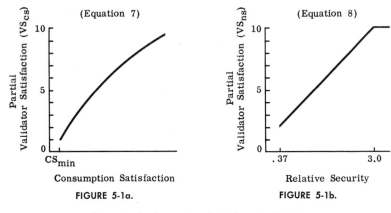

FIGURE 5-1a.   FIGURE 5-1b.

Bases for the Generation of Validator Satisfaction.

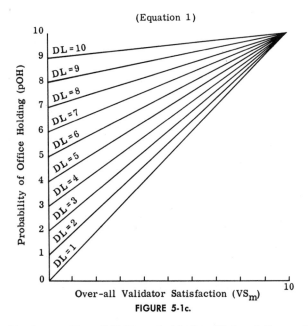

FIGURE 5-1c.

Relationships Between Over-all Validator Satisfaction (VS_m) and Chances for Holding Office (pOH) for Varying Levels of Decision Latitude (DL).

TABLE 5-1 | SCALES FOR (a) THE MEASUREMENT OF VALIDATOR SATISFACTION AND (b) PROBABILITY OF OFFICE-HOLDING

(a)

VALIDATOR
SATISFACTION
(VS)

10   maximum satisfaction

9⎫
8⎬ high satisfaction
7⎭

6   moderately high satisfaction

5   indifference

4   moderately low satisfaction (moderate dissatisfaction)
___ [revolution threshold, p. 118 ff.]

3⎫
2⎬ low satisfaction (high dissatisfaction)
1⎭

0   minimum satisfaction (maximum dissatisfaction)

(Same scale is used for VS_m , VS_{c8} , and VS_{n8})

(b)

PROBABILITY
OF OFFICE-
HOLDING
(pOH)

10   certainty of office-holding

9⎫
8⎬ high likelihood of office-holding
7⎭

6   moderately high likelihood of office-holding

5   even likelihood of holding or losing office

4   moderately low likelihood of office-holding

3⎫
2⎬ low likelihood of office-holding
1⎭

0   certainty of losing office

The transformation displayed in Figure 5-1c is explained as the relationship of Table 5-1a to Table 5-1b. When over-all validator satisfaction is high, likelihood of retaining office tends to be greater;

when over-all validator satisfaction is low, the likelihood of retaining office tends to be less.

Programmed Assumption No. 2: Relations of Over-all Validation to Component Validations. The validators are satisfied to the extent to which their national security and standards of living are realized.

$$VS_m = (eVS_{cs} + gVS_{ns}) \qquad (2)$$

where VS_{cs} represents consumption satisfaction for validators deriving from their living standards, and VS_{ns} represents satisfactions deriving from national security. These terms will be defined in more detail below, pp. 124 and 126. The parameters e and g were set at .5 in the exploratory runs in 1957-1959.

It is possible to inject some of the effects of an opposition party into the simulation through the use of a participant who makes critiques of the performance of the decision-makers serving as office-holders. In Noel's description of the January, 1959 runs, he explains how we asked individuals to stand by, ready to take over when the decision-makers lost office. In his International Organizations course, Alger has worked out procedures to consummate a transfer of power to an opposition group. An aspirant office-holder makes his own decisions, parallel to those made by the office-holders. He functions without the operating responsibilities imposed on the official decision-makers. The extent to which the aspirant's decisions prove to be potentially more adequate in meeting the needs of the validators serves as an indicator of the amount to which validator satisfactions provided by the central decision-makers are diluted because of alternatives provided by an opposition.

The validation process is an example of our endeavor to build essentials into the simulation by the use of so-called "prototypic" variables. The probability that particular individuals will continue in office in real life is an elaborate, ill-understood process. Yet, it seems that decision-making in domestic and foreign affairs is dependent upon a number of factors, two of which we intuitively assert may be taken as representative of a wider gamut. The decision-makers may endeavor to retain office by favoring one source of validation over another—representing the way in which practical politicians may cater to one validating group rather than another. A running competition with the aspirant decision-maker would make it necessary for those in office not only to satisfy their validators, but to come to decisions which compare favorably with the promises of an opposition that has none of the responsibilities of office-holding. In this way, the simulation creates a conceptual environment for the decision-makers, which typifies variables that are seen as motivating office-holding in political life.

DECISION LATITUDE

In the real world the relationship between validator satisfaction and office-holding varies widely from nation to nation, depending upon the forms of the internal government. In some cases, the decision-makers for certain periods of time have wide latitude in making their decisions, regardless of how their validators respond. In other instances, the decision-makers have little latitude; they find their office-holding is very sensitive to changes in the over-all satisfaction of their validators.

These differences in decision latitude are represented in the simulation by varying the functions relating satisfaction and office holding in Figure 5-1c. The participants are given a scale which indicates the sensitivity of their validators to their decisions, as presented in Table 5-2.

TABLE 5-2 | SCALE FOR REPRESENTATION OF DECISION LATITUDE

DECISION
LATITUDE
(DL)

10 complete decision latitude
9⎫
8⎭ high decision latitude

7⎫
6⎪
5⎬ moderate decision latitude
4⎭

3⎫
2⎭ low decision latitude

1   no decision latitude

Core Variable: Decision Latitude (DL). The degree to which the probability of office-holding of the decision-makers depends on changes in validator satisfaction.

Programmed Assumption No. 3: Relation of Office-Holding to Decision Latitude. The higher the decision latitude, the less immediately is office-holding subject to validator satisfaction.

This assumption is incorporated in Equation 1, when *DL* now is allowed to vary. This equation is linear with respect to variations in

DL, if VS_m is considered to be a constant, as the following rearrangement of the terms of Equation 1 indicates. Multiplying out the constants in Equation 1 yields:

$$pOH = abVS_m - a(DL)(VS_m) + cDL - cd$$

Then by regrouping the terms one obtains the following linear equation:

$$pOH = (c - aVS_m)DL + (abVS_m - cd) \tag{1'}$$

The nation's decision latitude changes slowly, sometimes being dependent upon factors quite beyond the control of the office-holders, and at other times responding directly to decisions made by the nation's principals. Changes in the freedom of the decision-makers due to exogenous factors are stochastically developed by the simulator. These are programmed to occur randomly, resulting in a change in the decision latitude of one unit either in an upward or downward direction. These changes in decision latitude may be thought of as occurring for reasons outside the control of the central decision-makers, such as shifts in leadership among the validators, changes in mass media that allow new ideologies to gain prominence among validating groups, and so forth.

Programmed Assumption No. 4: Variations in Decision Latitude by Validators. During each period there is random modification in the decision latitude of each nation.

Changes of plus or minus one unit or zero are equally probable. But the central decision-maker himself may attempt to induce changes in decision latitude, never exceeding one unit down or up in a period. Unless he is willing to apply political pressure, a situation to be considered later (see pp. 127 ff.), conditions generated by the validators predominate.

Programmed Assumption No. 5: The Predominant Character of the Validators in Producing Changes in Decision Latitude. When pressure is not used to implement changes in decision latitude desired by the central decision-maker, the validators' preferences are effected.

Even when there is agreement between the validators and the decision-makers with respect to the changes in decision latitude, there is no augmentation of the magnitude of the change. By not programming an additive effect, rapid and abrupt changes in decision latitude are avoided, thus representing nonrevolutionary change situations with more adequacy.

The decision to vest authority in an individual rather than a small internal group is dictated by our interest being centered on the interrelations among the nations, rather than in the internal functioning of each of the states. However, an effort was made to represent constraints upon these decision-makers, constraints which seem always to exist in national political systems, whether they be totalitarian or democratic, through the limitations on office-holding as extended by the validators and through restrictions in decision latitude. Thus, the validation and decision latitude functions are designed to represent such constraints as those imposed by courts, legislative bodies, and bureaucratic inflexibilities.

The use of stochastic processes in these programs is analogous to their use by operations research analysts in their simulation of physical systems. Whenever the variables involved in a given consequence are numerous and complicated—and thereby at times little understood—it is possible to represent the resultant by a probability distribution of random numbers. This stochastic representation later may be replaced by a more adequately detailed program which gives rise to the desired consequence by other than random means. Our use of prototypic variables to represent a complex network of poorly delineated variables parallels this employment of stochastic or random determinations in the inter-nation simulation.

ORDERLY AND DISORDERLY TRANSFERENCE OF POWER

The mechanisms of the transference of power from one set of public office-holders to another is of central interest to the political scientist. When over-all validator satisfaction is quite low, there would be some chance that disorder might occur, possibly with immediate loss of office. When over-all validator satisfaction is high, more orderly and regularized devices for the transfer of power from one set of office-holders to the next would prevail. Yet, even when there is great likelihood of losing office, decision-makers in the real world retain office because of nonpredictable circumstances. These hypotheses again are embodied in the simulation by the use of probabilistic devices—this time for the determination of office loss.

Core Variable: Determination of Office-Holding (pOH_m). At periodic or intermittent times, a determination of office-holding is made within each nation. This determination may result in continuation of the same decision-makers in office or provide for their replacement.

Core Variable: Determination of Occurrence of Revolution (pR). When a determination of revolution is made, the result may be revolution or no revolution.

Core Variable: Determination of Outcome of Revolution (pSR).
When a revolution occurs, the decision-makers may or may not lose
office.

The simulation is divided into periods. To date, we have employed
periods ranging from forty-five to seventy-five minutes in length.
At the beginning of each period the office-holders are informed of
the likelihood of retaining office. To simulate more routine, orderly
shifts in the occupants of positions of power in a nation, regular
biperiod or triperiod determinations of office-holding have been
employed.

*Programmed Assumption No. 6: Office Retention or Loss De-
termined by Average of Probabilities of Office-Holding.* Whether the
central decision-makers of a nation continue in office or lose office
at the regular determinations depends upon the average of the probabilities of office-holding during preceding periods.

The ruling is made on the basis of the average likelihood of office-
holding over a given number of periods, as follows:

$$pOH_m = \sum_i^j pOH/j - i \qquad (3)$$

where the ith period precedes the jth period.

In the runs of the inter-nation simulation during our exploratory
work, the average was determined over the last two or three periods.

The span over two or three periods gives the participant the
ability to take short-run gambles with his validators, if in the longer
run he believes that he can maintain an average of satisfactions high
enough to keep his chances for holding office sufficiently great. But
even when his chances are high at the times of these regular determinations, there still will be some occasions when office is lost.
For example, in a run in 1958, the central decision-maker of P lost
office when the random numbers were applied, even though his
scale value of "9" indicated nine chances out of ten that he would
retain office. Due to the vagaries of politics—"perhaps there was a
scandal of political import in his immediate family"—he lost office,
even though his decision-making had induced much satisfaction in
his validators.

A risk of revolution is encountered within a nation when over-all
validator satisfaction drops to or below a threshold of three units
(see "Revolution Threshold" in Table 5-1a). The impact of disorder
is determined immediately on a probability basis. If there is no

revolution, the decision-makers retain office and the orderly process for the transfer of power prevails, despite the low validator satisfaction. If disorder terminates in revolution, then a second stochastic calculation is involved to determine the outcome of the revolution itself.

Programmed Assumption No. 7: Relation of Regularity in Office Determination to Validator Satisfaction. If the satisfaction of the validators is above the critical threshold of three units, there is periodic determination of office at regular intervals.

Programmed Assumption No. 8: Relation of Occurrence of Revolution to Validator Satisfaction. If the satisfaction of the validators is below the critical threshold, three units, there is an immediate determination of whether a revolution has occurred.

Note how the combination of programs for the determination of office-holding and revolution imply that although a government in the short run may be threatened by revolution, if it should maintain immediate power during the disorder, its chances for holding office might still be relatively good because of the past satisfactions of its validators. The choice of the levels of probability involved in determining the outcome of revolution will be explained in detail in a later discussion of the use which may be made of force capabilities. It is enough to indicate here that internal controls may be applied by the decision-makers to lessen the chances of the success of the revolution, no matter how immediately dissatisfied are their validators.

If the change in office is induced by orderly or disorderly procedures, once the calculation produces office loss, the central participant yields his decision-making office and is replaced in the simulation by another. Perhaps the greatest impact of the motivational setting of the simulation is felt in this situation. When the office-holders are strangers to each other except for the interaction that occurs in the simulation itself, less than powerful motivations are aroused. But when the simulation consists of adults who make their profession in foreign policy decision-making, their interest in retaining office is keen. Loss of office is loss of face among participant-colleagues with whom they will be in contact over the years ahead. Long-term operation of one's nation was taken as a sign of outstanding decision-making ability in one run of the simulation involving such professionals.

The stochastic determinations in the simulation represent the full scope of causes which may terminate office-holding in real life. The rarer events—such as ill health or death in office from assassination

—occur even when there is much over-all support for a regime. The common causes of office loss, such as coups d'état and narrow losses of elections, occur when there is less than full support for a particular set of office-holders. By varying the probabilities of office-holding, these differences in real-world situations are reflected in the inter-nation simulation.

Unprogrammed Hypothesis: Because the associated decision-makers of a government hold office on the authority of the central decision-maker, there is a tendency to replace at least some of the associated decision-makers upon transfer of power from one central decision-maker to another.

In establishing and maintaining the relations of their nation to others, the decision-makers seek to use the results to keep themselves in office. These efforts may indeed redound to the well-being of the nation's population, as when a comparative advantage arises from foreign trade to increase validator satisfaction. Or the external effort may simply reinforce the leaders' élite position with concomitant decreases in the well-being of their peoples, *e.g.*, through the display of great force which thereby assures an increase in the probability of office-holding. External relations, then, may be motivated by a felt need for office-holding, regardless of the consequences for the external system.

Free Variable: Decisions on External Affairs. A decision with respect to relations of the nation to other nations.

Free Variable: Office-Holding Needs. Considerations thought important by decision-makers in retaining office.

Unprogrammed Hypothesis: The considerations related to office-holding tend to dominate the considerations deriving from external relations in national decision-making.

There is controversy as to the genesis of policy change in foreign affairs, some arguing that basic policy shifts come only through change in the office-holders. The fact that office-holders are transient —often in the short and at least in the long run—is important in the relations among nations. Because the nation's interests and policies implementing them are subject to the interpretations of its office-holders, national goals and strategies are subject to change as the office-holders change. As individuals with different personality needs and different political ideologies take office, the goals and strategies of the nation in its relation to other states reflect such changes.

Free Variable: National Goals. The objectives, implicit or explicit, toward which the decision-makers attempt to direct their nation's behavior.

Free Variable: National Strategies. The plan of means, implicit or explicit, by which the decision-makers attempt to achieve national goals.

Unprogrammed Hypothesis: When different decision-makers take office, national goals and strategies change.

Unprogrammed Hypothesis: When different decision-makers take office, over-all satisfaction of the validators may be developed through changed emphasis on the components of validator satisfaction.

The fact of constant flux produces powerful pressures within international systems for "staying" until there are shifts in the office-holders of the other nations, *vis-à-vis* one's capacity to retain office. "Staying" tends to induce important limits and potentials in the relations of nations. Because office often is retained by continuation of the same general pattern of external relations that have aided office retention in the past, remaining in office tends to produce conservative, status quo tendencies. Because change of office-holders often is accompanied by changes in the bases for office retention, it is at this time that rearrangements of the complex relations among states may be attempted.

Free Variable: Continuation in Office. Number of consecutive periods during which a decision-maker holds office.

Free Variable: Similarity of Decisions. The extent to which the substance of decisions is repetitious in content, from time to time.

Unprogrammed Hypothesis: The longer decision-makers continue in office, the greater the tendency for similar decisions.

Many consequences of the changes in office-holding flow from uncertainties introduced into complex organizations by personnel changes. Role expectations are generated not only in terms of position demands, but also in terms of the personal characteristics and styles of the nation's representatives in their behavior in bilateral and multilateral contacts. Changes destabilize expectations in the larger system. These uncertainties in expectation make prediction of the behaviors of opposite numbers difficult. Hence, errors in decision-making are more likely.

Free Variable: Stability of Behavior Expectations. The extent of constancy which is expected in the anticipated behaviors of a unit.

Unprogrammed Hypothesis: The longer decision-makers continue in office, the more constant will others expect their behaviors to be.

Unprogrammed Hypothesis: The longer decision-makers continue in office, the greater is their adequacy in achieving their national goals in inter-nation affairs.

Unprogrammed Hypothesis: The more unstable the expected be-havior of others, the greater is the chance of error in the nation's decision-making.

NATIONAL CAPABILITIES

All kinds of resources, physical and human, are subsumed in the inter-nation simulation under the concept of "basic capability." The size of a nation's accumulation of basic capabilities reflects the nation's over-all ability to produce all goods and services, be they used for consumption or for the exercise of physical force in internal or external affairs.

Units of basic capability at the disposal of the nation's decision-makers may be allocated to the development of further basic capa-bility (as exploration for oil fields, investment in more efficient fac-tories, or the training of scientists and engineers), or for research and development. Because of obsolescence, deterioration, and re-source exhaustion, all nations must devote parts of their basic capa-bility to regeneration, if they desire to maintain constant standards. Growth, stagnation, and retrogression will occur, depending upon the amounts allocated over time to the development and renewal of the nation's basic capabilities.

Core Variable: Basic Capability (BC). The nation's over-all ability to produce goods and services, be they used for replacement of or for addition to the basic capability itself, to satisfy consumption needs and wants, or to produce arms.

Core Variable: Generation Rates. The rates at which basic capa-bility allocated to different sectors of the economy generate (with a lag of one period) new basic capability units, force capability units, and consumption satisfaction units.

Core Variable: Depreciation of Basic Capability. The rate at which basic capability depreciates each period, due to depletion, obsolescence, and deterioration.

Programmed Assumption No. 9: Stochastic Variation in Depreci-ation of Basic Capability. In each period, depreciation may occur in the amount of basic capability. The values 2, 5, and 10 per cent used during the exploratory runs for the depreciation rate are equiprobable. The relative magnitude of the depreciation has no relation to the amount of basic capability possessed by the nation.

The nation consumes its own goods and services at varying standards of living. A minimum portion of the nation's basic capa-bility must be devoted each period to the production of goods and services for consumption. This minimum changes from time to time, increasing as the basic capability of the nation increases and decreasing as the nation becomes depressed. The increases, however, are programmed to be a decreasing percentage of the total, as the gross national product increases. The minimum consumption represents that allocated of necessity, to provide for the supply and manning of the nation's productive capability. The minimum requirement further represents the amount of consumption which the peoples of the nation, despite government action, are able to devote to their own maintenance, as in the peasants' hidden poultry or grains, and in the laborers' pilfering of clothes or fuel. These minima are such that they yield little validator satisfaction. For consumption above the minimum the validator satisfaction increases with the ratio of consumption to the minimum consumption standard. The goods created for use in living are conceived in the simulation as being entirely expended, with no carry-over from period to period.

Core Variable: Consumption Standards (CS). Quantity of goods produced and utilized in the nation for consumption purposes.

Core Variable: Minimum Consumption Standards (CS_{min}). At least minimal consumption standards for its people must be provided.

Programmed Variable: Maximum Consumption Standards (CS_{max}). The maximum units of consumption which could be allocated by the nation in a given period to consumption standards; *i.e.*, $CS_{max} = $ all BC's $\times$ Generation Rate for CS's.

Programmed Assumption No. 10: Relation of Consumption Satisfaction to Utilization. The goods and services produced through the nation's basic capability are completely expended at the end of any period, without holdover.

In designing the programs involving consumption standards, an effort was made to include two effects, namely, (1) that as the basic capability of the nation increased, the minimum standards of the nation's population would rise; and (2) simultaneously, the rise of aspirations for increases in the minimum standards would be slow enough so that increasingly large amounts of basic capability might be devoted to activities other than consumption.

Programmed Assumption No. 11: Relation of Minimum Consumption Standards to Basic Capability. The minimum consumption standards of the nation increase as the basic capability of the nation increases in its ability to produce satisfying goods and services.

Programmed Assumption No. 12: Proportion of Basic Capability Needed to Fulfill Minimum Consumption Standard. The percentage of the realized basic capability required to fulfill minimum living standards decreases as the nation's basic capability increases.

Programmed Assumptions Nos. 11 and 12 may be represented simultaneously in a single equation.

$$CS_{min} = (1 - \frac{CS_{max}}{k})CS_{max} \tag{4}$$

where k equals 380,000 CS Units.

The constant k was chosen to be considerably larger than the values which CS_{max} reached during the runs before 1960. This constraint assures that Equation 4 is a monotonically increasing relation between CS_{min} and CS_{max}, as asserted in Programmed Assumption No. 11. When CS_{max} is quite small compared with k, then $CS_{min} \cong CS_{max}$, for CS_{max}/k tends to zero. Contrariwise, when CS_{max} gradually increases, the percentage of basic capability needed for CS_{min} gradually decreases. This may be seen as follows: Divide both sides of Equation 4 by CS_{max}:

$$\frac{CS_{min}}{CS_{max}} = 1 - \frac{CS_{max}}{k} \tag{4'}$$

Note how the ratio CS_{min}/CS_{max} decreases with increases in CS_{max}, thus meeting the assertion of Programmed Assumption No. 12.

Programmed Variable: Validator Satisfaction with Respect to Consumption Satisfaction (VS_{cs}). The satisfactions attained by the nation's validators from the amount and distribution of goods and services.

Programmed Assumption No. 13: Relation of Validator Satisfaction to Consumption Satisfaction. This assumption consists of three parts:

1. For consumption near minimum consumption standards, validator satisfaction depends on the relation of consumption satisfaction to minimum consumption standards.
2. Once minimum consumption standards have been met, larger and larger increases in consumption are necessary to produce corresponding changes in validator satisfaction.
3. This saturation effect is more prominent for wealthier nations.

The effects of Programmed Assumption No. 13 are incorporated in a quadratic equation in the inter-nation simulation.

It is conceived that when minimum living standards are but barely met (*i.e.*, when the CS in any period equals CS_{min}), the validators are minimally satisfied (*i.e.*, $VS_{cs} = 1$). Part 1 of the assumption then may be represented as the first term of a quadratic equation, that is:

$$VS_{cs} \cong r\frac{CS}{CS_{min}} + s \tag{5}$$

when consumption is near minimum consumption standards. When VS_{cs} equals 1, and CS/CS_{min} equals 1 (as $CS = CS_{min}$), then Equation 5 becomes $1 = r + s$. By transposing terms, $s = 1 - r$. Using this value for s and rearranging terms, Equation 5 for Part 1 of Programmed Assumption No. 13 may be stated as:

$$VS_{cs} \cong 1 + r\left(\frac{CS}{CS_{min}} - 1\right) \tag{5'}$$

As CS increases above CS_{min}, the saturation effect of Part 2 may be represented by subtracting a squared term from Equation 5' as follows:

$$VS_{cs} = 1 + r\left(\frac{CS}{CS_{min}} - 1\right) - u\left(\frac{CS}{CS_{min}} - 1\right)^2 \tag{6}$$

According to Part 3 of our assumption, however, the effect is more prominent for wealthier nations, so that the constant u then should be made to depend upon the relation of CS_{min} to CS_{max}. This may be done, so that the final quadratic expression for Programmed Assumption No. 13, including all three of its parts with appropriate constants, is as follows:

$$VS_{cs} = 1 + r\left(\frac{CS}{CS_{min}} - 1\right) - v\frac{CS_{max}}{CS_{min}}\left(\frac{CS}{CS_{min}} - 1\right)^2 \tag{7}$$

where $r = 55$ and $v = 41$ during the exploratory runs.

Although the decision-makers must meet the bare minimum consumption standards for survival of their nation, their allocations of basic capability for strategic purposes may vary from zero to amounts determined by the nation's security needs. The ability of the nation to use force as a threat or for actual warfare depends upon its current level of "strategic capability." Although one's strategic capabilities may be carried over from period to period, the loss in each period is considerable because of high obsolescence and operating costs. The reductions are erratic, depending upon military breakthroughs, weapon developments, and so forth. Because there is lag in the conversion of basic capability to strategic capabilities, preparedness policies demand standing forces, despite their drain on the nation's resources. Validator satisfaction is based on the strength of a nation and its allies in relation to the strength of the non-allies.

Core Variable: Force Capability (FC). Coercion available for the control of external and internal affairs.

Core Variable: Internal Controls (FC_{ic}). Force capability which is applied internally for purposes of reducing the chances of revolutions being successful.

Core Variable: Military Costs. The obsolescence and wear (depreciation) as well as the resources consumed and labor involved in operating a military establishment.

Programmed Assumption No. 14: Relation of Levels of Force Capability to Military Costs. The costs of the force capability of the nation change over a period of time, the percentage amounts varying randomly with given ranges from time to time. The values of 20, 30, and 40 per cent for the rate of depreciation of force capability within a period are equiprobable.

Programmed Assumption No. 15: Time Lag in the Availability of Force Capability. Although there is a period lag involved in the creation of force capability, the force in existence at any time is available for immediate use.

Programmed Variable: Validator Satisfaction with Respect to National Strength (VS_{ns}). The extent to which a nation's validators feel secure in their military position in relation to other nations.

Programmed Assumption No. 16: Relation of Validator Satisfaction to Level of Force Capability. Validator satisfaction is directly related, within limits, to the ratio of the force strength of the nation and its allies *vis-à-vis* the strongest nation or group of nations not allied with it, as follows:

1. Top limit: when a nation with its allies is many times stronger than nonally nations or groups
2. Bottom limit: when a nation with its allies is insignificant in its strength by comparison to its nonallies.

$$VS_{ns} = w \frac{\overset{\text{allies}}{\sum}(FC - FC_{ic} + a'BC)}{\underset{\text{others}}{\sum}(FC - FC_{ic} + a'BC)} + b' \tag{8}$$

where $w = 3$ and $b' = 1.3$ are arbitrary constants. The FC units without subscript represent the total coercive power of the nation, from which is subtracted that part which is devoted to internal controls (FC_{ic}), a variable already defined above. The force capability available for external use plus a measure of the over-all basic capability of the nation are added for the nation and its allies, constituting the numerator of the ratio of strength represented in Equation 8. The constant a' was set at .5 during the exploratory runs reported in other chapters of this book. The corresponding sum, which supplies the denominator for the comparison, is gathered for all non-allies. If the nation has no allies, the comparison is made between itself and the total of all the other nations. When the ratio is greater than 3, VS_{ns} is considered to have reached its maximum. When the relative level of a nation's FC's is less than .37 the nation is considered disengaged from the armaments race, as is represented by the cut-off in Figure 5-1b. Its VS_m then is made directly equivalent to VS_{cs} rather than the combination of VS_{cs} and Vs_{ns} assumed in Equation 2 (p. 114).

The underlying capability decisions made each period by the central decision-maker, therefore, are interdependent. The sum of the allocations made each period to consumption, force, and renewal or improvement of the basic capability is constrained always by the basic capability available from the previous period. In this way, the simulation attempts to represent the allocative choices facing top decision-makers concerned with domestic and foreign affairs.

Unprogrammed Hypothesis: The decision-makers of a nation will allocate their various capabilities so as to increase their chances of retaining office and of implementing their nation's goals.

CONSEQUENCES OF PRESSURED CHANGES IN DECISION LATITUDE

What happens when the validators (through the stochastic process postulated in Programmed Assumption No. 4) wish to contest the desires of the decision-makers with respect to the nation's decision latitude? Then political pressure may be used to contravene the predominance of their validators. The consequences of the use of such pressure in these circumstances were programmed as follows:

Programmed Assumption No. 17: Relation of Changes in Decision Latitude to Validator Satisfaction. Increases in decision latitude initiated by the decision-maker induce temporary decreases in validator satisfaction proportional to the difference between the decision-maker's induced change and that desired by the validators.

$$\triangle VS_m = c'(\triangle DL - \triangle DL_v) \tag{9}$$

with the restriction that $VS_m \leq 0$.

The delta signs indicate unit changes in the decision latitude, as actually effected by the central decision-maker (DL without suffix) and as proposed by Programmed Assumption No. 4 for the validators (DL_v). The constant c' may take the value of -1 or -2, as given below in Programmed Assumption No. 20.

Programmed Assumption No. 17 represents a situation in which the central decision-maker applies pressure for an increase in decision latitude against the wishes of the validators. Such a move, however, incurs a temporary decrease in validator satisfaction, as represented in Equation 9. The decrease, however, dissipates during the period, as the validators become accustomed to the new state of affairs.

But the pressured change in decision latitude is not without side consequences. Three programmed assumptions were introduced to portray these effects, as follows:

Programmed Assumption No. 18: The Relation of Pressured Changes in Decision Latitude to Dissipation of Basic Capabilities. Changes in decision latitude effected by central decision-makers against the intention of their validators proportionally decrease the basic capabilities of the nation.

$$\frac{\triangle BC}{BC} = c'd' \; (\triangle DL - \triangle DL_v) \tag{10}$$

where c' takes values as described in Programmed Assumption No. 20 and where $d' = .05$.

These losses in the nation's basic capabilities represent the inefficiencies introduced into the economic system by protest movements, work stoppages, and other forms of political activity aroused by the conflicts between validators and decision-makers with respect to decision latitude.

Programmed Assumption No. 19: The Relation of Pressured Changes in Decision Latitude in Terms of Force Capabilities. Changes in decision latitude effected by central decision-makers against the intention of the validators incur a proportional cost of force capabilities.

$$\frac{\triangle FC}{FC} = c'e' \; (\triangle DL - \triangle DL_v) \tag{11}$$

where c' again takes values as described in Programmed Assumption No. 20 and where $e' = .10$.

These dissipations in force capabilities of the nations represent the side effects of disagreement between decision-makers and validators, as might be expressed in loss of troop morale, as well as in the more tangible forms of reduction in output of munitions factories and inefficiencies of the military support services manned by civilians.

The decreases programmed in Equation 11 indicate that there is less force capability available for external purposes, as so typically occurs when a nation is preoccupied with internal matters. On the other hand, the side effects of such disagreement are not as severe as during revolution when force capability must be employed internally to suppress rioting, as is programmed in Equation 14 (see p. 131).

The changes in c' from -1 to -2, depending upon the level of the decision latitude, may be stated as an explicit assumption, as follows:

Programmed Assumption No. 20: Relation of Decision Latitude to Sensitivity of Validators to Forced Changes in Decision Latitude. The side effect of pressured changes in decision latitude increase when the absolute level of the decision latitude is already very high.

$$c' = -1, \quad \text{when } 1 \leq DL < 8$$

$$c' = -2, \quad \text{when } 8 \leq DL \leq 10 \tag{12}$$

This assumption represents the difficulties governments historically have in gaining complete control over their peoples, even though they may have been able to consolidate their internal powers during the more moderate days of their regime.

Programmed Assumptions Nos. 17, 18, and 19 may be thought of as the costs involved to the decision-makers in imposing their wishes upon their peoples. Note the similarity of form of the three equations, indicating that all costs are hypothesized as proportional to the magnitude of the differences between the decision latitude effected by the central decision-maker and the intended change generated stochastically by the validation process.

These four Programmed Assumptions (Nos. 17 through 20) are complementary to Programmed Assumptions Nos. 4 and 5. Taken together, the over-all operation of the sources for changes in decision latitude are meshed, so that although the validators in general predominate in controlling their relations to the decision-makers, it is possible for the central decision-maker to contravene, when he is willing to pay the costs involved. The elaborateness of the programs illustrates how refined one may become in the development of details of the simulation, should the researcher be so inclined. It seems that these elaborations represent the extreme to which one can usefully go, unless many other components of the simulation are analogously differentiated.

OCCURRENCE AND CONSEQUENCES OF REVOLUTION

Now that capabilities have been described, it is possible to enumerate further details about one of the important political processes within the simulation—revolution. As noted above, when the validator satisfactions descend below the revolution threshold, a two-step program is invoked: first a determination is made of whether there is or is not a revolution and then if there is a revolution, its outcome is decided.

The chances of having a revolution, once the critical threshold of validator dissatisfaction is reached, are determined stochastically in the simulation, the probability of revolution varying directly with the insensitivity of the decision-makers to their validators, that is, varying with decision latitude. When the decision-makers are not sensitive to the validators, then attempts at revolution are substituted for more orderly political processes. But the likelihood of revolutionaries precipitating upheaval will also depend upon the chances that they might succeed in taking over the government.

Programmed Assumption No. 21: Relation of Occurrence of Revolution to Decision Latitude and Outcome of a Revolution. The risk of having a revolution, be it eventually successful or unsuccessful, is related directly to the nation's decision latitude and the chances of the revolution being successful.

$$pR = (g' DL + pSR)/h' \qquad (13)$$

where $g' = .1$ and $h' = 2$. The programmed variables DL (decision latitude) and pSR (probability of a successful revolution) have been defined above (pp. 115 and 118).

The chance of being successful in a revolution, should one occur, is also determined stochastically in the simulation. However, it is possible for the central decision-makers to use the nation's force capability to increase the government's chances of crushing a revolution. The central decision-maker may reserve up to 30 per cent of his force capability for application as internal control measures during any period of the simulation. The application of force units to control the demands of the rebelling validators during periods of upheaval represents such devices as riot suppression forces, secret police, and paramilitary activity.

Programmed Assumption No. 22: Relation of Outcome of Revolution to Internal Controls. The chances for a revolution to be successful, should one occur, are reduced directly by the percentage of force capability that is applied to internal controls.

$$pSR = 1 - k'(FC_{ic}/FC) \qquad (14)$$

where $k' = 3.3$.

This last hypothesis indicates that although reduction in validator satisfaction may release or trip a revolution, its outcome actually is not dependent upon the level of validator satisfaction. The potential success of the revolution is specified as dependent upon the amount of forceful opposition the government is prepared to give to the revolutionary effort, as defined by FC_{ic} on page 126. Because of the tendency of the armed services to participate in revolutions in many parts of the real world, the effectiveness of the forces loyal to the office-holders is expressed as a percentage of the total forces in existence (FC_{ic}/FC).

Costs of the force capability, as programmed in Programmed Assumption No. 14, remain the same whether the force is applied to internal controls or used for purposes of foreign affairs. Should a revolution occur, the entire allocation of force units is consumed.

Programmed Assumption No. 23: Utilization of Internal Force During Revolution. When a revolution occurs, the whole force capability devoted to internal controls is expended during the revolution.

Note the flexibility in policy that decision-makers have with respect to their validators, regarding the possibility of revolution within their nation. By keeping validator satisfaction high, the government may almost insure its perpetuation in office—at most incurring orderly changes. By operating their government so as to insure themselves sufficient decision latitude, approaches to the revolution threshold may be forestalled (Equation 1). Or should revolutionary outbreaks occur, the decision-makers within a nation may apply direct force internally, thereby attempting to suppress the revolt (Equation 14).

Unprogrammed Hypothesis: Decision-makers will tend to prevent the outbreak of revolutions in the first place, rather than depend upon their suppressive force to control revolution once it has been set in motion.

But revolutions are not without cost, even should they be successfully suppressed. Not only is there a loss of the force capability which was applied internally, but the economic life of the nation is disrupted so that its basic capability is reduced.

Programmed Assumption No. 24: Depletion of Basic Capability Due to Revolution. The basic capability of a nation is depleted by a given amount at the conclusion of each revolution.

$$\triangle BC = r' \, BC \tag{15}$$

where $r' = 20$ per cent during the exploratory runs reported in this book.

Revolutions also yield benefits. After each revolution, there is an immediate increase in over-all validator satisfaction, part of which continues during the subsequent period. In the case of a revolution that has been crushed, the rise in over-all satisfaction occurs because the opposition has been silenced and suppressed. In the case of a revolution that has been won, the rise in over-all satisfaction occurs because the new government now is operated by men of greater popularity. Eventually, however, these revolutionary gains are dissipated, as when the decision-makers confront their validators during more normal times.

Programmed Assumption No. 25: Increase in Validator Satisfaction Due to Revolution. At the conclusion of each revolution, there is a rise in validator satisfaction.

$$\triangle VS_{mi} = + 2 \text{ units} \qquad \triangle VS_{m(i+1)} = + 1 \text{ unit} \tag{16}$$

During the period i immediately after the revolution, the over-all validator satisfaction computed by Equation 2 for this period (VS_{mi}) was increased by two units during the exploratory runs; during the second period after the revolution (period $i + 1$), only one unit was added to the computed $VS_{m(i+1)}$

A "silent" revolution already was programmed within the simulation. Consider again the contest between a stochastically induced decrease in decision latitude and the status quo, or even an increase desired by the decision-makers of a nation, as described on pages 129 and 130. If the stochastic process resulting in decreases in latitude for the decision-makers (Programmed Assumption No. 4, p. 116) is considered as an effort by the validators to gain internal freedoms, then the consequences involved in Programmed Assumptions Nos. 17 through 20 (pp. 127 ff.) represent the resistance of the ruled to their rulers. This silent revolution is controlled, however, by the decision-makers when they are willing to utilize political pressures other than those force capabilities already allocated for stand-by against violent revolution. By the application of police measures, resistance to the status quo or to increases in decision latitude may be suppressed.

NATIONALISM

An important ingredient in validator satisfaction within nations is the esteem with which nations are held by the peoples of the world. A constellation of variables is invoked in explaining the role of world opinion, nationalism, and other social processes in building esteem. To date, we have no core variables in the simulation with which to program the feedback of national pride into the validation process. Our two failures in programming feedbacks from the internation system itself into validator satisfactions are described by Noel in Chapter Four.

However, there are unprogrammed feedbacks from the interaction to the decision-makers themselves. The participants become strongly identified with their own nations, feel intense rivalries and are sensitive to grievances. Among the external decision-makers representing different nations, status hierarchies develop based on such considerations as the nation's capabilities, the skill of the decision-makers in the conduct of their nation's affairs, and the ideological force with which the nation's diplomacy is conducted. These feelings of esteem extend beyond that of friendship, since sometimes a *coup de maître* is the beginning step in a switch of allies.

The following hypotheses suggest the rich isomorphism to reality that has been produced by unprogrammed developments in runs of the simulation:

Unprogrammed Hypothesis: The greater the feeling of identification of the decision-makers with the importance of their states, the greater sensitivity will they feel about their status relations within the inter-nation system.

Unprogrammed Hypothesis: The less secure the decision-makers feel about their tenure in office, the greater sensitivity will they feel about their status relations within the inter-nation system.

Unprogrammed Hypothesis: The greater the esteem with which a nation is regarded in the inter-nation system, the greater are the chances that developments in the inter-nation system may redound indirectly to increase the probability of continuation in office by its decision-makers.

Can one gain perspective on the way in which the model has been constructed to this point by examining the differentiation between the programmed assumptions and the unprogrammed hypotheses? The distinction between the core and free variables discussed above is analogous to the differences between the programmed and unprogrammed relationships among the variables. The programmed assumptions are hypotheses structured into the foundation of the simulation. Although they constitute the basic postulations of the operations which constitute the simulation, they can be changed from time to time, should they prove at variance with increases in our understanding of processes within the real world to which they are supposedly isomorphic. The unprogrammed hypotheses are speculative formulations of the way in which self-developed features of the simulation operate.

It would be possible to transform some of the unprogrammed hypotheses into the simulation as programmed assumptions. For instance, one might develop a program rule for increasing the nation's decision latitude whenever there was rapid decrease in validator satisfaction, a not unreasonable proposal in that governments often take self-defense measures which inhibit orderly change procedures when their populations begin creating public disorders. Contrariwise, it would be possible to relax an assumption, allowing the variables involved to operate without a structured program. An instance might be developed by eliminating a program which imposes costs in basic capabilities whenever there is an increase in decision latitude, as now is operative in Assumption No. 18. Were this made the case, an unprogrammed relation between basic capabilities and decision latitude could develop, nevertheless. Decision-makers generally might be prone to operate with higher decision latitudes, were they able to obtain latitude without cost. This in turn might induce them to take more risks with their nation's basic capabilities, inasmuch as with more latitude they would need to be less sensitive to the standards of living of their people. Such risks might pay off well —or result in impoverishment of the nation's basic capabilities. Thus, although a programmed assumption was eliminated, the same core variables might still be related to each other through unprogrammed processes.

Is it possible to program a free variable into a core variable, by making an appropriate assumption? For example, could one formally link the esteem variable with the probability of office-holding, as possibly intimated in the last mentioned unprogrammed hypothesis (p. 133)? It seems the answer is negative. Although one can speculate about the impact of core variables on free variables (and vice versa) by means of unprogrammed hypotheses, one cannot program one's hunches into the simulation unless one already has defined core variables for incorporation into the new assumptions. It will be noted that the programmed assumptions of this chapter consist of relationships only between core variables.

III. Relations Among Nations

Our effort has been confined so far to a description of the nations and the variables—both core and free—through which the decision-makers operate within the simulation. Now attention may be turned to relations among the nations. At first, focus will be placed upon the interaction processes themselves in the political, economic, and military spheres. Later the development of supranational institutions will be examined. On occasion in the first part of this chapter, the interrelations among nations were incorporated integrally into the operation of the simulation, as in the dependence of satisfaction with respect to national security upon the levels of arms of one's neighbors (Programmed Assumption No. 16). But in the main, with the exception of the rules for communication and war, interaction between states is generated in unprogrammed ways by the decision-makers themselves, as this section demonstrates.

COMMUNICATIONS

Characteristics of the communications existing between states yield important consequences for their behaviors. Implicit in our description of the simulation to this point has been the existence of communication within nations and between them. An attempt has been made within each run to have all the communications between nations, whether oral or written, routed through external decision-makers. Ten to thirty decision-makers send a tremendous number of messages over a period of fifteen to forty-five hours. If the decision-makers do not organize themselves adequately within their nation, the unit becomes paper-bogged and there are consequent failures in communication. Sometimes the neglect of requests by other powers is interpreted as disrespect and an indication that the notes from a nation are considered insignificant, or not worthy of top-level attention.

Core Variable: Conferences. Oral communications involving two or more decision-makers within the same nation and between nations.

Core Variable: Messages. Written communications from one decision-maker to another, within the same nation and between nations.

An important difference between sets of inter-nation communication patterns is whether they are bilateral or multilateral. In the former, the communications are restricted to the two nations involved. When the multilateral exchanges include less than all the nations, as in the case of the trilateral exchanges, decision-makers often are unaware of what is going on in the other parts of the system. This tendency toward ignorance sometimes is strengthened by a division of labor among the two to five decision-makers within the nation, so that even though one of the participants receives a message from another nation, his failure to communicate it internally to others in his government may result in important errors of omission in the actions of the other decision-makers.

These areas of ignorance induced the experimenters to augment the direct exchanges among the decision-makers with a communications system external to the nations themselves—a world newspaper. Journalists were introduced into the simulation to present information about inter-nation events to all decision-makers simultaneously through a mass medium. Issues of the world newspaper, published every fifteen to thirty minutes during the run, provided communications among the decision-makers which otherwise only the most elaborate and costly intelligence operations could have assembled.

The mass media provide knowledge about the international system, so that most decision-makers know the rough outlines of what is going on within the world. Space is given for the insertion of press releases and communiques by the decision-makers of any nation. The development of nonsecret treaties are publicized through issues of the press, be they concerned with economic, military, or ideological matters. The proceedings of open conferences are reported in summary so that nonattenders may receive dispatches of progress being made or learn of stalemates and conflict. A special statistical supplement is included in the report from time to time, summarizing the information on changes in validator satisfaction, in economic well-being, and some statistics on force capability. Extra editions are prepared when there is turnover in government. Although no radio or television apparatus was used in the simulation, the printed media served as a surrogate for the mass media.

Core Variable: Mass Media. Regular reports containing information about states of the inter-nation system, as well as releases issued by the decision-makers; its contents are open and circulated to all members of all nations.

During one of the runs, professional editors operated two competing presses. By taking sides with particular blocs, the two papers helped develop propaganda quarrels among the nations. In fact, when one of the blocs was conquered through a devastating war, the deposed decision-makers continued participating in the world complex by starting a rebel newspaper.

Some information circulates in the communication nets among the decision-makers as rumors or secret reports. It is possible for the decision-makers to issue messages which are false or merely speculative. Decision-makers classify some of their messages as RESTRICTED. Receivers sometimes find it advantageous to violate the secrecy. At times this creates severe distrust, especially when strategies are divulged in the course of current negotiations. A stochastic leakage of restricted messages is part of the newspaper operation. Without favoring any particular nation, these intelligence reports allow decision-makers to weave a web of conjecture from partial information which is gleaned by tapping one out of every five of the restricted exchanges.

Core Variable: Restricted Messages. Messages whose existence and contents are not known by other than the sender and receiver.

Programmed Assumption No. 26: Relation of Leakage of Restricted Messages to Volume of Messages. Inasmuch as restricted messages are leaked stochastically, the greater the volume of restricted messages, the greater will be the revelation of secret information to the mass media. The message leakage rate was set at 20 per cent, that is, every fifth message.

Although no formal espionage operation is included in the simulation, it is fascinating to see how external decision-makers attempt to gain information by posting "observers" at conferences, even when they refuse to have formal representation of their nation at the conference table for reasons of diplomacy. An external decision-maker at times will attempt to ingratiate himself with an ally by communicating supposedly secret information obtained from nonmembers of the alliance.

Because news is communicated in terms of who said what, when, and to whom, the internal and external communication systems help create prestige hierarchies among the decision-makers. These hierarchies of esteem have great import for the operation of influence patterns in the simulation world, as they do within the real world. It is revealing to note how a prestigious nation, once its central decision-maker has spoken, can change the policies of less influential nations.

Unprogrammed Hypothesis: Communication failures due to over-load are interpreted by decision-makers as deliberate signs of dis-respect and neglect.

Unprogrammed Hypothesis: When there is a preponderant use of bilateral rather than multilateral and mass media channels for com-munication, there is more distrust and suspicion among the decision-makers of the world.

Unprogrammed Hypothesis: Standards for judgment of national achievement develop in the course of inter-nation communication, thereby defining the "social realities" of the system.

INEQUALITIES AMONG NATIONS

To anyone surveying the more than one hundred independent countries of the real world, an outstanding characteristic of the array is found in their differences. An attempt has been made to incor-porate some of this rich variety of the real world in the simulation. The nations may be distinguished from each other by virtue of dif-ferent weightings of the core factors. Basic differences may be reflected in variations in decision latitude. Authority might be shared instead of centralized in one decision-maker. Some nations might be designated as having higher or lower thresholds for revolution than others. In some, the office-holder determinations might be made at regular, relatively short intervals—while in others, the determination might be made only after revolutions, following (for example) life-tenured monarchies. It is possible to distinguish one nation from the others through the validation process, by using different weights for the contributions of the components of satisfaction to office-holding (Figure 5-1). One nation, for example, might have a more demand-ing consumption standard. The validators in another nation might want higher levels of national security.

Different weightings are employed to symbolize inequalities among the nations with respect to their capabilities. Some of the na-tions are construed as "have-nots" with meagre capabilities; others are rich. These differences among the nations are induced in two ways—by starting the nations with different accumulations of basic and force capability, and by assigning differential generation rates for the production of goods and services used for the standard of consumption and for strategic purposes. For example, in one run the initial conditions characterizing nation Erga were designated as 10,000 basic capability units, with an accumulation of 500 force units. The analogous parameters for nation Ingo were 16,000 and

2400. The rates at which these nations could generate consumption satisfaction units from their basic capability units were 1.0 and 1.5, respectively; the generation rates for force units were .5 and 2.00. In the programmed equations constituting the intra-nation system, some thirty parameters are utilized.

These inequalities among the nations produce important differences in the unprogrammed relations among the nations. Further inequalities, of course, emerge from the ways in which the decision-makers use their resources. In one run, the decision-makers in nation S lost their top position as wealthiest nation. In another run, nation M rose to a position as one of the two nations with the dominant strategic capabilities. It is feasible to go farther by introducing slowly—or suddenly, to correspond to an important technological breakthrough—changes in the generation rates during the course of the historical development of nations. For example, during an exploratory run, a middle-sized nation was allowed to "develop" nuclear power, which increased tenfold its force capabilities.

The employment of differences in the weightings yields important leverage for using the simulation in the study of international relations. By setting the weightings to correspond to the configurations found in today's system of nations, contemporary problems in foreign affairs may be studied. By resetting the weightings, it is possible to represent historical situations. Perhaps as important is the potential development of simulation analyses based on weightings that have not yet existed in the real world. This latter possibility may be the most significant heuristic value to be obtained from the simulation. Research leading to better understanding of the possible in the development of world affairs, unbounded by current practices, may lead to unimagined innovations in international relations.

Although at first the participants within a nation feel they are the United States, or nineteenth-century Britain, or perhaps contemporary Yugoslavia, these identifications with historical or existing nations gradually lose their potency. The simulated nations seem to take on color and characteristics unique in themselves. Then the participants vividly contrast their own nations with those of the real world. Suppose we attempt to set the weightings in our functions as they are found in real nations. Further, suppose each nation is manned by persons of the nationality of the nation being represented. Then, if the model simulates adequately, participants of a given nationality should feel themselves conceptually to be operating in their own "home country" when they serve as decision-makers for their home nations.

ARMAMENTS: DEFENSIVE AND AGGRESSIVE USE OF FORCE

In the exploratory runs undertaken to the first of 1960, the decision-makers tended to make great use of their force capabilities in handling their external problems. As noted earlier, validator satisfaction derives from a given level of strength, because a nation is programmed to depend upon its relation to the strength of its non-allies (Assumption No. 16). The relationship, however, is considered to have a ceiling effect in that validator satisfaction reaches its maximum when the strength of a nation is three or more times that of its strongest potential enemies. Likewise, there is a floor effect, because when the nation's strategic capability is small, its validators become indifferent to the nation's strategic capability in world affairs.

Free Variable: Alliance. Written treaty explicitly authorized by central decision-makers to provide military aid and/or support to another nation in case of the latter's involvement in military activity. (There is no enforcement of these treaties by the simulation director.)

The effectiveness of strength as a factor in foreign relations depends on the uses to which it may be put. The simulation provides opportunities for its symbolic employment both in aggressive and defensive ways. The decision-makers within each nation project war plans of an offensive and/or defensive nature, which may be revised from period to period. These plans specify the amounts of force which may be directed against particular nations. The plans provide for target selection, directed toward the basic capability of the other unit and/or toward his military forces.

The attack, counterattack, and defense plans may be kept quite secret or they may be exhibited as part of a deterrent strategy. Sometimes the nations will stage war exercises or make displays of strength. The central decision-makers systematize response plans analogous to the von Schlieffen plan—or they may develop automatic response plans, resembling those contemplated for mid-twentieth-century nuclear warfare. The arrangement allows significant variation in the use of force in both limited or more global ways. Since the decision-makers are allowed to ally themselves freely, the possible combinations are great. By building war into its programmed rules, the simulation accommodates a range of use of strength for purposes of threat and intimidation.

The war programs of the inter-nation simulation are still in need of marked revision. However, a general outline of the waging and consequences of war in these exercises can be sketched at this time.

In the making of war, the routines may be phased so that there are opportunities for varying levels of engagement in battle. When a nation goes to war, rallying to the national cause is portrayed through increases in validator satisfaction. The war itself may engage less than the total resources of the system, so that during its conduct there is time for threats and counterthreats, for peace proposals and counterproposals. During these periods, other nations come to decisions as to whether they will or will not enter the struggle. Sometimes a "neutral" will attempt to mediate the conflict.

Core Variable: War. The use of force capability by one or more nations against one or more other nations.

Programmed Assumption No. 27: The Relation of the Making of War to Validator Satisfaction. Whenever a nation makes war against another (or others), its validator satisfaction is temporarily increased.

$$\triangle VS_m = s' \tag{17}$$

where s' was taken as 2 in the exploratory runs.

The hardware intricacies of war itself are abbreviated in the simulation because interest does not center on nonpolitical aspects of violent conflict. The outcomes of the contests of strength depend stochastically upon the relative basic (BC) and force (FC) capabilities of the nations. It is possible to allow consequences to vary in their severity, from partial to total destruction. If the nation is not totally destroyed, its decision-makers may surrender, negotiate an armistice, and eventually sign a peace treaty with the victor(s). An occupation may be arranged, in which the winning power exercises authority within another nation, through implementation of its decisions with respect to the internal and external functioning of the nation. Included among these decisions is the possibility of reparations and tribute. Of course, there is internal opposition to the occupying force, which in time may become acute enough to engaged the revolution mechanism against the occupying power as it sometimes is evoked against an indigenous national government. The rules also permit other nations to throw out the occupying forces through a war of liberation.

Core Variable: Determination of Outcome of War (pOW). When a determination of the outcome of war is made, the result may be victory or defeat.

Programmed Assumption No. 28: Outcome of War as Related to Relative Strengths. The winning or losing in each phase of a war is determined stochastically, with the chances for winning proportional to the relative strength of one's opponent at the beginning of each phase of the war.

$$pOW = \frac{(FC - FC_{ic} + \acute{a}\,BC)_{ad}}{\sum_{all} (FC - FC_{ic} + \acute{a}\,BC)} \tag{18}$$

where "ad" is defined as "adversary" and "all" is defined as "all nations in war."

The adversary may be a single nation or a group of allied nations. In the exploratory runs a' was set again at .5, as in Equation 8 (p. 126).

Core Variable: War Destruction (WD). The amounts of the basic and force capabilities of a nation which are destroyed during each phase of a war are proportional to the force capabilities applied to one's self by the adversary in the course of each phase.

Programmed Assumption No. 29: War Destruction as Related to Force Capabilities Applied in Course of War. The war destruction suffered by any nation is proportional to the force capabilities applied by its adversary.

$$\frac{\triangle FC}{FC_{tar}} \text{ and } \frac{\triangle BC}{BC} = \frac{FC_{ad}}{\sum_{all} FC} \tag{19}$$

where "tar" is defined as "in target nation." Whether the percentage destruction is suffered in FC's or BC's, or both, depends upon the targeting decision of the adversary.

Unprogrammed Hypothesis: When the members of a coalition are historically unified in terms of ideology, they will come to the defense of one of their members when the latter is attacked by outside forces, either directly through participation in a current war or later through a war of liberation.

The following example of the above unprogrammed hypothesis was found in one run in which three nations operated as tightly reigned states, as reflected in their high decision latitudes. When one of their number clashed with a democratic nation, the other two immediately came to its aid. The decision-makers in the totalitarian bloc simply could not understand why the other nations, which continued to operate with low decision latitudes period after period despite opportunities for increasing their decisional latitudes, wished to remain democratic.

Perhaps the intertwining of the internal and external processes within an inter-nation system is nowhere as well represented in the

simulation as in the utilization of the force capabilities of the nations. As has been demonstrated in the history of military aid in the
real world, the arms of a country may be used by its decision-makers
to control its own peoples, as well as against the peoples of other
nations. The intimacy of the reciprocity of domestic and foreign
policy is embodied in the inter-nation simulation in the internal
control and war programs.

INTERACTION PATTERNS: CONFLICT AND COOPERATION IN WAR AND PEACE

Interest in developing an operating model of inter-nation relations stemmed in part from the belief that mathematical and vernac-
ular languages as they exist today seem to limit, for different reasons, our ability to handle abstractions. It was hoped that the
central heuristic value of this kind of exercise would reside in its
representation of intergroup processes, which we simply are unable
to program adequately, given our present state of knowledge.

Enfolded within the capabilities are the sinews of war and peace.
Quests for high standards of living, given differential rates of production, may result in trade, loans, or aid. Anxiety for national
security may produce alliances and arms races. Although the capabilities seem at first directed only toward fulfillment of validator
satisfactions, they too become significant bases for external activity.

There are variations in the degree to which interactions stabilize
in the form of structured organizations. Let us now explore the way
in which the interactions involving peace and war yield entanglements in the relations among our simulated nations. In the following section, the more formalized, complex organizations that may
evolve in the simulation will be discussed.

The decision-makers can and do make informal and formal agreements on many subjects. Sometimes these agreements are simply
de facto working arrangements which develop tacitly in the course
of the interactions. For example, in an early exploration run one of
the external decision-makers in state P informally helped an external
decision-maker of state G arrange a multilateral conference among
the nations. Sometimes the agreements are more formal, being
registered with each nation's signature. Some of the treaties are
secret and some are publicized. Some treaties even involve definite
commitments of force capability units to other nations, for purposes
of aggression against another nation or group of nations or for
collective security purposes.

Unprogrammed Hypothesis: When agreements are openly de-

veloped and widely publicized throughout the international system, there is less miscalculation of national intentions.

Much interaction is generated among the nations because of the differences in their abilities to transform one capability into another. The economic "law of comparative advantage" induces trade, which is often sporadic but sometimes takes a more stable, long-term form with formal exchange agreements. Because of the impoverishment of some nations, loans are arranged between them and the wealthier countries. These loans may be interest-bearing or free. Agreements may be made to provide that basic capability be sent abroad to generate returns at the rates of the nation within which the investment is made. During our exploratory runs, outright grants of aid were made—sometimes military (in force capability units) or economic (in basic capability units) in form, and sometimes of an emergency nature (in consumption satisfaction units). The aid arrangements at times became part and parcel of security alliances.

Unprogrammed Hypothesis: The more mutual trust among nations, the more likely is the law of comparative advantage to operate.

No attempt was made to further complicate the economic features of the simulation by introducing a formal monetary system. With three "commodities" (basic capability, consumption satisfactions, and force capability), transactions by barter seem to be made without awkwardness. In one exploratory run the basic capability units operated for the nations' decision-makers as a gold standard in determining prices used in international transactions. Since there is no explicit private sector of the national economies, the usual need of governmental decision-makers for trade restrictions in the forms of tariffs, exchange controls, and quotas is not present.

Trust and suspicion are generated in these interactions. Some nations become reliable and trustworthy; others are suspect and perceived as crafty. During the course of the simulation runs, it is possible at the end of each period to ask the decision-makers to rate each other nation in terms of its trustworthiness. Mutual trust can be generated, even when the decision-makers are overtly unconcerned with each other's welfare when certain situational conditions hold. One such condition is that in which there is opportunity for each party to know what the other will do before committing itself to irrevocable choice. The entanglements arising from economic and military matters generate ideologies among the nations, which seem in some cases to have created much trust, and in other cases considerable hostility and feelings of threat.

Unprogrammed Hypothesis: At any level of congruence or conflict of national goals, the greater knowledge each nation has of the other's action, the greater the mutual trust.

INTER-NATION ORGANIZATIONS

When the volume of transactions among the nations becomes stable and sufficiently large and is spread over considerable time periods, the interactions occur through formal inter-nation organizations.

Unprogrammed Hypothesis: Members of an alliance which exists but for a single purpose under ad hoc conditions gradually will begin meeting periodically for increasingly broad purposes.

It is intriguing to note how inter-nation collectivities thus evolved tend to develop an autonomy of their own, so that the delegate members no longer act solely in terms of their national reference groups but develop bases of action within the international organization itself. The organization may be consultative or it may be given decision-making power of its own by delegation of national power from the member states. The evolutions sometimes are followed by devolutions so that an over-all effect of waxing and waning is experienced.

Free Unit: Inter-Nation Organization. A formally chartered supra-unit among three or more nations (see p. 107).

Unprogrammed Hypothesis: Inter-nation organizations tend over a period of time to develop an increasing amount of autonomy to the extent that they are successful in achieving their substantive goals.

In the course of a pair of exploratory runs, two formal inter-nation organizations were created by the external decision-makers acting in behalf of their nations. During one run, an underdeveloped nation induced all but one of the other nations of the world to establish an international bank. Each period the member nations made contributions in basic capabilities to a fund thereafter to be controlled entirely by the bank's board, consisting of external ministers from the contributing states. Before the simulation was terminated, the poorer countries of the world had been given loans, resulting in decided increases in the stability of their governments. During another run, two large powers established an international grant-in-aid corporation to which the dissident smaller powers, flirting with aggressive national policies, might apply for help. The external ministers who manned the corporation, however, squabbled so much among themselves that, before the terms of the grants were formulated, the smaller countries experienced internal disorders, with many changes in their decision-makers. The disagreements among the great powers and the disorders within the smaller powers resulted in a world war. It was interesting to note that the subsequent post-war peace treaty provided, among other things, for re-establishment of an international grant-in-aid corporation—this time with a world-wide membership on its board. During a run in Alger's International Organizations course, the students found themselves unable to build a viable international bank, even though considerable effort was devoted to the enterprise.

Unprogrammed Hypothesis: More basic changes in the international system take place when there are simultaneous changes in office-holders within several of the nations.

Unprogrammed Hypothesis: When there are changes in office-holders within the several nations within a short period of time, the decision-makers find the behavior of each other more unpredictable.

Because of the relatively short duration of our runs up to this point in the exploration, there has been little time for the international organizations to consolidate. Each of our nations has needed opportunity to worry through its internal problems first. Although both the bank and the development corporation began establishing rules for their own internal operation, no attempts have been made yet to erect a court or legislature for the establishment of inter-nation law. When the runs are extended in duration, the nations may develop unifunctional versus multifunctional organizations. It also is possible that regional organizations may emerge to compete with universal complexes. Patterns of interrelationship will develop among the various inter-nation organizations themselves. It should even be possible to note how world community norms develop ahead of, or lag behind, the building of legal and political institutions among the nations. Because the central decision-makers may turn over parts or even all of their decision-making to supranational groups, it is possible to have federations and/or world governments.

Unprogrammed Hypothesis: When the decision-makers of a nation are intensely involved in meeting internal problems, there is little growth of inter-nation organizations.

Unprogrammed Hypothesis: Inter-nation organizations established for single purposes tend to be less viable than those established for multipurposes.

Unprogrammed Hypothesis: The norms of conduct of states which develop within an inter-nation organization tend to be applied to relations among all states, whether they are members or not.

The relation of the decision-makers to their own nations plays an important role at the international level. In the simulation runs to date, we have evidence of the problems involved in the relation of the foreign mission to the home foreign office. When the external environment is rich with international activities, how can the external ministers adequately communicate to their internal ministers? One of the external decision-makers for state K had much trouble in a particular run because he acted as a plenipotentiary. The reactions of other states to nation K's inconsistency in policy lost K its membership in a newly forming alliance.

IV. Discussion

One chapter cannot handle all the problems which the construction of the simulation raises. But some of these are so pressing that it may be useful to mention them, even if they cannot be solved at present.

Although no explicit reference has been made to the scholarly literature of international relations, the constructors of this operating model have steeped themselves in this body of speculation. Hence, we have borrowed freely from many others as guides to our formulation. Perhaps more attention should have been devoted within the chapter to justification of our decisions, indicating the rationale employed in making each of the individual choices. As yet, no formalized criteria have emerged to provide guidance for our exploitations of the work of others. For instance, no sampling technique seemed appropriate to guide our selection of core variables. Detailed rationalizations of the choices must be provided eventually. It is important that a firmer embedding of our model within the studies of international relations be attempted, so that an almost total reliance upon an intuitive grasp of this literature may be circumvented.

Has the choice of simulation which mixes men with computed programs been sound? An all-computer simulation would obviate the implicit contents introduced in the inter-nation simulation by the use of human decision-makers. An all-man simulation without intra-nation programs, on the other hand, perhaps would bring the form of the simulation too close to a face-to-face group. As the simulation stands now, it seems to be a composition of computer and men so that the intergroup relations which emerge from its operation are somewhat isomorphic, from a subjective point of view, to the phenomena one encounters in the interrelations of real nations.

But have not our omissions of important features of the real world developed incapacitating artificialities within the simulation? How can the motivational stress of a game be compared with the deadly struggles for power which exist within and among the governments of the world? For example, has not our positing of authority within the central decision-maker induced an unrealistic security for the holders of power? And how is the impact of geography displayed? Because of the short time duration of the simulation, are not the historical factors—especially as they operate through tradition—being short-circuited? Perhaps most puzzling of all, how does the mixture of men and computers distort the time relations within the system? The participants function in terms of biological, or real time. The machines compress time so that some seventy minutes of game time are made analogous to a year of life time. These problems certainly must be given close attention.

If the simulation is to be of heuristic value, as Snyder contends in his introductory chapter to this book, its ability to produce unprogrammed consequences that are isomorphic to reality must be checked thoroughly. For example, Alger unexpectedly found that in several underdeveloped nations in the runs in his International Relations course, the aspirant decision-makers consolidated their efforts with those of the decision-makers in office, evolving one-party nations. It seems that such nations felt they could not afford the luxury of opposition among their decision-making groups. Work on the validity of the simulation is imperative at this time. When such validity is demonstrated, then one's use of the simulation for exploration in uncharted areas, such as the N-country problem, will be more justifiable.

The task of making explicit the implicit contents generated by the programmed assumptions within the inter-nation simulation is a large one. It will be worthwhile only if the simulation demonstrates its potential as a heuristic device in the acquisition and application of reliable knowledge about international relations.

V. Summary

Individual and group components of the inter-nation simulation are meshed into an operating model through both structured programs and free, self-developing interactive processes. In general, programmed assumptions are used for setting the foundations of the simulation, serving to provide operating rules for the decision-makers whereby they may handle the political, economic, and military aspects of their nations. On the other hand, with the exception of the rules for the conduct of war, there are no programs prescribing the relations among nations. The basic strategy used in the construction of the simulation has been to allow free development of the inter-nation relations, without restrictions other than those implicit in the characteristics of the nations themselves. Illustrative hypotheses are offered to indicate the richness of the relations of the structured programs to the free activities within the inter-nation simulation.

Chapter Six

Use of the Inter-Nation Simulation in Undergraduate Teaching

Chadwick F. Alger

Although the simulation was developed as an aid to research, its potential as a teaching device soon became apparent through testimonials by participants on the learning value of their simulation experience. Since some of these unsolicited comments on learning came from undergraduates, it was natural that the use of the simulation in undergraduate teaching should be considered. At the time of this report it is being used in undergraduate courses taught by the writer at Northwestern for the third year. In 1959 and 1960 the students in an international organization course participated in a three-hour simulation once a week for eight weeks. The eight sessions were in effect a continuous twenty-four hour development of the simulation, since each session began where the previous one had stopped. In 1961 the simulation was used in both an international relations and international organization course that were offered in sequence. A ten-week simulation was used, again in weekly three-hour sessions. The simulation bridged both courses, with five sessions in each.

In this chapter the writer will perform five main tasks:

1. Place the Northwestern educational use of simulation in the context of other educational uses, both in international relations and other kinds of human behavior.
2. Describe the teaching goals of the international relations courses in which the simulation is used in the context of trends in the study of international relations.
3. Show how the simulation has been integrated into college courses.
4. Give a brief account of the kinds of events that students create and encounter in their simulation experiences as decision-makers.
5. Report student responses to their simulation experiences.

I. Educational Uses of Simulation

The Northwestern use of simulation for educational purposes is, of course, not a new departure. Mock trials have been a part of the educational program for lawyers for a number of years. The use of simulation devices for business training has become so extensive that a national symposium on management games was held in 1959. The proceedings of the symposium list twenty-one games (Proceedings of the National Symposium on Management Games). War games have been used for many years in military training programs as well as in strategy planning. In recent years there has been a growing interest in extending simulation beyond military factors and into the general field of international relations.

Although the educational benefits of simulation have not been rigorously measured, numerous testimonials assert that simulation participation has significant educational benefits. Such claims are made for international relations simulations developed by RAND and the Massachusetts Institute of Technology. Herbert Goldhamer and Hans Speier of RAND write: "We believed when we began our work in gaming that the political game would prove to be a useful educational device. Our experience (and that of academic institutions with which we have collaborated) has increased our conviction in this regard" (Goldhamer and Speier, p. 79). Lincoln Bloomfield and Norman Padelford indicate that, when properly integrated into a college course, the MIT simulation

> . . . can produce tangible results over and above what can be taught and learned about politics by more usual methods of instruction. We are sufficiently convinced of the productive results to have decided that this technique should be tried, on varying bases, in other courses, and be made more or less a standing part of the curriculum in International Politics and American Diplomacy (Bloomfield and Padelford, p. 1112).

Users of simulation for educational purposes have employed a variety of kinds of simulations and have observed a number of types of educational benefits. A survey of the reports of a number of these users has provided a long list of claimed benefits which can be summarized under four headings:

1. It is reported that *simulation heightens the interest and motivation of students in several ways.* First, the activity of most simulations appears to be more enjoyable than customary kinds of learning. Reporting on written student reactions to a 1961 simulation in an international relations course at MIT, Norman Padelford reports that "the comment that the 'game was fun' seemed to represent a near consensus" (Padelford, *et al.*, 1961, p. 8). Although some have argued that anything enjoyable could not possibly be educational, psychologists assert that pleasure in the laboratory task brings important reinforcement to learning. Second, it is difficult in most cases for students to avoid extensive involvement in the simulation. They are put in predicaments where they have to act, and they are stimulated to learn because of the immediate application they can make of relevant knowledge. Third, simulation participants have a mutually shared experience which stimulates discussion with fellow-students outside of class far more than normal course work. As a result of experience with a management game, Richard H. Rawdon has written that simulation "seems to be a catalytic agent among people playing in a group, providing them with more objectives for the exchange of background information" (Proceedings of the National Symposium on Management Games, p. I-16).

2. It is claimed that *simulation offers an opportunity for applying and testing knowledge* gained from reading done in connection with the course and from other sources as well. Reporting on a Carnegie Tech management game, William R. Dill reports that it "provides a laboratory in which students can apply a wide variety of concepts, tools, and strategies they have learned elsewhere—from books, from professors or from fellow students" (Cohen, *et al.*, February, 1961, p. A-1). He indicates, for example, that students can consider in "real-life terms the meaning of phrases like 'lines of communication' or 'lines of authority'" (Cohen, *et al.*, February, 1961, p. A-2). Some simulation reports suggest that there is not only application of individual parcels of knowledge but also integration of materials. A 1958 report on RAND experiences with an international simulation states that participants "draw together, organize and apply existing knowledge of past and present political events in rigorous fashion to problems of the future" (Social Science Division, p. 10).

3. There are numerous ways in which simulation experience is reported to give participants *greater understanding of the world as seen and experienced by the decision-maker.* The highlights of these reports can be summarized in three categories. First, in most simulations the participant is part of a group involved in making decisions. He experiences the ways in which decisions are shaped by group relationships and by the way roles are defined within the group. Second, experience is gained in actually making decisions about the problems under study rather than simply evaluating the decisions of others. William Dill points out the value to the participant of being required, in a long-running simulation, "to plan and carry through sequences of analysis and decision" (Cohen, *et al.*, February, 1961, p. A-2). In a simulation used by the Pillsbury Company to train managers, Seymour Levy emphasizes the importance of "feedback upon the economic judgments of the manager" (Proceedings of the National Symposium on Management Games, p. IV-5). Richard M. Cyert of Carnegie Tech aptly observes: "The student must be prepared to live with his decisions" (Cohen, *et al.*, February, 1961, p. C-2). Third, it is also claimed that simulation experience offers insights into aspects of the decision-maker's predicament that are assumed to be peculiar to the institutions being simulated. A few examples from international relations simulations are particularly relevant here. Goldhamer and Speier of RAND suggest that participants acquire "new insights into the pressures, the uncertainties, and the moral and intellectual difficulties under which foreign policy de-

cisions are made" (Goldhamer and Speier, p. 79). Bloomfield and Padelford report that even the international relations scholar can learn from simulation participation since it can increase [his] appreciation of the operator's predicament and of the extraneous issues that tend to impinge on him" (Bloomfield and Padelford, p. 1113).

4. *Most simulations provide a miniature world that is easier for the participant to comprehend as a whole than are the real institutions themselves.* Discussing a business management simulation, Seymour Levy believes that it helps participants to "better estimate the economic relationship among variables" (Proceedings of the National Symposium on Management Games, p. IV-5). Levy is critical of games that become "too complex for the people to grasp the economic regularities," asserting that "you need simplicity to assist in the analysis of the process" (*Ibid.*, p. IV-8). Reporting on the RAND international relations simulation, Goldhamer and Speier observe that simulation may even provide an enlightening overview "for individuals with considerable political training and knowledge." They write "that the game provided excellent opportunities and incentives for such participants to acquire an overview of a political situation and to amass relevant information that the ordinary intellectual division of labor and specialization by area or discipline do not make available" (Goldhamer and Speier, p. 79).

The educational use of simulation has been motivated by two kinds of training objectives. On the one hand the objective is to train simulation participants for performing the actual roles that they are simulating. This is usually the case for simulation employed in the training of lawyers, military men, and business men. Sometimes simulation training is given before the real roles are performed. On other occasions simulation is used for in-service training of officials already playing the roles they simulate.

Simulation is also used to enhance the knowledge of students about roles that they may never assume themselves. It is in this sense that simulation is used in undergraduate courses in international relations at Northwestern. It was not the first to use simulation in university international relations courses and it is not the only school engaged in such utilization at the time of this writing. For example, Waldo Chamberlin and Thomas Hovet have used simulation for many years at New York University in a course on "The United Nations at Work." In this two-semester course the students simulate the main councils and committees of the United Nations. International relations simulations are now being utilized in college teaching at the Air Force Academy, the Massachusetts Institute of Technology, and the University of Wisconsin. The simulations at the Air Force Academy (Lackman), MIT, and Wisconsin (Bernard Cohen) require the participants to take the part of decision-makers of real nations. In all of these simulations action begins at a date some months in the future. The instructional staff provides descriptions of events that lead up to the beginning of the simulation. In both the MIT and Wisconsin cases, the participants are faced with a crisis situation. The MIT effort has been of longer duration than the other two, having begun in the 1958-1959 academic year. The yearly efforts by MIT since that time have been usefully described and evaluated in written documents by the institute's instructional staff. This documentation of the MIT effort provides more opportunity for comparison between the Northwestern and MIT teaching applications of simulation than among the others (Bloomfield, 1958, 1960, 1961; Bloomfield and Padelford; Padelford *et al.*, 1961).

There are four key differences between the Northwestern educational application of simulation and the other efforts. First, all the other simulations employ nations with names and characteristics of real world nations, whereas the Northwestern simulation has nations that do not have counterparts in the real world. This does not mean, however, that students participating in the Northwestern simulation find themselves in decision-making situations that are necessarily less real than those students who are simulating countries with real world names. Both kinds of simulation attempt to simulate the same world. The difference is in the categories of data that are selected from this world for simulation. In the one case an effort is made to recreate aspects of particular nation-states deemed most significant for international relations—crucial decisions have to be made about what to include and what to exclude, since abstractions are made from total reality. The same kind of decisions have to be made in constructing the Northwestern simulation where the attempt is made to abstract from the same reality those factors having the most important impact on the way foreign policy makers design and conduct their relations with other nations. To the degree that this effort is successful, the student decision-maker finds himself influenced by and attempting to manipulate the same factors as decision-makers in the real world.

Second, the Wisconsin and MIT efforts, although not that of the Air Force Academy, simulate a particular kind of international rela-

tions situation—the international crisis. The Northwestern effort has
not selected a particular kind of situation but has allowed the simulated international system to develop varieties of situations. In each
educational use of the simulation, crises have developed, but they
have been only a part of the total history of the simulations. And
when they have occurred, they have developed out of situations created by the participants.

Third, the Air Force Academy, MIT, and Wisconsin simulations
all assign prominent roles to an umpire. The rules for the umpire in
the Air Force Academy simulation state, for example: "The Umpire
reserves the right to rule out any move by any state on the grounds
of implausibility. Your moves in the game should be reasonably in
character for the state which you are playing." In addition to ruling
on plausibility of moves, Bloomfield and Padelford report that the
umpires in the MIT simulation give advice to decision-makers, and
"act as 'Nature,' inserting new 'facts,' passing on confidential information from one party to another, playing the role of a party not
otherwise represented in the exercise, or leaking rumors of anticipated team moves in order to speed up action or lend an air of sus-
pense" (Bloomfield and Padelford, p. 1110). By contrast the Northwestern simulation does not have actors in the system aside from the
student decision-makers. The simulated world is designed so that
decision-makers are in predicaments which in their basic characteristics are as much as possible like the real world. Therefore, to the
extent that this effort is successful, they can only do plausible things.
Furthermore, the instructional staff has never attempted to manipulate events in order to change the pace or create excitement.

Fourth, MIT and Wisconsin simulations have been concentrated
in one spot in the courses in which used. On the other hand, the
Northwestern simulation has been made an integral part of the entire course, with a three-hour laboratory period each week devoted
to preparing and running the simulation and to conducting a post-
analysis and discussion of it. In the spring of 1961 the Air Force
Academy used a simulation in a defense policy course that ran
throughout the term.

The four characteristics that distinguish the Northwestern simulation from other simulations used in teaching are importantly related
to the teaching goals of courses in which the Northwestern simulation has been used. After a discussion of these teaching goals in the
context of developments in the discipline of international relations,
the significance of the four characteristics to the teaching goals will
be discussed.

II. Teaching Goals in International Relations

The selection of a particular kind of simulation and the mode of its use, as well as the decision whether to use simulation at all, depends upon the teaching goals. Important also is the state of our knowledge about international relations and the expectations about the study of international relations that students bring to the classroom. The development of international relations simulation is an expression of the general intellectual ferment that has occurred among international relations scholars since the early thirties and has reached a crescendo since World War II (Snyder, Bruck, and Sapin, pp. 35-51). New demands have been placed upon these scholars by a world preoccupied with problems of war and peace. These demands themselves, as well as research advances in response to them, have stimulated much self-criticism on the part of teachers of international relations (Fox, Goodwin, Kirk, Lerche and Sapin, Manning, and Van Dyke, 1957).

In the 1920's courses in international relations were usually courses on the League of Nations (Fifield, p. 1191) and tended to be reformist in orientation. The appearance of Frederick L. Schuman's textbook, *International Politics,* in 1933 is evidence that a revolt against what has been termed "idealism" in favor of "realism" had begun. Since that time there has been a growing chorus of scholars and teachers who conceive that their primary mission is to propagate knowledge about the real world rather than to act as missionaries for reform. In the years after World War II Hans Morgenthau has become the most eloquent spokesman for "realism," largely through his widely used textbook, now in its third edition, *Politics Among Nations.*

The turn to realism, as represented by Morgenthau, has had a salutary effect on the study of international relations; it has accentuated the fact that the development of successful strategies for reform must be preceded by accurate knowledge of the area to be reformed. But this realism has maintained a mixture of the normative and empirical that perpetuates the same inhibition to sound scholarship which characterized the idealists. Professor Morgenthau describes his realism in this way:

> Political realism contains not only a theoretical but also a normative element. . . . Hence, it is no argument against the theory here presented that actual foreign policy does not or cannot live up to it. That argument misunderstands the intention of this book, which is to present not an indiscriminate description of political

reality, but a rational theory of international politics. Far from being invalidated by the fact that, for instance, a perfect balance
of power policy will scarcely be found in reality, it assumes that
reality, being deficient in this respect, must be understood and
evaluated as an approximation to an ideal system of balance of
power (Morgenthau, p. 8).

Thus, in the influential pen of Morgenthau, realism became something quite different from an attempt to describe and explain international relations. Although the policies it advocates are quite different from those of the idealist, Morgenthau's realism also mixes
analysis and reform. The realism-idealism dichotomy has come to
be two syndromes each containing a mixture of prescription, description, and explanation. This ordering of the field has so pervaded
both scholarly and nonscholarly writing that the college teacher cannot ignore it—it is part of the culture in which the student develops
his first impressions of international relations. Writing in 1955,
Quincy Wright has made this trenchant commentary on the pattern
of international relations teaching:

> There has been a degree of indoctrination in American under-
> graduate education in international relations hardly compatible
> with the theory of what education should be in a liberal democracy.
> During a half century college education has successively and in a
> measure, successfully guided opinion in the United States toward
> isolationism, toward international organization and toward power
> politics as the central theme of American foreign policy (Wright,
> p. 72).

There is a growing conviction among international relations
scholars that students cannot be effectively equipped to handle international relations problems, either as citizens or professionals, unless they are to some degree able to apply the procedures of scientific inquiry to these problems. A cardinal principle of the scientific
method is that the normative preferences of the analyst are con-
scientiously prohibited from intruding on his analysis of the state of
affairs. The scientific method provides a set of procedures for developing reliable knowledge about any phenomena that can be experienced with the senses. Nevertheless, the university teacher of
international relations normally confronts a class which includes a
number of students who find the application of the scientific method
to the understanding of international relations a strange and even
ridiculous enterprise.

But this should not be surprising. Their misgivings are shared by
such men as George F. Kennan. In 1953 in an address at Princeton

University on "The Teaching of International Relations" this scholar-diplomat spoke as follows:

> . . . let the international affairs course stand as an addendum to basic instruction in the humanities. . . . International relations are not a science. And there is no understanding of international affairs that does not embrace understanding of the human individual. . . . If men on this campus want to prepare themselves for work in the international field, then, I would say: let them read their Bible and their Shakespeare, their Plutarch and their Gibbon, perhaps even their Latin and their Greek, and let them guard as the most precious of their possessions that concept of personal conduct which has grown up in this institution around the honor system, but of which the honor system is only a part and a symbol (Kennan, p. 11).

It is perhaps the writings of such men as Kennan that have perpetuated the notion, held by many undergraduates, that abilities bordering on the mystical are required in order to comprehend the alchemy of the world of the diplomat.

Nevertheless, growing numbers of university teachers of international relations are advocating the belief that their subject is but another branch of social science amenable to study through the same tools used for study in sister disciplines. For example, a 1958 textbook by A. F. K. Organski states that "this book approaches international relations in the tradition of the sciences rather than that of the humanities or the arts" (Organski, p. 5). The issue for scholars such as Organski is not whether the study of international relations is a science, but how it can become a more adequate one.[1]

An examination of recent international relations textbooks clearly reveals a trend away from using historical narrative and current problems as focuses for the presentation of the field to the student. In the preface to *Principles of International Politics,* Charles O. Lerche, Jr., writes that if these courses "are to be anything more than a discussion of current events with only limited educational value to the student, the factual data must be given perspective, form, and meaning. Such insights in the student are forthcoming only if it is possible to provide him with a framework of systematic theory" (Lerche, vii; see also, Haas and Whiting, vii; Organski, vii; Padelford and Lincoln, vi; Van Dyke, v.).

But the attempt to deal with "the factual data" in a more rigorous way is having consequences beyond the reordering of these facts.

---

[1] For an exposition of this point of view see Herbert McClosky, p. 282.

Systematic analysis is revealing that there are significant gaps in the data. In particular, an examination of any international relations textbook reveals inadequate links among gross data on geography, population, resources, military capability, etc., and the actions of and relations among officials who carry on international relations. Filling in these gaps in our knowledge offers a stimulating challenge to researchers.

But what does the writer or teacher who wishes to offer the student a general survey of the field do with the empty data boxes? In the introduction to the sixth edition of his highly successful textbook, *International Politics*, Frederick L. Schuman describes his reaction to the problem:

> The teaching of World Politics should aim at a systematic application and synthesis of what have come to be called the "behavioral sciences." This I believe, albeit conceding the formidable difficulties of the enterprise. But I do not believe that the time is ripe to essay such a venture in a textbook. Wise teachers can do much in this direction in the classroom. A textbook can suggest interrelationships and implications. But its primary function, as I see it, is still that of presenting in well ordered and readable fashion the basic factual data of contacts among nations and stimulating new thinking about policy-making in the face of the dilemma of the 20th Century (Schuman, p. x).

It is disappointing that Professor Schuman did not bring his extensive background and talents to bear in writing the kind of textbook that he believes is needed. The writer has no evidence that the task is easier in the classroom than in the writing of a textbook. Furthermore, the discipline is the loser by not having the differently "ordered" data and the different body of "basic factual data" that the task would have required Schuman to provide in his stimulating book.

There is another method of handling the problem of the empty data boxes as demonstrated by Ernst Haas and Allen Whiting in their *Dynamics of International Relations*. Finding that certain kinds of "empirical material is frequently unavailable or inaccessible" they warn the reader that:

> Some of the generalizations in Part I, therefore, are closer to the abstract "model" type of treatment than to detailed empirical formulation. Chapter 4 is especially open to the charge of being an overly abstract statement of processes for which there is no unambiguous empirical support. If our formulation errs, therefore, we hope that the effort will act as a stimulus to further and more precise investigation (Haas and Whiting, p. vii).

The solution of Haas and Whiting is clearly more useful to the teacher who shares both Schuman's and Haas and Whiting's eventual goal than is Schuman's method. His strategy still requires the presentation by the teacher of parts of the field that are supported by inadequate empirical data, but it is not easy to integrate this material with a text that provides "basic factual data" that is arranged according to implicit rather than explicit models.

But whether originating in textbook, lecture or both, it is not an easy task for the teacher to communicate the significance of explicit models to undergraduate students of international relations. First, their expectations make them more receptive to factual detail about stirring world events. Thus their criteria for choosing significant data are drama and excitement rather than explicit theory or hypothesis. Second, as has been discussed earlier, the explicit theories and hypotheses of the scientific method may not seem relevant because of widespread attitudes against using this method for acquiring reliable knowledge about international relations. Third, the task of the teacher may also be made difficult because of the distance of the events in international relations from the realm of student experience. Many students have been to Congress and state legislatures and have had first-hand experiences with local governing agencies. But they have not had such contact with agencies that make foreign policy, nor have they been able to watch international conferences. Thus they do not have a feel for the significance of models such as those that Haas and Whiting have constructed because they have not yet had the experiences that brought these scholars to the point where they saw the need for them.

Given this set of problems, how does the teacher of international relations accomplish his task? As reflected in a number of recent textbooks, this task is not to provide information on a particular set of international relations events or data on the foreign policies of particular countries. The goal is to help the student to acquire an analytic scheme that will enable him to analyze any international relations event and any foreign policy—even when the content of these phenomena is different from that of today. This analytic scheme is a model that links into one system the propositions and hypotheses that inquiry up to this time has either confirmed or believed to be potentially fruitful. This scheme serves as a map to tell the student what factors are significant and how they are related. But in order for the teacher to stimulate the student to acquire such a model, he must convince him of its usefulness and give him meaningful opportunities to use it. This is the problem that led the writer to the use of simulation in teaching.

The simulation, as has been described in earlier chapters, is a model of what appear to be the essential factors that affect relations among nations. In order to participate in the simulation, the student must learn this model. As he first approaches the simulation that learning is not an end in itself but is a means toward effective participation. Nevertheless, the concepts in the model, although initially quite unfamiliar, become a part of his vocabulary; and his success as an official in one of the simulated nations depends on his learning the relationships among the variables in the simulation. The gap between the student's experience and the world of international relations is removed at least partially through the experiences that the student has in the simulated world of international relations decision-makers. The phenomena that lie between the basic capabilities of states and the behavior of decision-makers can be observed and experienced by the student from his vantage point inside the process.

Before concluding this discussion of teaching goals, we must fulfill our promise to discuss the relationship between these goals and the four factors that distinguish the Northwestern simulation from other simulations used in undergraduate teaching. First is the contrast that results from the construction of contrived countries rather than the simulation of real countries. It would be possible to simulate real countries, but the use of contrived ones tends to move the attention of the student away from particular nations and to focus it on the factors that affect the policies of nations and on the conditions that affect the relationship between these policies. The development of *explicit* analytic tools for the analysis of international relations is quite a different task from collecting information about the foreign policies and problems of specific countries. An examination of recent textbooks reveals that this emphasis is in harmony with trends within the discipline. For example, Vernon Van Dyke states in the introduction to his *International Politics:*

> The questions posed are dealt with on a general basis rather than in relation to specific countries. . . . Once the study of history has progressed far enough to provide generalizations (or the basis for them), as it obviously has, it seems best to seize upon them and use them, always testing them to determine the extent to which they provide reliable guides to an understanding of actual events, and always trying to perfect them so as to provide a basis for prediction (Van Dyke, p. v).

The student in the simulation finds, for example, that the latitude of decision of policy-makers is a factor in the development of foreign policies and in the interaction of foreign policies. In policy decisions where latitude is great, certain consequences occur, and when it is narrow other consequences follow—no matter whether the nation concerned is Great Britain, Mali, Hungary, or Argentina.

Second, the inter-nation simulation does not assign a major role to an umpire who decides whether actions of decision-makers are plausible. All actions that conform to the simulation rules are permitted. This lends more reality to the decision-making experience of the participants, since umpires are not an element in the environment of real-world decision-makers. A simulation that permits implausible decisions until ruled out by the umpire has failed to provide the stimuli that are present in the real world. The intervention of umpires would add unreal actors—"gods"—to the simulation and might inhibit its use as an analytic tool for understanding the real world. As Guetzkow has noted earlier in this book, the programmed characteristics of the simulation allow many unprogrammed features to develop without intention or self-awareness on the part of the participants, by virtue of the fact that the simulation contains basic components which "spontaneously" generate representation of international phenomena. Thus, it is not necessary that students role-play countries under the supervision of coaches to produce a dramatization of international affairs.

Third, the Northwestern simulation allows relationships between nations to develop out of nation characteristics and the behavior of decision-makers. There is no attempt to simulate crises or to intervene in order to create drama and excitement. Simulation of crises alone would, of course, teach students much about international relations under crisis conditions. But allowing crises to develop out of the system brings insights into how crises emerge. In addition, both students and scholars are perhaps already more attentive to dramatic crises such as Berlin, Korea, Suez, and Hungary than they are to the long-term characteristics of the international system. A simulation not focused on crises alone draws the student's attention to the significance of these long-term characteristics and stimulates him to develop criteria of significance that are different from those of the journalistic norms that play such an important role in defining what events constitute a crisis.

Fourth, the Northwestern simulation is built into courses as a weekly laboratory period rather than offered as an exercise at a single point in the course. The primary reason for this is that the simulation is a model of the field being studied. As such it can be used effectively throughout the course as a map through which the student may locate the relationship between material in current reading assignments and lectures, and other areas of the field. On the other hand, the readings offer constant opportunities for the student to challenge the validity of the simulation. By having simulation throughout the term, the student is stimulated to conduct a continuous dialogue between it and material in readings and lectures that may facilitate his understanding of both.

The integration of the simulation into an undergraduate course obviously requires more than scheduling simulation sessions throughout the term. It requires the selection of readings that help the student to relate the simulation to the real world. The teacher must use the simulation as an analytic model in class discussion. And papers and exams must be devised so that students can build intellectual bridges between the simulation and the world it represents. We will now describe the way in which the simulation has been incorporated into university courses.

III. Using the Simulation as a Laboratory Period

As has been indicated, for three years the simulation has provided the framework for a weekly three-hour laboratory in undergraduate courses at Northwestern. In 1959 and 1960 the simulation was used in a course in international organization. In addition to the simulation session, two one-hour seminars were held each week. The same schedule was used in an international relations course and in an international organization course in 1961. Each of the three international organization courses had an enrollment of approximately twenty-five; the international relations course involved sixty-four students.

For the laboratory session the instructor has the aid of a graduate assistant who monitors the flow of decision forms during the simulation. He is also responsible for the operation of the calculations center and setting up the simulation rooms with the necessary chairs, tables, and other equipment. These last two functions are actually performed by an undergraduate assistant. This undergraduate is a political science major who has no special training in mathematics or statistics to perform his calculations responsibilities. He requires three assistants to help make the necessary computations.[2]

Depending on the size of the class, students have been distributed equally among five to seven nations. At least one person in each nation is out of office at all times. This permits someone to be brought in to head the nation from outside the government when the chief of state loses office through election or revolution. Students not in office act as couriers, handle space arrangements for international conferences, and run the newspaper. If the class is large enough, two newspapers are operated. When there is an international organization requiring a secretariat, students not in office, if acceptable to the organization, are assigned this function. Even when there is no office change of the central decision-maker as a result of election loss or revolution, his subordinates occasionally are rotated in and out of the nongovernmental roles. This distributes the miscellaneous duties among the class members and also simulates personnel turnover in each nation's bureaucracy.

The central decision-maker has complete authority to assign his available personnel to perform the various tasks that must be handled if the nation is to function. He may discharge any official at any time and may delegate as little or as much authority as he desires. He is consulted before members of his staff are rotated to nongovernmental roles.

The space requirements of the simulation exceed those of lectures or seminars. In the three courses in which enrollment was approximately twenty-five students, each decision-maker was located in a separate small room of Northwestern's social psychology laboratory. In addition, several small rooms were available for bilateral conferences, the production of the newspaper, and calculators. A larger room was used for the international organization. It was divided so that separate space was available for sessions of the organization, for offices of permanent representatives and secretariat, and for a lounge for informal contact among persons assigned to the international organization. Private rooms for decision-makers are not essen-

---

[2] At an hourly wage scale of $3.00 for the graduate assistant, $1.50 for the undergraduate assistant and $1.25 for the three calculations assistants, labor for the laboratory sessions in which the simulation was being run cost approximately $55.00 per session. The graduate assistant averaged approximately eleven hours per simulation session, and the undergraduate assistant about five hours. The calculations assistants each worked only the three hours that the simulation was in operation. In addition, supplies cost approximately $10.00 per session. This includes secretarial help for the preparing of necessary forms.

tial; however, experience with the class of sixty-four has shown that it is necessary to have decision-makers separated at least by room dividers. Although conferences among decision-makers of one nation are permitted, their partial isolation from each other, with use of written as well as oral communication, permits the simulation of national bureaucracies with specialization and coordination problems. Finally, locations where inter-nation conferences can be held in secret must be available.

Undergraduates in the international relations and international organization courses in which the simulation has been used have not had previous courses in these subjects. Therefore, particular care has been required to insure that students approach the simulation as a tool for understanding the real world rather than as an end in itself. This is done by stimulating the student to build intellectual bridges between the simulation and the real world that he experiences through course readings and international relations encountered in the press, radio, and TV. The bridges are built by encouraging the student to analyze the real world through the analytic scheme that the simulation provides and to test the validity of the simulation by challenging it with real events. This is accomplished in class sessions, papers, and examinations.

It is not difficult to get students to test the simulation against the real world. Even before they have done course readings they raise numerous objections to the model when it appears to fail to portray what their background knowledge tells them are important characteristics of international relations. There is great initial skepticism because the concepts in the model are new to the students and also because they are not accustomed to making their theories of international relations explicit. This skepticism, providing the student with a set of questions, offers a fruitful basis for teaching. The student is encouraged to maintain his skepticism and thus to continue to relate the simulation to the real world by challenging this model of reality.

Although it is not always feasible or desirable to add dimensions to the simulation that students suggest, they are encouraged to participate in the construction of the simulation by building models of aspects of international relations in which they believe the simulation to be inadequate. The international organization component of the simulation has been primarily developed through class discussion and student invention in simulation laboratory sessions.

Students have also become participants in the building of the simulation through the use of laboratory sessions. The differentiation of military capability into conventional and nuclear components and the incorporation of the opportunity for nations to invest in research and development are two prominent examples. In the 1961 international relations course, aspiring decision-makers were established in each nation for the first time. The class played an active part in experimenting with and developing this role. In this innovation the aspiring central decision-maker, in conjunction with a deputy, fills out decision forms each time the government does. If these decisions are more attractive to the validators than those of the government, the aspirants sometimes take office.

In reverse fashion, the students are encouraged to use the simulation as an analytic scheme to aid them in understanding the real world as experienced both in course readings and the news media. The simulation provides the student with a set of explicit questions to ask of the mass of data he encounters. As a result of participation in the simulation, the model is quickly learned and is almost spontaneously used as an analytic scheme by some students. But the teacher, in class lecture and discussion, can hasten the process and aid students not initially able to see simulation-real world relationships.

Previous discussion stressed that the simulation is used not only as a strategy to stimulate students to learn and use an explicit model of international relations, but also to overcome the student's feeling of distance from the events being studied and to enable him to have contact with and even perform research exercises with kinds of international relations data that are not normally accessible to undergraduates. The student gets more out of his first-hand experience as an international decision-maker if he is able to discuss the experience with others and have his decisions criticized as well as to criticize the decisions of others. This cannot be done while the simulation is in progress because decision-makers would be most unwilling to reveal honestly details of their goals, strategies, etc., to decision-makers of other countries. Therefore, final laboratory sessions are devoted to a discussion of the simulation events.[3] In preparation for the postsimulation discussions, decision-makers of each nation are required to write a history of their nation. Histories of the press and international organization also are written. Copies of these histories are distributed to each participant before the first postsimulation

---

[3] Reporting on experiences with MIT's international "political exercise," Lincoln Bloomfield says that "practically all who have taken part in these experiments agree that the post-mortem session following the game is perhaps the most valuable event of the political exercise" (Bloomfield, 1960, p. 63).

session. Further material for the discussions is provided by documents prepared by each nation before each laboratory session setting forth the goals of the nation, plans for achieving these goals, and predictions of success. At the time they are written, the purpose of these documents is to encourage thoughtful and explicit planning on the part of decision-makers. It is not until the simulation is completed that these documents are reproduced and circulated to all members of the class.

The postsimulation sessions vary, but several recurrent factors make deep impressions on students. First are the different perspectives and varied interpretations that historians from different nations give the same events. Not only do these differences result in varying histories for the simulation, but it can be seen that these differing perspectives were important factors in the design of national policies. Second, the session usually uncovers factors of great significance when the course of events that are not in the histories of the participants is revealed. In one case the real reason why a nation entered a war, explained in the history as fulfillment of a treaty obligation, did not come out until a lengthy seminar on the causes of the war was held. In a number of instances two nations have had amazingly different perceptions of the goals and intentions of a third nation. Only in the postsimulation sessions have some nations learned of the images they conveyed to some decision-makers of other nations and of the importance of these images to the course of events. Third, the postsimulation materials reveal to the students how partial their knowledge of the events of the simulation has been. Discussion of these events with decision-makers having different partial knowledge shows the role that the distribution of information has had on events.

Closing the events of the simulation before the end of the course also permits students to transform their roles from decision-maker to researcher. The simulation documents, with all secret messages now open for inspection, the revelations of postsimulation discussion, and access to all decision-makers give the student an opportunity to perform a kind of international relations research that cannot be attempted when the raw material is limited to the resources of the university library. Thus, the laboratory sessions provide not only a laboratory for international decision-making but a laboratory for international relations research as well. Although the documentation for a single simulation run sometimes seems staggering to the student, it is extremely small compared with that of the real world. With this advantage as well as the easy accessibility to data, the student can do a thorough examination of a meaningful problem in a relatively short space of time.

In these research projects almost any international relations interest could be pursued, but a worthwhile strategy is to use the research phase as another opportunity to integrate the simulation with course readings. A very useful approach is to have students explore basic propositions in the literature through examining data from their simulated world. This is not done with the intent of saying whether these propositions are or are not true in the real world, but rather to provide an exercise in the use of scientific methods in the analysis of international relations data. The student has a first-hand experience in trying to verify a significant generalization. In addition, the concepts and the relationships between these generalizations become more meaningful as the student works with them than is the case when the theories of international relations are but words to be mouthed from a textbook.

Two examples of the kind of inquiry students have done might be of interest. In the international relations course, investigation has been made of a basic proposition in A. F. K. Organski's textbook *World Politics* which asserts that "an approximate balance of power increases the danger of war" (Organski, p. 440). In the international organization course, investigation has been made of the basic conclusions reached by Karl Deutsch and his associates in the stimulating volume that came out of Richard Van Wagenen's project in the 1950's at Princeton: *Political Community in the North Atlantic Area*. After the examination of a number of instances of successful and unsuccessful political integration, the writers of this book assert that certain conditions make possible communities of political units that do not prepare to make war on each other. Students have examined the degree to which such conditions as "mutual responsiveness," "compatibility of major values," and "predictability" were present in the simulation. After an effort to actually use Deutsch's concepts in research, students find these concepts much more meaningful and can make more mature evaluations of the contributions of this book.

IV. What Happens in the Simulation?

A brief account of the simulation events created by students in laboratory sessions may help the reader to understand better the kinds of experiences students acquire. The 1959 and 1960 events are summarized, but for the sake of brevity the 1961 simulations are described only to the extent required to demonstrate the varieties of international situations that occur. The total of sixteen three-hour simulation sessions in 1959 and 1960 can be treated in a single historical account, since the 1960 class began their simulation approximately where the 1959 class had finished. The histories written by the 1959 participants provided historical background material for the 1960 group.

When the decision-makers of the five nations assumed their positions during the first period of the simulation in 1959, they found that two nations (Omne and Utro) were wealthy and that the other three (Algo, Erga, and Ingo) had quite limited economic potential. It became apparent rather early that improvement for the three nations of lesser economic competence would be a long-range task. In comparison to the wealthier nations they actually were getting poorer. The growing military competence of one of the two wealthy nations (Omne) was becoming a matter of concern to all.

The external decision-maker of one of the smaller nations (Erga) responded to this situation by calling an international conference. This decision-maker indicated that he thought the economic problems of the small nations, as well as the problem created by the developing military threat, could be solved if all the nations could just get around a conference table and talk things over. Taking leadership in the conference, this decision-maker advocated the establishment of an international bank through which wealthy countries would aid the poorer ones. The multilateral consideration of this proposal lasted several hours and eventually involved the external decision-makers and heads of state of all nations. The wealthy nations developed resistance to the proposal; and although a unanimous resolution, supporting in principle the establishment of a bank, was finally passed, the bank actually was never created. The rich nations were willing to extend some aid to the less wealthy ones, but through bilateral rather than multilateral channels.

For the remainder of the 1959 simulation, with one exception, universal conferences were not again used as a diplomatic technique. Suspicious of the reasons for Omne's growing military capability, Utro began to arm. Eventually two blocs developed as a result of secret alliances: Omne-Ingo and Utro-Erga. Both large nations wanted to insure that the entire world would not join the other against them. The small nations wanted the military security of an alliance and were using their alliance to obtain economic favors.

Algo, the poorest nation of all, was left out of the alliance system, thereby becoming exceedingly fearful of its eventual fate. Omne, in a bilateral conference, suggested to Ingo that Algo be requested to join their alliance, but Ingo suppressed the idea by casting suspicion on Algo's dependability as an ally. Ingo feared that Algo might get some of the economic favors from Omne that Ingo was getting if the alliance was extended to three nations. At the same time, however, Ingo was expressing great friendship and sympathy for Algo in bilateral conferences.

Algo's decision-makers became more and more concerned about their military vulnerability and their declining economic status. Finally they decided that only a radical change in the world system could save them, and they devised a plan to incite a realignment. A fabricated message from Erga to its ally Utro was written by Algo, in which it was indicated that Erga and Utro planned to attack Ingo. It was then arranged for this message to fall into the hands of Ingo's decision-makers. In response to the threat Ingo pressed for federation with Omne. Ingo then called an international conference to reveal the plot to the world.

At a dramatic conference session that ended the 1959 simulation and extended beyond the three-hour laboratory period, Erga denied authorship of the note. When an investigation became imminent Algo voluntarily admitted authorship of the note—proclaiming that it was a means to incite the calling of a universal international conference in order to save the world from its declining state of affairs. Since the conference had been assembled and the fabricated note had not plunged the world into war, Algo asserted that its deception was vindicated. In their history, however, the decision-makers of Algo admitted that they had other objectives in writing the note. They "hoped that Algo could gain its rightful place in world affairs through offering its services as mediator; or, should this prove unacceptable, it would remain at peace and emerge from the conflict ahead of the war-torn countries." Ironically, during the course of the conference it became known that after Algo's dramatic attempt to change the international system had been perpetrated, Algo had been able to obtain a secret military pact and economic aid from Omne. Omne preferred to keep it secret and use Algo as a potential neutral listening post for information on its strongest enemy, Utro.

The 1960 simulation began where the 1959 class ended with the exception of the alliance structure; the 1960 group was given the opportunity to develop its own system of external relationships. Thus Omne and Utro were still far ahead of the other nations in military and economic capability. Early in the 1960 term Utro suffered a revolution because of its failure to allocate sufficient resources to consumer goods while concentrating on the arms competition with Omne. This revolution was costly to Utro in that its temporary internal difficulties allowed Omne to pull considerably ahead in the arms race.

As in 1959, universal meetings were held to discuss the establishment of an international organization that could help the nations to avert war and to solve the economic problems of the poorer nations. These meetings took place at both the head of state and external decision-maker level. The external decision-makers were eventually successful in drafting an agreement to form an international organization that was signed by all heads of state during the fifth session of the simulation. This organization was authorized to establish economic institutions such as "a world bank or loan fund"; and the two nuclear nations, Omne and Utro, agreed to turn their nuclear weapons over to the organization. In addition, two-thirds of each nation's conventional weapons were to be transferred to the organization. It was stipulated that the international organization could use these weapons for only one purpose—to resist military aggressors.

Much of the initiative for the establishment of the international organization came from Omne. However, the superior economic and military position of Omne gave her an influence in world affairs that irritated other nations. Despite the constant assurance by Omne that its only interest was in the establishment of institutions that would guarantee peace and opportunity for all to prosper, there was suspicion that Omne had other intentions. Utro in particular was dissatisfied at finding itself destined to remain the number two nation. Utro felt that Omne was using its influence to establish international institutions that would enable it to perpetuate its dominant position. In the postsimulation session Utro's decision-makers indicated on several occasions that a world order in which they would remain perpetually number two was not attractive to them. They energetically applied themselves to designing a strategy that would enable them to avoid this fate.

Representatives to the international organization designed an inspection system to enforce the disarmament provisions of the international agreement that established the organization. The inspection function was assigned to the Secretary General of the organization. Inspection was carried out by an examination of decision forms, immediately after they were filled out by each nation, to see whether they had transferred existing weapons to the organization as agreed and to assure that resources were not being devoted to the manufacture of new weapons. Despite the agreement and energetic bilateral negotiations between the Secretary General and all heads of state, existing stocks of weapons were never turned over to the organization. There was not sufficient trust in other nations, nor in the disarmament system, for nations to be willing to comply.

Utro decided to use this period, in which there was a disarmament agreement but confusion in regard to implementation, to obtain the security that it thought the role of dominant power would offer. It hastily put all available resources into nuclear weapons, undetected by the still ineffective inspection system. Then with military superiority over Omne it offered an ultimatum which essentially demanded immediate amalgamation of the two nations, under the domination of Utro's leaders, or destruction of Omne. The bilateral negotiations that followed this ultimatum ran for more than two hours. Determined not to yield, the chief Omne negotiator cleverly prolonged the negotiations by using an imaginative range of delaying tactics. Finally, with Utro's patience exhausted, Omne was attacked and suffered damage that reduced it to the level of the three minor powers.

Utro then turned to the task of constructing a world order that, in the absence of the threat of Omne, it thought would be just and profitable for all. But Utro did not realize that once it had resorted to arms the degree of trust of its intentions by other nations would be even less than that which it formerly had for Omne. Fearful of their fate in the absence of a strong Omne to restrain Utro, the other three nations federated and used their combined resources to develop nuclear weapons. While Utro was concentrating on developing the new Utro-Omne economy and designing plans for a new world order of peace and prosperity, the Federation launched a preemptive attack on Utro. In this attack Utro was destroyed. But in accordance with a defensive war plan that Utro had in operation in case of an attack from Erga, a member of the Federation, Erga was destroyed by nuclear devices launched from Utro before the latter's destruction. As a result of these military adventures, distrust and suspicion permeated the relations among the surviving nations as the simulation ended.

The 1961 simulations, composed of ten sessions split equally between an international relations and international organization course that ran in sequence, also allow a single historical account. The histories written by the students in the first course served as background for students in the second, many of whom had taken the initial course during the preceding term. The number of laboratory sessions devoted to the simulation were cut down because the 1959 and 1960 experiences suggested that the educational benefits of the simulation could be increased if the postsimulation discussion and research activities were extended. Thus in 1961, operating in a ten-week college term, the first two laboratory sessions were spent in training the students, five in operation of the inter-nation simulation and the last three in postsimulation activity.

Primarily because of the larger class in the first term, the number of nations was increased to seven. More nations could have been established, but additional personnel were used instead in establishing a second newspaper and in assigning two aspirant decision-makers to each nation—an aspiring central decision-maker and his deputy. Once again the simulation world had two wealthy nations possessing nuclear weapons, the remainder of the nations trailing far behind. As before, the poorer nations found themselves unable to close the gap between themselves and the two rich nations. Their uneasiness at their predicament was converted into suspicion of the intentions of Utro and Omne, when the latter two nations arranged a surprise amalgamation that made the new nation economically and militarily superior to all other nations combined.

The decision-makers of Erga were particularly disturbed by their inability to get a significant economic development program under way. Finding that peaceful measures, through investment, trade, and aid, were not providing the progress that they desired, they decided to use force. They attacked Zena, destroying only a portion of Zena's military capability; they hoped then to be able to acquire, either through amalgamation or through tribute, a portion of Zena's economic capability. They predicted that their war could be limited to two countries, although Erga did not inform any other nation of her plan. Contrary to Erga's expectations, Ingo and Yora came to the aid of Zena and attacked Erga (the fifth smaller nation, Algo, had disarmed). At this point Utro-Omne entered the war and attacked Ingo and Yora. As a result Utro-Omne was in even greater dominance. Erga had the satisfaction of being unchallenged as the second strongest nation, although the gap between it and Utro-Omne was even wider. As the simulation ended a summit meeting was being held to determine the exact nature of the postwar world, with the central decision-maker of Utro-Omne making little effort to hide the ability of his nation to design the new world order.

Although the histories of the first term provided historical background for the second, it was assumed in the 1961 runs that events had transpired in the simulation world between the two terms. In

the interim period Erga was assumed to have become a close chal-
lenger of Utro-Omne, and Algo had developed into a middle-level
nation, with Ingo, Yora, and Zena still in relative poverty. Desiring
to give the students in the international organization course experiences with an organization in the world system, the instructor asked
each nation to send an official to offices created for permanent representatives to an international organization. These representatives
were not required to conduct business and any nation had the right
to withdraw their representative at any time.

During the second term, an international organization was developed, with a General Assembly, Security Council, and Secretariat.
Its achievements were mostly in the economic area. A clearing house
was established to facilitate the discovery and execution of advantageous trades, and capabilities to be used for the economic development of the poorer nations were acquired by a 1 per cent assessment of all nations. But lengthy negotiations on disarmament in the
international organization were unsuccessful. The negotiations were
principally devoted to attempting to achieve a system for the
elimination of the nuclear capability of Utro-Omne and Erga. However, a plan was never devised to which those nations would agree,
despite their support for the idea that nuclear disarmament and
even total disarmament was desirable. Plans for inspection to insure
compliance with disarmament received much attention. Particularly
troublesome was the attempt to design in advance adequate response to lack of cooperation with inspection, some negotiators
desiring to consider it aggression and provide the international
organization with military competence for immediate retaliation.

These negotiations were of particular interest to Algo, the middle-
level nation at the beginning of the second term. Through heavy
investment in research and development Algo had made significant
gains and had achieved the level of development required for
production of nuclear weapons. Possibly because of its past tradition of disarmament, however, Algo chose not to build nuclear
weapons in the hope that the disarmament negotiations would be
successful. As the quarter ended Algo had become suspicious of the
unwillingness of the nuclear nations to accept disarmament proposals and began producing its own nuclear weapons.

One of the most interesting aspects of the postsimulation sessions
was the discovery of the variety of perspectives on the disarmament
question. In general, those in the international organization who
were engaged in the negotiations expected their efforts eventually
to be successful. The representatives from the nuclear nations did,

however, report personal difficulty in fully supporting any particular proposal when the possibility of signing an agreement drew near because of the "finality" of the dismantling of their nation's nuclear competence and because of each representative's fear that other nations might not keep the agreement. The decision-makers in the home governments, however, were never as hopeful that negotiations would bring nuclear disarmament as were the international organization representatives. This was particularly so in the case of the decision-makers of the nuclear nations. But the postsimulation discussions revealed that at least two of the home officials saw the advantage to their nation of having optimistic negotiators because of the image of sincere pursuit of disarmament which they gave to other nations. For this reason, Algo did not inform its international organization representative of the decision to build nuclear weapons until after the project was actually under way.

V. Student Response to the Simulation

The following assessment of student reaction to the simulation is based partly on oral student comments—in the class discussions and seminars, during the simulation sessions, and during conferences on student papers. In addition, students turned in written evaluations of the simulation at the end of courses. It is quite clear that students enjoy the simulation and believe that they obtain valuable learning from the experience. There have been numerous requests that the time devoted to simulation be expanded.

In any one class there have never been more than two students who have submitted basically negative evaluations. Excerpts from the two negative responses in the international organization class of twenty-four who participated in the simulation in 1961 will provide examples of the rationale for this kind of response. A senior wrote:

> I enjoyed the simulation—especially the first three or four weeks. It was a novelty then, but later it became a mechanical drudgery. . . . Were the course an introductory one, I would readily acknowledge the importance of the simulation. However, I personally would have benefitted much more by having an extra two or three hours of lecture on the various international organizations other than the United Nations, i.e., NATO, SEATO, OAS, Warsaw Pact, Arab League, etc.

The evaluation of a sophomore stated:

> I enjoyed the simulation immensely, and I am sure that it is of untold value for purposes of research. However, I really don't feel that it taught me any more than I could have gleaned from a

lecture or a book. I should definitely have liked more opportunity for discussion of reading on the United Nations and was
looking forward to studying the OAS, Arab League, SEATO,
NATO, etc.

More positive evaluations, of course, have included suggestions for
improving the simulation. These suggestions have played an important role in the development of the simulation as a model as well
as in improving procedures for integrating it into an academic
course.

The general enthusiasm that students develop for the simulation
is not present from the beginning. Although students are initially
intrigued with the opportunity and eager to participate, they are
puzzled by its unfamiliarity. They arrive at the laboratory for their
first encounter with the simulation expecting it to be something like
the model United Nations most of them have observed and in which
many have participated. How can there be a world without the
United States and the Soviet Union? Reflecting on their initial reactions, students write comments such as these:

> When the simulation began, I did not seem to be getting a thing
> from the experience. Then as the strangeness of the terminology
> became familiar and the decision form took on meaning, I began
> to see a nation at work.

> Owing to the newness of the simulation I was somewhat bewil-
> dered at first, but it didn't take long to adapt to the new role I
> was expected to assume as central decision-maker of Utro.

The students soon become thoroughly acquainted with the concepts and procedures of the simulation. It cannot be otherwise if they
are to make decisions that will enable them to avoid losing office.
And students do have a great desire to stay in office and do develop
loyalty to their nation.

The degree to which students develop nationalistic feelings for
the nations of the simulation is one of the unexpected features of
the study. The students too are somewhat surprised, as is indicated
in this comment:

> It was difficult to imagine, upon hearing about the simulation,
> that loyalties and concern for a nation's existence could really
> materialize. But it does and did happen. I actually felt great
> *relief* and deep appreciation when the news arrived that Yora
> and Ingo would support our attacked nation of Zena.

One of the most fervent nationalists wrote as follows:

> I feel like an Omnian! In other words, I have developed a na-
> tionalistic patriotism (pride in Omne's achievements and distress

over its failures) which in many ways is just as strong as my American patriotism.

The development of nationalism is not only useful in helping the simulation nations to develop characteristics of the real world, but some students seem to find that close observation of the birth of nationalism is helpful to their understanding of international relations:

> The simulation sessions have given participants an idea of how patriotism and love of one's homeland evolves. At first, a number of wry comments were heard about the nations of Omne, Utro, Zena and the others. But the feeling toward the simulation fatherlands soon changed. Students who considered the whole set-up an object of ridicule began to defend the position of their country to the press and to the "citizens" of other nation-states. Rationalizations for the behavior of the various units were stated to the newspapers.

> It is interesting to note how much real feeling was generated by the simulation. When a student who represents a mythical country can get so emotional about the world situation, it is easy to see why Organski says that the nation-state will continue to be the significant unit in international relations.

The desire of students to stay in office as well as the development of nationalism are both evidence of the degree to which students become involved in the simulation. Occasional comments in the written evaluations indicate that the identification is quite intense: "I got all involved, emotionally involved." And: "I was a nervous wreck most of the time."

In 1961 the class of sixty-four was asked to evaluate their simulation experience after four laboratory sessions. They were asked: "In what ways has your simulation experience helped you to better understand international relations?" The main themes in these responses have been tabulated and will be reported below, with extracts from student responses. The purpose of these open-ended evaluations is to develop knowledge of the educational value of simulation from the student's perspective—independent of the goals of the teacher. As a result, potential teaching values of the simulation are emerging that were not anticipated by the teacher. It should be made clear to the reader that the following values cited by students are in no sense confirmation of the superiority of simulation over other teaching methods. A rigorous evaluation of the simulation in contrast to other methods will have to be made to determine whether this is the case. Now that reasonably satisfactory methods for incorporating the simulation in courses have been devised,

Northwestern feels an obligation to make a more rigorous evaluation. This evaluation is now in progress (Robinson).

The six most often cited themes in student response to the question stated in the above paragraph were the following, with the number in parentheses indicating the number of students mentioning each theme:

1. Provides vividness and understanding beyond what one gets from a textbook. (38)
2. Gives one a realization of the complexities and/or the lack of simple solutions to international relations problems. (22)
3. Indicates the importance of having reliable knowledge and the importance of communication in international relations. (17)
4. Develops better understanding of the problems and goals of nations not like the United States. (16)
5. Experience in decision-making enables one to better understand the problems of the decision-maker. (14)
6. Demonstrates the difficulties of balancing the requirements of internal and external affairs. (14)

Since these themes were volunteered by students in their responses, the number in parentheses does not indicate the number of students who might think the simulation useful in that regard in answer to a direct question about it. Short extracts from student responses will help further the goal of this section of the chapter, which is to help the reader assess the value of the simulation for students of international relations.

General statements about the understanding that the simulation gives indicate that the simulation does help to diminish the previously mentioned hiatus between the events and officials of international relations and the world of student experience.

> The awareness of the vast number and the complexity of the factors which must be considered by a nation, could never have been as vivid from reading a book as they are after the simulation experience.

> The simulation helped me a great deal in understanding what the authors were trying to tell me. In a great many cases something I read would just "sorta hang there" until I came across it in the simulation and then I would understand it much more.

> In my two terms in the simulation, the thing which has become most imbedded in my mind is the impossibility of making a value

judgment of a decision by considering only that decision. It is necessary to put the decision into its context, to study all the factors that effected it, before any valid judgment can be made. This understanding could never have come from reading textbooks on international relations. It came from being put into a system similar to the atmosphere that surrounds real world decision-makers. Only in this way, I think, can one come to understand the very real limitations on decision-making and the decision-making process.

Simulation was most valuable in that it enabled abstract concepts to come to life.

The frequent student comments about the unexpected complexity of international relations problems may be partially explained by two factors. First, the miniature world that the simulation creates initially seems extremely simple to the student. But as the model becomes clothed in layers of history and inhabited by human beings, each student possesses only partial knowledge of the events of the simulation. Second, many students are accustomed to selecting ideal solutions for international relations problems in the real world on the basis of whatever knowledge chance has brought their way. As decision-makers, however, they are stimulated to design feasible policies and to make a more concerted effort to obtain information about the environment in which the policies will be implemented. In the course of performing these activities an area of simple choice becomes one in which the pathways to utopia appear to be more complex.

Simulation increased my awareness of the complexity of factors which seem to operate in the world, and increased my appreciation of the difficulty in making decisions when all the factors are not known, or cannot be evaluated.

I was frankly astonished at the complexity of international relations when embroiled in the simulation. As a detached observer of the real world it is dangerously easy to blame and criticize, especially in retrospect. When involved in the process, the conflicting demands of internal and external policy-making, the numbers of people attempting to formulate some working harmony, left one rather breathless, not to say confused.

Undergraduate students are so accustomed to explaining international relations events in terms of ideology and factors subsumed under the power concept that it is often not easy to develop their sensitivity to information distribution and characteristics of the international communications system as factors of importance in international relations. This makes the citation of these factors by more than one-quarter of the respondents to the question somewhat surprising.

One becomes aware of how incomplete his knowledge of events really is and how his interpretations of events can be quite different from others' interpretations.

One is impressed by the limits imposed upon the individual decision-maker by the information that is available to him. The relative isolation which is imposed upon a nation has major effects upon the course of inter-nation relationships. The fact that a head of state cannot ever be assured of complete information in respect to a given circumstance is an important insight which the simulation underscores. The importance of adequate information and the consequences of precipitating action on the basis of incorrect or inadequate information was dramatically demonstrated in the case of the Erga-Zena war. Knowledge of a defensive alliance involving Zena would have certainly produced a different course of action on the part of Erga. The ensuing military defeat of Erga was a direct result of a failure to realize the limitations of her information gathering facilities.

Experience as decision-makers of small and economically underdeveloped nations in the simulation is often an enlightening experience for United States undergraduates. Despite their determined efforts to catch up with the wealthier and more developed nations, they usually find their nation dropping even further behind.

First of all (and most enlightening to me) was the understanding I obtained of the point of view of small nations. Being a citizen of Algo was quite a change from being a citizen of the United States. I can now see why small nations tend toward neutralism; I can see why they have great fear of becoming economically or politically dependent on any one nation. I understand why they fear embroilment with any large power no matter what purposes it professes. Finally, I know why all small nations want large powers to disarm. This chance to study the small nation viewpoint somewhat mellowed my distaste for fence-riding neutrals in the real world.

I gained a perspective, by belonging to a smaller country, which I never had before, as problems and feelings incurred through inferiority were made readily apparent. Everyone should get the opportunity to be a small-nation member; this alone, as an educational experience, made the simulation well worthwhile.

Finally, another important thing I now understand better is communism. I realized to my amazement when we made out the decision sheet for Ingo that even those of us who claimed to be staunch conservatives were advocating pushing economic development as hard as we could, disregarding as far as we dared the validators. Our "motto" was to bring the people as close as possible to starvation without there being a revolution. Now I can see why communism has such an appeal among the underdeveloped nations of the world. The temptation to move swiftly ahead at all costs is a strong one indeed, and this is especially true if you have nothing to conserve (thus why be conservative?).

Mark Twain once said that "a fellow who takes a bull by the tail once gets as much as sixty or seventy times the information as one who doesn't." As with simulation experiences in other fields, students who participate in the inter-nation simulation find that the experience gives them deeper understanding of the predicament of the decision-maker.

It is hard to explain to someone who has not participated in the simulation the difficulty of making decisions that could possibly destroy your country. One has to experience this role himself to be able to appreciate and understand the problems that face decision-makers in the real world.

A person can read a large amount of material, but until he is actually called upon to act, certain factors exist to which one is blind. Those factors which are missing in reading become evident when one performs the functions. A person can read about the effect of various factors on the success of a nation, but only when anxiety arising from past errors is present can one feel the gravity of the various factors, for example, the decreasing of validator satisfaction, being attacked by another nation, deciding how to allocate your basic capability. It is in the above way—basically the anxiety arising from past errors in the simulation, when combined with the principles learned from experts like Organski, Morgenthau, Haas and Whiting, etc.—that one is better aided in understanding the processes of international relations.

The simulation is designed so that some decision-makers must make not only foreign policy decisions but also domestic decisions related to their internal security, economic development, expenditures for consumer goods, and decision latitude in relation to the validators. These decision-makers face not only external threats but the possibility of losing office because of the unpopularity of their internal policies. Some students obtained insight into the relationship between domestic and foreign policy by having to weigh the often conflicting demands of these two areas of the decision-maker's environment in the simulation.

It was exciting to see how the problems of intranational and international relationships and decisions are so intricately woven together and must be closely coordinated in order to maintain validator satisfaction as well as world position—it is no easy task to accomplish both simultaneously.

Another helpful and interesting facet of the simulation was the relationship it showed between internal and external affairs. From this experience in the simulation, I can better understand the importance of internal factors on external decisions in the real world.

Student comments confirm Guetzkow's assertion in Chapter Two that the simulation is not a "small group" exercise. Acknowledging that the problems faced in the simulation are extremely complex, students claim that the experience helps them to understand better the multifaceted world that is described and explained in their textbooks. It also is indicated by their awareness of information gaps between nations and by dramatic differences between the personal experiences described by members of poor as contrasted to members of rich nations. Thus, they assert that the simulation is not a "small group" but consists of a number of separate units with a complex system of relationships. Members of these units only partially perceive other units, and different units provide quite different experiences for their personnel.

It is instructive to examine the way in which students have explicated in their comments the educational benefits claimed by users of a variety of simulations in the opening pages of this chapter. Indication that the simulation provides "a miniature model of factors that can be more readily observed and understood" is supplied by the students' claims that they now realize the "importance of reliable knowledge and the importance of communication in international relations," as well as by their realization of the relationship between internal and external affairs. Students indicate that a simulation laboratory provides for the application and testing of knowledge by stating that simulation experience provides them with a deeper understanding of assigned readings. The simulation furnishes "insight into the decision-maker's predicament," according to our students, by providing "experience in decision-making" which "enables one to better understand the problems of the decision-maker." It was unforeseen that the students would emphasize that such insight was realized concretely in the development of "better understanding of the problems and goals of nations not like the United States." Heightened "interest and motivation of students" is reflected in the "vividness in understanding" they feel they obtain "beyond what one gets from a textbook." It is also indicated by the strong nationalistic feelings they develop toward their simulation nation.

No longer are the students passive spectators of international affairs. They are challenged to utilize their learning of principles in creative ways, as they actively endeavor to solve the problems of their simulated worlds.

VI. Teaching Potential of the Simulation at Other Academic Levels

This discussion has been limited to the use of the simulation on the undergraduate level, although it may have educational value for other groups as well. Modified versions of the simulation have been used in international relations courses by two high school teachers with success. [During the three years of Northwestern's Workshop in International Relations for High School Teachers, Professor George I. Blanksten and I found the simulation of increasing interest to high school teachers. This workshop was cosponsored by the Foreign Relations Project of the North Central Association of Secondary Schools and Colleges during the summers of 1958-59-60.] The participation of more than 350 high school students in research runs of the simulation in the summer of 1960 shows some promise for use at this level. These students were quite able to perform the simulation roles. There were indications that some of the students found the experience educationally rewarding.

Although it is not feasible to introduce the simulation into graduate courses at Northwestern because classes are not large enough, participation in the simulation also has educational potential at this level. Comments of graduate students who have participated in research runs of the simulation are similar to those of undergraduates. Both MIT and RAND report that even more advanced scholars gain through participation in their simulations. An MIT report states that "senior scholars have reported eye-opening perceptions of elements in their own field of specialty" and also that participation helps scholars identify new research areas (Bloomfield, 1960, p. 61). Goldhamer and Speier of RAND report that "the game provided excellent opportunities and incentives for such participants to acquire an overview of a political situation and to amass relevant information that the ordinary intellectual division of labor and specialization by area or discipline do not make available" (Goldhamer and Speier, p. 79).

The simulation may also have value as a training device for career foreign service personnel. Reports on the participation of professionals in the MIT and RAND simulations maintain that these simulations of actual countries have value for practitioners. Professor Bloomfield of MIT claims that "one of the most useful purposes of the serious professional 'reality game' is to help clarify premises which underlie thinking and planning but which are not often if ever put to the actual test of events. Lacking such a test of events, the game sets up a laboratory in which those events can be lived through experimentally" (Bloomfield, 1960, p. 61). Reporting on a RAND experience Joseph M. Goldsen states that "the participants from the Department of State were particularly emphatic in their belief that much had been learned" (Goldsen, p. 36). The MIT and RAND simulations appear to have value in exploring the potential consequences of specific policies and searching for new alternatives. Participation in the simulation of contrived countries, as critics and developers of the simulation as well as in the role of decision-makers, might also stimulate practitioners to develop their analytic skills.

As has been pointed out by Greene and Sisson as a result of their experience with business simulations, the educational benefits of simulation extend to the teacher as well (Greene and Sisson, p. 2). In designing a simulation and modifying it as a result of class discussion and of new findings in the literature, the teacher is required to make his model of the field explicit, to subject it to constant challenge and, when necessary, to make revisions. In working with the model the teacher must devote some attention to international relations as a whole; thus he is less likely to concentrate only on the part of the field with which he is most familiar or with which he enjoys working the most. Furthermore, the model stimulates the selection of readings that are relevant to it and that illuminate the variables and relationships that it incorporates. This provides explicit and theoretically meaningful criteria for selection of readings rather than selection on the basis of what is customarily used or what is readily accessible.

VII. Summary

To summarize briefly, a survey of reports by educational users of simulation indicates that the main claims for the educational value of simulation are (1) it increases student interest and motivation; (2) it serves as a laboratory for student application and testing of knowledge; (3) it provides insight into the decision-makers predicament; (4) it offers a miniature but rich model that facilitates comprehension of world realities. In the Northwestern use of simulation in international relations teaching, there is particular interest in purposes (2) and (4), the simulation being a device for encouraging students to acquire an analytic scheme that can then be used as a tool for analysis. In addition, the simulation through benefit (3) helps remove the student's feeling of distance between international relations and his own life experience and permits contact with kinds of data that are now inadequately covered in the literature. It was pointed out how the use of contrived rather than real nations serves these educational purposes by increasing the objectivity of the student as he approaches controversial problems in international affairs.

Three years of experimentation with the simulation in laboratory sessions of undergraduate courses has shown that its successful use requires careful integration of the simulation with course readings, papers, lectures, and seminars. This integration is achieved by scheduling a laboratory throughout the term devoted to preparation for running the simulation, actual runs, and discussion stimulating the student to build intellectual bridges between the simulation and the real world.

Student response to the simulation was reported as positive. The six most cited student gains were: (1) obtaining vividness and understanding beyond that provided by texts; (2) appreciation of the unexpected complexities of international relations; (3) learning the importance of reliable knowledge and of communication factors; (4) understanding the problems and goals of nations unlike the United States, particularly the underdeveloped nation; (5) better appreciation of the problems of the decision-maker; (6) learning the difficulties of balancing internal and external factors in devising foreign policy.

Finally, it should be quite clear that judgment of the educational value of a simulation that attempts to portray the essential characteristics of all international systems must be made independently of an evaluation of the particular simulation described in this volume. The propositions about reality that are incorporated in this simulation must be evaluated by rigorous study of reality. Whether or not to have a simulation laboratory in a course requires a decision as to how one can most effectively enable a class to comprehend and use a list of essential propositions—whether they be those proposed in this book or others. And even if a teacher begins with the model in this book he will make changes over a period of time. In a field that is in its scientific infancy, as well as one in which additions to knowledge are being made rapidly, a scholar's summary of the essentials of international relations can hardly remain static.

VIII. References

Bloomfield, L. P., *The Political Exercise—A Progress Report*. Center for International Studies, Massachusetts Institute of Technology, March, 1961, mimeographed.

———, "Political Gaming," *United States Naval Institute Proceedings*, LXXXVI (1960), 57-64.

———, "Report and Analysis of Political Exercise," C/58 (revised ditto) Center for International Studies, Massachusetts Institute of Technology, September, 1958.

——— and N. J. Padelford, "Three Experiments in Political Gaming," *The American Political Science Review*, LIII (1959), 1105-1115.

Center for Research in Business, *Proceedings of the National Symposium on Management Games*, University of Kansas, May, 1959.

Cohen, B. C., "Political Gaming in the Classroom," *Journal of Politics*, XXIV (1962), 367-381.

Cohen, K. J., R. M. Cyert, W. R. Dill, and M. H. Miller, "Four Discussion Papers on the Carnegie Management Game," Graduate School of Industrial Administration, Carnegie Institute of Technology, February, 1961.

Deutsch, K. W. and R. W. Van Wagenen, *et al.*, *Political Community in the North Atlantic Area*. Princeton: Princeton University Press, 1957.

Fifield, R. H., "The Introductory Course in International Relations," *The American Political Science Review*, XLII (1948), 1189-1196.

Fox, W. T. R. and A. B. Fox, "The Teaching of International Relations in the United States," *World Politics*, XIII (1961), 339-359.

Goldhamer, H. and H. Speier, "Some Observations on Political Gaming," *World Politics*, XII (1959), 71-83.

Goldsen, J. M., *The Political Exercise: An Assessment of the Fourth Round*. Washington, D.C.: The RAND Corporation, D-3640-RC, May 30, 1956, mimeographed.

Goodwin, G. L. (ed.), *The University Teaching of International Relations*, Oxford: H. Blackwell, Ltd., 1951.

Greene, J. R. and R. L. Sisson, *Dynamic Management Decision Games*. New York: John Wiley & Sons, Inc., 1959.

Guetzkow, H., R. A. Brody, M. J. Driver, and P. F. Beach, *An Experiment on the N-Country Problem Through Inter-Nation Simulation: Two Case Study Examples*. Social Science Institute, Washington University, St. Louis, November 28, 1960, mimeographed.

Haas, E. B. and A. S. Whiting, *Dynamics of International Relations*. New York: McGraw-Hill Book Co., Inc., 1956.

Kennan, G. F., "The Teaching of International Relations," *Princeton Alumni Weekly,* (March 6, 1953), 10-12.

Kirk, G. L., *The Study of International Relations in American Colleges and Universities.* New York: Council on Foreign Relations, 1947.

Lackman, W. F., Jr., "Political Game Academic Year 1959-1960," United States Air Force Academy, Department of Political Science, Colorado Springs, April 18, 1960, mimeographed.

Lerche, C. O., Jr., *Principles of International Politics.* New York: Oxford University Press, 1956.

————— and B. M. Sapin, *Some Problems in the Study and Teaching of International Politics, Outlines Stemming from a Faculty Seminar on the Teaching of International Politics.* Atlanta: Emory University, 1958.

Manning, C. A. W., *The University Teaching of Social Sciences.* International Relations: A Report Prepared on Behalf of the International Studies Conference. Paris: UNESCO, 1954.

McClosky, H., "Concerning Strategies for a Science of International Politics," *World Politics,* VIII (1956), 281-295.

Morgenthau, H. J., *Politics Among Nations: The Struggle for Power and Peace,* 3rd ed. New York: Alfred A. Knopf, Inc., 1960.

Organski, A. F. K., *World Politics.* New York: Alfred A. Knopf, Inc., 1958.

Padelford, N. J. and G. A. Lincoln, *International Politics, Foundation of International Relations.* New York: The Macmillan Co., 1954.

—————, G. H. Sewell, and T. Harrison, *Report on Political Exercise on Simulated Far Eastern Situation.* Political Science Section, Massachusetts Institute of Technology, January, 1961, mimeographed.

Rawdon, R. H., *Learning Management Skills from Simulation Gaming.* Bureau of Industrial Relations, University of Michigan, December, 1960.

Robinson, J. A., "A Research Design for Comparing Simulation with Case Studies and Problem Papers in Teaching Political Science," *Proceedings of the Conference on Business Games as Teaching Devices,* New Orleans, April 26-28, 1961, 123-129 (revised in U.S. Office of Education, Project No. 1568, 1962).

Schuman, F. L., *International Politics: The Western State System and the World Community,* 6th ed. New York: McGraw-Hill Book Co., Inc., 1958.

Snyder, R. C., H. W. Bruck, and B. Sapin (eds.), *Foreign Policy Decision-Making.* New York: The Free Press of Glencoe, Inc., 1962.

Social Science Division, *Experimental Research on Political Gaming.* Santa Monica: The RAND Corporation, RAND Report P-1540-RC, November 10, 1958.

Van Dyke, V., *International Politics.* New York: Appleton-Century-Crofts, Inc., 1957.

—————, *A Report Concerning a Seminar for the Improvement of Teach-*

ing in International Relations. Iowa City: State University of Iowa, September 1, 1955, mimeographed.

————, *Some Approaches Used in the Teaching of International Politics.* Iowa City: State University of Iowa, 1957, mimeographed.

Wright, Q., "Educational and Research Objectives," *The Study of International Relations.* New York: Appleton-Century-Crofts, Inc., 1955, pp. 65-80.

Chapter Seven

Varieties of Simulations in International Relations Research

Richard A. Brody

In the past decade and a half increasing attention has been paid to the development of methods for the study of politics. The voter-attitude studies have adapted survey research techniques in order to gain further understanding of the process of voter decision-making. Decision-making case studies, employing techniques drawn primarily from social psychology, have attempted to add the weight of rigor to the arguments of those political theorists who postulate a "group theory of politics." Content analyses have been employed by political scientists to examine the theoretical foundations of their own literature as well as to analyze systematically governmental documents and other political data. Simulation, or gaming, as a method of analyzing political interaction processes, is another of these postwar developments.

The Northwestern inter-nation simulation is but one among a growing number that have been developed by students of international relations. Our task now is to describe a number of these and to examine the purposes for which they have been constructed and operated. In order to ground the discussion in the growing concern over scientific method, the logic of simulation will be considered briefly. Since political simulations are a type of "operating model," the concept of "model" will be explored first.

I. Models in Science

A model is a collection of assertions about some reality—past, present, or predicted. It is a set of statements which purports to describe patterns of relationships holding between components—units and variables—of that reality. But a model is less than a total representation of the details of the phenomena of interest to the model builder. Otherwise, the scientist would work directly with the phenomena themselves in their total richness. Model building is an attempt to achieve parsimony in the representation of a range of unique and particular phenomena.

A model is a scientific tool. If a model is to be useful for description, explanation, or prediction, there must be some manner of correspondence between the model and the reality it represents. Developing a model involves abstracting from reality those components and relationships which are hypothesized as crucial to what is being modeled. Important detail is included in the model with the exclusion of redundant and distracting detail. "The better the theory, the more knowledge we have about the conditions under which neglected variables do or do not make a difference" (Brodbeck, 1959, p. 381). Do outcomes in the model resemble outcomes in the reality it purports to represent closely enough to warrant making inferences about aspects of the reality by using the model? The confirmation or disconfirmation of a model via this pragmatic test informs the theorist about the adequacy of his abstraction and thus about the usefulness of his abbreviated theory to cope with reality.

II. Types of Models

It seems useful to distinguish between classes of models. The four types identified here—pictorial, verbal, mathematical, and simulational—are those commonly found in use in the social sciences, but they do not exhaust the possible models.

PICTORIAL

Pictorial (or iconic) models have enjoyed wide currency among social scientists. Consider, for example, the numerous organization charts found in a basic political science text. Here, by the use of a few symbols (lines for channels and boxes for units), patterns of authority and subordination are described, the path that a bill follows through the House is traced, or certain aspects of the interrelations of the branches of government are illustrated. "Since early times," Deutsch points out, "men have tended to order their thoughts in terms of pictorial models. The model itself . . . served, more or less efficiently, to order and correlate men's acquired habits and experiences, and perhaps to suggest a selection of new guesses and behavior patterns for unfamiliar situations" (1951, p. 232).

Pictorial models seem to be used primarily for description. They are essentially static and do not yield easily to the deductive logic necessary for prediction. While they can be very useful for depicting order and flow, as Meadows points out, "in the long-run . . . it is not possible to evade this limitation on all pictorial models. Relations cannot be readily pictorial" (1957, p. 7).

It is interesting to note that pictorial models usually need to be elucidated with words. Often the social scientist uses a verbal model to construct a "metatheory" within which the pictorial model explicates limited and particular features of a broader schematization. Hence, the common use of diagrams in texts, which exploits the iconic features of a two-dimensional representation, simultaneously remedies its defect by complementary verbal material.

VERBAL

Verbal models, if they are more than just word pictures, have several advantages over pictorial models. It is, for example, possible to describe relationships between units in ordinary language which could not be pictured. Furthermore, it is possible to imbue verbal models with a logical consistency which admits deductive predictions.

Verbal models abound in political science. The *Republic* is a verbal model of Plato's conception of the ideal state. Beyond this, it contains descriptions of an actual state of affairs. It proposes a series of steps which, it predicts, if followed would accomplish the transformation of the present reality into the ideal system. In recent times, Easton, Dahl, Key, and other authors have contributed to the store of verbal models at the disposal of the political scientist—unquestionably this type of model has been the principal tool of the discipline. Bentley and Truman offer similar but separable models of political process. Here the units are groups of individuals; the models purport to describe the relationships between these units with the end of explaining and predicting the process.

Despite the advantages of verbal models over pictorial models, they also suffer from significant disadvantages. It is difficult, for example, to draw cumulative knowledge from verbal models because of the ambiguities of the symbol system. The same word, in the system of two different theorists, may have substantially different meanings. The terms of relationship (*e.g.*, more than, before, correlates with) are suggestive but without precision. Moreover, the development of crucial experiments from verbal models generally involves the translation of the verbal symbols into a more explicit symbol system. One result of this type of translation can be a mathematical model of the system formerly described by the verbal model.

MATHEMATICAL

Mathematical models of political systems are of relatively recent origin. They are, as Beshers puts it, ". . . constructed by abstracting the properties of some data by measurement, and by expressing these properties in a set of symbolic statements that include the logical relationships that hold for the entire set of statements" (1957, p. 33). Richardson's "Mathematical Psychology of War," although published in 1919, lay unnoticed until quite recently. In the past few years several authors, including Dahl, Downs, Matthews, Shubert, and Simon, have contributed to our meager stock of mathematical representations of political phenomena.

To utilize mathematical models, the human behavior symbolically represented in its equations must be so structured that the relationships among the units and variables involved do produce consequences isomorphic to the reality one portrays. Sometimes one seeks to have the very rules of relationship which constitute the axioms of whatever calculus is being used correspond to the social processes themselves. Whenever the consequences fail to produce the reality

—or under the more rigorous requirement, whenever the processes as well as the consequences fail to mirror the empirical social system one is attempting to represent—alternative calculi may be sought, so that the model may become a more adequate representation of the system of human behavior being considered.

Where appropriate mathematical models can be found, they are powerful scientific tools. The abstractness of the symbol system facilitates the recognition of similarities and congruences between models and, therefore, between the realities they represent. In this way the process of accumulating knowledge may be expedited.

Beyond this advantage, mathematical models can be made to yield information about a variety of states of the system without changing the basic model. The question, "What happens when the 'size' [or 'power,' or some other variable] of a unit changes with respect to the system?" can be explored in the model. And this question can be asked and examined for many combinations of units and variables.

In order to derive full benefit from this feature of mathematical models, it is desirable to be able to try a large number of parametric values or to try one set of parameters over spans of time. To facilitate this kind of manipulation, mathematical models can be programmed on high-speed computing equipment, the mathematical model thereby becoming one type of operating model—in this instance, a "computer simulation."

The heavy reliance of mathematical models upon verbal supplements is noteworthy. The variables posited in the equations are often explicated through verbal language. The measurements used to secure precision in handling these variables are operationalized in verbal language, too. And sometimes the relationships among the equations, especially when discontinuities and contingencies are being handled, are expounded by verbal means. Often the invocation of "simplifying assumptions" when the mathematics become intractable is explained by verbal metatheoretical considerations.

SIMULATIONAL

Simulations are physical and/or biological representations of systems which attempt to replicate sociopolitical processes. They are models which yield information about unit and variable changes over time. The theories they incorporate, therefore, include propositions about time-change in the system.

As empirical social systems are difficult to manipulate, the social theorist perforce is dependent upon the "natural" experiment or some substitute in carrying out his confirmatory studies. The natural experiment has the advantage of providing data from the empirical system itself. Here the researcher can observe the operation not of a model but of the actual system; validity is assured. Natural experiments, however, have two serious drawbacks from the point of view of the requirements of a scientific methodology: (1) An experimental situation cannot always be found in nature which definitively confirms or unconfirms hypotheses; and (2) when natural experiments are found, it is unlikely that they will be found in sufficient number to provide statistically useful samples; reliability becomes a problem (Campbell and Stanley, 1962).

"A *simulation* . . . model," according to Shubik, "is amenable to manipulations which would be impossible or impractical to perform on the entity it portrays. The operation of the model can be studied, and from it, properties concerning the . . . actual system or organism [can be] . . . inferred" (1958, p. 1). The fact that manipulation takes place in a *model* of reality can itself be considered an advantage. Changes in a system can be tried in a "pilot plant," for example, which might prove excessively expensive and dangerous if they were introduced into the full-scale operation. Simulation allows the study of induced variable change in situations where it might be otherwise difficult or undesirable to induce this change—which might be the case for many, if not most, social systems. With simulations, the problem of numbers can be solved by replication of runs. The number of runs is limited primarily by the resources, and the stamina, of the researcher.

The manipulation of simulation models has been termed "pseudo-experimentation" by Helmer and Rescher—" 'pseudo,' because the experiments are carried out in the model, not in reality" (1959, p. 48). They contend that:

> . . . pseudo-experimentation may effectively annul the oft-regretted infeasibility of carrying out experiments proper in the social sciences by providing an acceptable substitute which, moveover, has been tried and proved in the applied physical sciences (1959, p. 49).

Simulation offers an advantage to the theorist working with models in which *time* is likely to be an important variable. The ability to compress or expand time in a controlled fashion offers an opportunity to study the effects of a given variation upon the system in a way which might be otherwise impossible. Thus it becomes feasible to study foreign policy decision-making in a series of situations in which the decision-makers have differentially timed deadlines. Decisions under "normal" circumstances may be different from those made in the face of "ultimata" or "crises."

The advantage of simulation techniques in theory-building and testing are summed up in the idea of "control." Because the researcher is to a large extent master of his system, he can work with many of the variables that interest him. He can study consequences of changes in particular subsystems or within the total model. He can evaluate the outcomes associated with a variety of alternative policies in relation to any given desired outcome; he can, in short, attempt to represent future states of the system.

Work in simulation involves the utilization of other modes of model building. Pictorial representation of computing procedures is widespread. The use of ordinary language throughout man-computer simulations places heavy reliance upon verbal models. In developing programs, the computer components in simulation models rely upon mathematical representations. As Guetzkow and Noel illustrate in their chapters, to work with simulation as a social science tool, it has been necessary to make metatheoretical explication of the hypotheses which are embodied in the operating representation itself. Hence, Noel presents by means of a verbal model in Chapter Four the changes made in evolving the inter-nation simulation. Guetzkow attempts to tighten his understanding of the simulation by using mathematical models to explicate the programmed hypotheses embodied in the simulation and by employing verbal hypotheses to exhibit the unprogrammed relationships that were implicitly incorporated in the game by its human participants. Although iconic, verbal, and mathematical devices are very useful in developing a simulation, their limitations are precisely the reason why one moves to an operating representation of the phenomena, using physical and/or biological means for the model construction.

III. Political Simulations in the Study of International Relations

Political simulations are developed and used in order to help the theorist explore hypotheses about political systems. Most commonly, political games have been used in working with international political systems. For the student of international relations the experimental manipulation of the object of his study is out of the question at present; he must rely on other methods.

Three subtypes of simulations may be identified: (1) machine or computer simulations; (2) man simulations or games; and (3) mixed or man-computer simulations. What varies here is the degree of involvement by human actors in the operation of the model (as units or subunits of the model, not as experimenters). The simulations of international political systems, which will be discussed below, come in all three varieties. The three subtypes show similar lines of development and similar *raisons d'être.*

Now let us examine the contributions of a number of the researchers who already have begun to employ simulation techniques in their studies of various aspects of international relations. A variety of simulations has been used with differing emphases on the two basic objectives, theory and training. But, because for either activity the simulation must approximate reality, these researchers have shown concern for furthering the state of knowledge of international relations.

COMPUTER SIMULATIONS

Machine simulations are operational models that have been programmed for high speed computing equipment. In these simulations humans are involved primarily in the role of experimenters. A model of decision-making behavior (so-called "rules of action") is included as part of the larger model to replace the human decision-makers found in man-machine simulations and games.

Among social scientists, economists have made the most use of this type of simulation. Milbrath (1958) has suggested the possible usefulness of voting simulation. The "Simple Diplomatic Game," developed by Oliver Benson (1958, 1959) at the University of Oklahoma, is perhaps the single instance of a primarily machine simulation dealing with international relations materials. However, more recently Howard (1961) at General Motors has developed an all-computer simulation of a colonial socioeconomic development system, and his colleague Kaehler (1961) has been preparing for the study of problems of international conflict with an analog computer.

The Benson development "is a computer simulation program . . . designed to reproduce in simplified form a number of features of the international political system" (1959, p. 1). Fundamentally, this simulation attempts to describe political counteractions to particular actions in given situations and the effects on situations of a given

action-counteraction cycle. The model consists of two sets of variables—action variables and situation variables—and a program that
specifies the relationship of variables to outcomes.

The action variables consist of nine possible acting nations, nine
possible target nations[1] and nine possible intensity levels of action.

> The nine actor states used initially are the nine major powers of
> the actual scene: The United States, Britain, the Soviet Union,
> Western Germany, France, Italy, India, China, and Japan. The
> nine target states are chosen from recent tension areas: Korea,
> Guatemala, Egypt, Lebanon, Hungary, Vietnam, Taiwan, Indo-
> nesia, and Iran. . . .
> The nine intensity levels of action . . . are defined in the program
> as representing from ten to ninety per cent of effort . . . roughly
> corresponding to a scale of increasingly serious action . . . (Ben-
> son, 1959, p. 2).[2]

The situational variables describe the "state of the system" at
any given moment when action is taking place. The relevant variables are: (1) national power expressed in terms of war potential;[3]
(2) distribution of this power;[4] (3) the interest level, i.e., the degree

---

[1] The number of acting states and target states is arbitrarily limited by
the storage capacity of the particular computer being programmed
(IBM 650, in this case). Theoretically, any number of states for which
the requisite data are available could be employed.

[2] "The nine intensity levels of action are named . . . to make [them]
more vivid":

    .100 Diplomatic protest
    .200 United Nations action
    .300 Severing diplomatic relations
    .400 Propaganda-subversion campaign
    .500 Boycott and/or reprisals
    .600 Troop movements
    .700 Full mobilization
    .800 Limited war
    .900 All-out war (Benson, 1959, p. 2)

[3] Eight determinants of war potential are used: ". . . military age manpower, transportation, gross national product, gross national product per
capita, energy production, steel production, literacy, and atomic capability" (Benson, 1959, p. 4).

[4] Based on ". . . power distribution. . . . If two coalitions are dominant
to the extent of controlling 75 per cent of the power, the universe is
called loose bipolar . . . if two coalitions are dominant to a marked
degree—controlling 90 per cent of the strength—the universe is tight
bipolar . . . If power distribution is even to a given degree [i.e., if less
than 75 per cent of the total power is controlled by any two coalitions]
the universe of action is defined as one of balance of power" (Benson,
1959, p. 4).

of involvement of one state with another;[5] and (4) the propensity to act (or counteract) of each actor state.[6]

Benson has developed his model by tentatively accepting certain propositions about the relationship of action inputs to outcomes, given various situations. For example, the "nature of the universe," as defined by the distribution of power, sets the counteraction behavior pattern of states by specifying the rules by which the game is being played. Benson has simplified and programmed the rules specified by Morton Kaplan (1957) for three "empirical" systems of action (balance of power, loose bipolar, and tight bipolar).

A set of "elementary if rigid assumptions" links the interest index into the system: ". . . the degree of interest of one state in another varies directly with the ratio of mutual trade to total trade and inversely with [geographic] distance, and is heightened by alliance and by possession of military bases in the second state" (Benson, 1959, p. 5).

Benson describes one action cycle as follows:

1. The action card [which names the state acting, the form of the action, and the place in which the action occurs] is entered in the machine as a "play." It informs us that a certain large state has taken an action of a given intensity level against a certain small state, or target . . .

2. Following the action card, the program automatically selects a logical counteraction for each of the other eight large states in the universe . . .

3. After the choice of counteractions, the program recomputes the relative strength of the nine actor states and assigns them new war potential indices. By comparing these with the original set, gain or loss from the cycle of activity is revealed.

4. At the choice of the user of the program, the action cycle may substitute the modified indices of power distribution resulting from the previous play for the original set, and use them as the basis for the selection of counteractions. This possibility gives

---

[5] "Interest" is ". . . determined . . . by an index . . . of four indicators of interest: trade, coalition membership, presence or absence of military bases of the actor in the target area, and geographic proximity" (Benson, 1959, p. 5).

[6] "Data on *propensity-to-act* (initially based on Q. Wright's field theory indices of internal social, economic and political conditions: such labels as aggressiveness, militarism, flexibility, tension, stability, violence, defensiveness, frustration, and internationalism will be arbitrarily attached to weights intended to measure probability of overt action)" (Benson, 1958, p. 2).

a mildly stochastic touch to the program, since the new array may also change the rules for selection of counteraction . . .

5. Also at the choice of the user, the program will hold the results of two successive cycles and compare them for relative advantage or disadvantage to the actor state or states. By this choice two persons or teams might operate the program as a competitive game, though this feature is intended to make possible the exploration of alternative strategies rather than simply to entertain (1959, pp. 2-3).

Despite the seeming rigidity of the simulation, the program is such that modifications can be introduced. The basic information defining the situation can be brought up to date or replaced with other data deemed more theoretically significant. It is also possible to modify the assumptions upon which the program is built to admit new hypotheses about the international system.

In this exercise, as in all computer simulations, the computer itself is a drudge. Any outcomes derived from the model can also result from paper-and-pencil operations. However, the principal argument for using computing equipment is that the full exploration of the model would be impractical without the capability of rapid repeated operation of the model that computers afford. The insights into the logical implications of the model can hardly be gained in another manner.

Benson's simulation, for all its virtues, has only slight provision for accommodating human decision-making. By design, once an action input has been selected, the outcome is in the lap of the computer. The competitive variation of the game holds the prospect of providing data on human reactions to various states of the international system. The further development of this variation will, however, alter the character of this game—it then becomes a man-machine simulation.

MAN SIMULATIONS

A Short, Simple Exercise

The polar opposite of Benson's "mostly machine, very little man" simulation is Charles McClelland's "mostly man, very little machine" World Politics Game. The purposes of these two operating games are also nearly opposite: Benson says that "the game as designed is a pattern for testing general subjective statements about the international behavior of states" (1958, p. 1). McClelland indicates that his simulation:

. . . is conceived as an educational exercise. It is intended to build interest in the geography of world affairs, to increase sensitivity to the disparities in the distribution among countries and regions of resources and capabilities and to provide simulated experience with some of the strategies of statecraft. Perhaps its most important function is to encourage imaginative and manipulative constructions of possible international systems (1959b, p. 1).

The McClelland exercise is played by two opposing teams (of from one to *n* players each). Play takes place on a map of the world which has been divided into twenty regions. Each team selects a "nucleus region" or home base and four additional associated regions; these two groups of five regions comprise the initial territory and resources of the opposing blocs. The remaining ten regions become the "targets" for a series of diplomatic-military "moves." A sequence of three moves completes a period or "decade."

> The decision-makers . . . are free to carry on several kinds of strategies according to their own preferences and hoped-for outcomes. A player can be aggressive or passive; he can attempt to cooperate or engage in conflict; he can back a "United World movement". . . . In general, the player decides the kind of action [he] . . . will pursue (1959b, p. 3).

There are four classes of moves: political crises, economic offensives, propaganda-subversion moves, and United World movements; these are roughly analogous to Benson's "intensity" levels. The style of play, the specific level of commitment and the reaction to a given move are determined by the decision-makers. If the teams have multiple memberships, the internal debate over initiatory and response strategies and the "feedbacks" from the outcomes of moves can perhaps add new dimensions to the student's perceptions of foreign policy-making.

Two classes of capabilities are employed in the game—basic capability[7] and military capability. A team's total capability is derived from the potential held in the nucleus region and the five associated regions.

During play a team makes a move—of a given intensity level—

---

[7] "Basic Capabilities. The real-life reference is to the material resources, government and social organization, industry, science, etc., that support a society. *BCs* are units of fundamental wealth and strength of the region. Each region also has *MCs* or Military Capabilities. The term military is defined broadly to include armed strength but also the persuasive and organized abilities that can be used to change, direct, or control the international behavior of the other [team]" (McClelland, 1959b, p. 2).

toward a target region, thereby establishing initiative in the area. By "bidding up," *i.e.*, by committing even more capacity, the opposing team can attempt to wrest the initiative. Since each team defines its own interests in a given region, it will also decide when it has made its ultimate bid—the team with the largest commitment in a region is the initiator of action. When action has ceased, a "crisis outcome" is determined. There are probabilities associated with possible outcomes and the determination of the outcome is made stochastically—an element of uncertainty is thus added to the game. For example, in the political crisis the "odds on the outcome cards are: 1 in 2—initiator wins; 1 in 4—defender wins; 1 in 6—war; 1 in 12 —status quo ante" (1959 b, p. 3).

The provisions in the simulation for decision-making in the face of uncertainty heighten the realism of the experience for the students. They also tend to make the game useful for checking certain hypotheses about strategic behavior, proposed by the "Theory of Games," against the actual behavior of participants in the game.

Role-Playing—Crisis-Playing Games

The type of political simulation represented by the RAND exercise has enjoyed the widest currency of any of the games reported in this volume. Variations on the basic RAND theme have been employed at MIT, Columbia University, West Point, University of Wisconsin, and the Air Force Academy. Because of the basic similarity between these exercises, the fundamental game will be discussed in the RAND context, with other variations being noted.

Beginning about 1954, the RAND Corporation began to develop a conception of political gaming which may be characterized as "Role-Playing—Crisis-Playing." "RAND's interest in political gaming grew out of work in political analysis and previous experimentation with the use of gaming techniques for other purposes" (Goldhamer and Speier, 1959, p. 72). Attempts at devising a quantifiable cold war game (presumably, some sort of machine simulation) were abandoned as "unproductive" according to Goldhamer and Speier. The present technique was settled upon.

Goldhamer and Speier offer the following description of the prototypic game:

> The government of each country was to be represented by a separate player or group of players. (In practice, of course, all countries never were represented, but only those regarded as most significant for the geographical or problem area around which the game was centered.)

In addition, "Nature" was to be represented by an individual or a team, and there was to be a team of referees. The role of "Nature" was to provide for events of the type that happen in the real world but are not under the control of any government: certain technological developments, the death of important people, nongovernmental political action, famines, popular disturbances, etc.

Participants in the game were to be area specialists who could draw upon their knowledge and accumulated area experience. With the exception of the American Team, all government teams were to act as they judged "their" governments would in the circumstances prevailing at any given time of the game ("predicted strategy"). The American Team was less restricted; it was permitted to pursue any strategy which it judged to be optimal; in particular, the United States Team was not required to follow the foreign policy line of any administration or to have special regard for the constraints placed upon American foreign policy in reality by domestic considerations. The game was thus designed to permit tests of a wide range of United States strategies.

The referees had the task of ruling on the feasibility of each move; that is, they were to disallow any move that they did not regard as within the constitutional or physical power of the government proposing it. For three reasons the referees also played the role of "Nature." This arrangement saved manpower; it restricted the number of arbitrary moves which might have been made had full-time players represented "Nature"; and it permitted the referees to make certain non-governmental moves which constituted indirect, partial evaluations of the state of affairs that had been reached at any chosen point of the game. For example, the referees could introduce such evaluations in the form of press roundups, trade union resolutions, intelligence reports, speeches made in the United Nations, etc. (The governmental players were permitted, however, to challenge the plausibility of such moves.)

Prior to the start of gaming, considerable time was spent on the preparation of a "scenario" and "strategy papers" (1959, pp. 73ff.).

The "scenario" and "strategy papers" are important devices for setting the stage for the game. In the first few runs the historical present was used as the starting point for the game; however, for several reasons—e.g., the overtaking of the game by real-world events and the consequent "noise" introduced by the nongame press—it became desirable to project the game further into the future. The scenario for the Fourth Game described a "future" some nine months hence which became the starting point for the exercise. The scenario and Nature team are useful for inducing the sense of urgency essential if strategic decision-making in crisis is to be simulated.

The strategy papers record both projected and actual moves of the teams. A set of these papers is prepared prior to the run, based on information contained in the scenario; during the run revisions in these papers can be made and/or totally new strategy papers can be executed.

The strategy papers are a major information variable in the game. By classifying or declassifying papers or by leaking or withholding their content, the Nature team and, to a lesser extent, the several government teams can control the amount of information extant in the system.

According to Goldhamer and Speier, "the game was so designed as to meet six main requirements":

1. *Minimal formalization:* The government teams were not limited to any prescribed set of moves . . . nor did the game contain any preestablished prescriptions automatically entailing certain consequences from particular types of moves . . .

2. *Simulation of incomplete and incorrect information:* In foreign affairs, state secrets, which all governments keep with varying degrees of success, are important obstacles in the process of decision-making. In our game the introduction of "game classified" moves and their unpredictable handling by the referees tried to take account of this factor.

3. *Simulation of contingent factors:* In political life many events are beyond the control of the most powerful actors, a fact designated in political theories by such terms as *fortuna*, "chance," "God's will," "changes in the environment," etc. We tried to simulate this fact by moves of "Nature."

4. *Plausibility of game events:* We vested insurance against implausible game events not only in the political judgment of the referees but also in that of the participants responsible for governmental moves . . .

5. *Clarification of issues:* Our aim was not to move on rapidly from point to point of the game but to clarify by discussion the issues raised in the course of play. Such discussions took place during the game within each team before a move was proposed or on occasion between a government team and the referees, and after the game among all participants . . .

6. *Exploration of novel strategies:* We tried to stimulate efforts to meet this requirement by prescribing "predicted" and "optimal" strategies respectively to various teams in advance of the play (1959, pp. 75 ff.).

There are a series of points-of-entry which admit variations in the RAND system. The particular variation used reflects the goals and facilities of the group conducting the simulation.

The most common variation has been in the "credentials" of the participants. Though RAND used "area experts" to staff the countries of their *expertise*, several similar exercises have not. When the primary goals of gaming have been pedagogical, students rather than experts have been the participants. Some of the MIT exercises have used graduate students; several of the games there and at other institutions have used undergraduates to staff the nations.

At MIT both the student participants and their instructors, who conducted the exercise, agreed on the value of political gaming for instructional purposes (Bloomfield and Padelford, 1959, p. 1114). Bernard Cohen reports similar positive results from his Wisconsin simulation in Spring, 1960.[8] However, he qualified his endorsement of the technique, noting that benefits seem to vary directly with the amount of background information one brings to the game. Thus far, there has been no performance comparison data upon which judgment can be based. Given the RAND conception, this is not really a question. Since the values of political gaming for RAND derive from the confrontation of expert-with-expert, the focus of nonexpert runs is, by definition, pedagogical.

A second source of variation in the basic game comes through the selection of differential "game times." The RAND runs were grounded in either the actual present or in the very near future. There is, however, no logical reason barring the choice of games further in the future, or, for that matter, in the historical past. Goldhamer and Speier have speculated that "such a game, removed from immediate political reality, could conceivably lead to the discovery of entirely new problems and to new insights and provide a greater emphasis on analytical results or generalizations" (1959, p. 82).

If the results of future-oriented games are to be more than merely suggestive, independent replication runs may become necessary. Thus far, the only example of the multiple gaming of a single scenario seems to be the runs conducted in 1960 by Lucien Pye (MIT), Warner Schilling (Columbia University), and Major Abbott Greenleaf (West Point) with undergraduates at their respective institutions. The results of this replication exercise, unfortunately, have not been reported as yet.

Professor Cohen's variation consists in increasing the impact of domestic considerations upon foreign policy-makers. This was ac-

---

[8] Bernard J. Cohen, personal communication, November, 1960. See also, Cohen, 1962.

complished by creating a game within the game; that is, within the over-all international relations game is a United States internal-political game. By this technique the players representing the American team in international affairs had to defend their policies not only to the referees but also to a Congress and an Executive within their own nation. Optimum strategies had to be found which would satisfy the values of national élites (who, in turn, had reference groups of their own) as well as the values of the policy-makers themselves. This is a more complex political environment than is ordinarily found in this type of game.

The exercise conducted at the Air Force Academy apparently modified another aspect of the RAND game. In this simulation no distinction appears to have been made between predicted and optimum strategies. With the relaxation of the requirement that all nations save the United States follow predicted strategies, the game becomes more flexible and, perhaps, more imaginative. It would probably be the case, in games not grounded in the present, that the tendency would be for *all* teams to follow optimum rather than predicted strategies.

Other variations on the basic theme are possible; scholars using the technique have suggested several but they are, as yet, untried. One of the striking features of simulations is that they are equally stimulating to the imagination of the theorist and the participant. New ideas come much faster than the opportunities to try them out.

The claims made for this style of political gaming have been cautious, even with respect to its use in the classroom. As a device for carrying out research, its prime virtue, it is asserted, resides in bringing together talented people and focusing their attention on problems in a more intense manner than would be the case with other methods. *The better the experts, the more thoroughly they become involved in the role and the closer the approximation of reality* seems to be the basic assumption of those who would use the RAND gaming technique for research.

It has happened that moves in the game, which have appeared to be of dubious legitimacy to the referees, subsequently have come to pass in the real-world equivalent situation. However, even when this kind of a prediction has resulted, systematic explanation has not. The focus of the RAND games has been on the exploration of strategies, not theories.[9]

---

[9] In many respects the RAND game approach is epistemologically related to "single case" studies of empirical systems. The approach exhibits the advantages and limitations of the single case method (Paige, 1959).

MAN-COMPUTER SIMULATIONS

It is quite possible to mix men with machines to develop complex forms of simulation, as has been done as a deliberate strategy in the Northwestern inter-nation simulation. In this way an effort is made to reap the benefits of both ways of constructing the operating model. Those parts of the theory in which knowledge is more adequately developed may be programmed for the computer; those aspects of the model which deal with the ambiguous or implicit may be represented by human participants. Just as the Benson system simulation represents the "mostly machine, very little man" end of a continuum, and the McClelland-RAND-Bloomfield-Padelford crisis games represent the other end, "mostly man, very little machine," so the simulations developed by the Operations Research Office (Harrison and Lee, 1960) and Northwestern (Guetzkow, 1959) may be located in the middle range of this continuum, "partly man, and partly machine."

It seems useful to describe the mixed simulation in the context of model building, contrasting these models with the all-man games developed by Schelling (1960) and by Kaplan, Burns, and Quandt (1960). Experience with simulations that have hypothesis testing as their primary focus has, thus far, been limited. In part, this reflects the relative youth of simulation methods. It also reflects the "state of the discipline" of international relations.

IV. Theory Playing—Simulation and the Exploration of Hypotheses

In this section four quasi-experimental simulations will be examined: (1) Morton Kaplan, Arthur Lee Burns, and Richard Quandt's use of gaming to study balance of power systems (Kaplan, *et al.,* 1960); (2) Thomas C. Schelling's study of bargaining and limited war (Schelling, 1961); (3) Joseph O. Harrison and Edward M. Lee's man-machine simulation of strategic (military-political) problems (Harrison and Lee, 1960); and (4) Harold Guetzkow and Richard A. Brody's exploration of the "N-country problem" with the inter-nation simulation (Brody, 1963; Guetzkow, *et al.,* 1960). The application of simulation techniques to systematic research in international relations is of such recent origin that no study (these four included) has as yet formally reported its complete data. The following presentation is based on the statements of the authors prior to the completion of their respective studies and is necessarily tentative in its conclusions:

Kaplan and his coauthors have as their major purpose to examine ". . . the 'balance of power' international system in terms of a restricted set of variables" (1960, p. 240) in order to build toward a theory of this system. More specifically, they are engaged in an attempt to "bring out and examine the stabilizing qualities and other potentialities attributed to the 'balance of power' system" (Kaplan, *et al.*, p. 240).

> The term "balance of power" has been used in the literature and makes intuitive sense if it is applied to the description of the international system that persisted throughout the eighteenth and nineteenth centuries and perhaps the early part of the twentieth century . . . The "balance of power" system is characterized by the following set of essential rules [which characterize the behavior of the national actors]:
>
> 1. Act to increase capabilities but negotiate rather than fight.
> 2. Fight rather than pass up an opportunity to increase capabilities.
> 3. Stop fighting rather than eliminate an essential national actor.
> 4. Act to oppose any coalition or single actor which tends to assume a position of predominance with respect to the rest of the system.
> 5. Act to constrain actors who subscribe to supranational organizing principles.
> 6. Permit defeated or constrained essential national actors to reenter the system as acceptable role partners or act to bring some previously inessential actor within the essential actor classification. Treat all essential actors as acceptable role partners (Kaplan, 1957, pp. 22 ff.) (cf. Brody, 1962, pp. 259 ff.).

Having thus described a balance of power system in this earlier work, Kaplan and his coauthors proceed to seek answers to questions about the stability of the system.

> Is the system stable—that is, does it have the property that it tends to be maintained as a system of independent nations, characterized by groupings into rival transient alliances; or does it tend to be transformed into a different system, either by a reduction in the number of states or by aggregation into a system of relatively permanent alliances? Or will the system be unstable or stable depending upon the conditions or assumptions built into the system? Is there some lower bound upon the number of nations necessary for stability? An upper bound? Since stability obviously depends in part upon the behavior of the members of the system, what motivations or mechanisms trigger the behavior that makes for stability? (Kaplan, *et al.*, 1960, p. 240.)

These questions, the authors feel, cannot be answered in the natural setting, *i.e.*, in the ongoing or historical international system. In order to develop answers, a competitive international political or balance of power game was constructed. In the authors' words, the game is

> a means of displaying the formal properties of any one of a family of models—*viz.*, of those which assume that the "balance of power" and other international systems are (i) essentially competitive and cooperative at once, (ii) essentially responsive to military force or the threat of it, and (iii) sensitive in the long run to changes in their constituents' economic potentials, from which alone their military forces are produced.

> The object of our game, therefore, must include both competitive and cooperative ends, though the proportion or mixture of these should be variable. The rules must allow for the possibility of making war . . . And last, the equivalents for "military force" to be displayed in the game must flow in the last resort from something equivalent to the instruments of production—the rate of flow again may be varied (1960, pp. 240 ff.).

The components of this model are the nation-states comprising the international system. For this study the nations were not differentiated internally, the implicit hypothesis being that the internal political system does not constrain the national actors from behaving in the manner prescribed by the rules of the international system. The model further assumes that no political impediments to the decision-making process exist, nor are there any constraints, save economic constraints, on the utilization of resources.

The decision-makers in the model have complete information about the economic and military resources of the other national actors. Simultaneously, uncertainty about the decisions made by the other nation-states, except when this information is voluntarily transmitted, is also a feature of the model.

The authors specify further assumptions about the nature of the national actors; these assumptions provide a further refinement of the essential rules of the system:

> . . . each nation dislikes uncertainty, that is, it prefers its present situation to a risky gamble that would improve its position, but [it] would also prefer a still less risky situation to its present one . . . each nation desires to maintain its position as an independent nation-state, that is, no economics of scale or values dictate either absorption into a larger organization or sacrifice for a different nation (Kaplan, *et al.*, 1960, p. 242).

The operating model is described by Arthur Lee Burns in an Appendix to the main body of the article. There is similarity between this game and the McClelland game discussed above. Both are "board" games with moves characterized by bidding. In the Appendix, Burns offers the following "brief description of the game":

> The players are Nations competing for pieces (chips or dice). Pieces represent units of resources; or they can be set aside as reserved forces which, when "deployed" on "frontiers" against other Nations, become "sources of firepower." Undeployed resources, *i.e.*, those neither deployed on frontiers nor in the reserve of forces, earn proportionate income, but in proportions that may vary by chance from round to round.

> Players take turns to move. A move can be passed; or it can be used to deploy, reserve, or withdraw forces, or to "make war" with forces already deployed. If at war, opposed pieces on a given frontier exchange at a rate determined by throwing the deployed dice and do so until one side's pieces deployed on that frontier are eliminated. The regular sequence of moves is suspended by warfare, until the initial conflict or battle is finished, the victor in that battle has taken some pieces from the defeated, and each contestant has had the opportunity to redeploy and to make war. Players know either that the game will be played to a finish or after a specific number of rounds it will conclude with a payoff which (in either case) will depend on the number of pieces then possessed.

> "Alliance" is supposed to consist in two or more Nations' reciprocal withdrawing of forces from a common frontier(s). "Pressure" consists in a Nation's increasing the forces it deploys against another. Degree of pressure is increasingly a matter of predominance at specific frontiers because of the Lanchester-type exchange-rate in war (1960, p. 247).

Generated from the model are hypotheses which presumably can be explored in the game. These hypotheses concern the stability of the balance of power system, the tendency for wars to be an outcome of political interaction in such a system, the tendency for alliances to form and for the members of the alliances to be rewarded, and finally, hypotheses about the relationship of the number of national actors to the stability of the system.

The following are included as examples of these hypotheses:

1. The stability of any balance of power, and the motivation it affords for alliances and other such balancing alternatives to war, are acutely sensitive to the form and intensity of the military exchange rate, and to the power of the weapons to destroy economic resources (Kaplan, *et al.*, 1960, p. 241).

2. There is a strong temptation to go to war in order to increase one's national strength in relation to at least some other nation's (Kaplan, *et al.*, 1960, p. 242).

3. . . . there is some tendency in the system for alliances to form and for alliances to culminate in at least limited wars (Kaplan, *et al.*, 1960, p. 243).

4. The nation to whom the alliance is offered knows that it can get a better deal from the nation that is left out. Since that nation does not want to be on the losing end of a war, it will accept less than a "fair" offer . . . [as the price of alignment] (Kaplan, *et al.*, 1960, p. 243).

The discussion in the article, unfortunately, does not present the research design by means of which the hypotheses about the balance of power are to be explored in the game. However, the constituents of the model are represented in the game. Research on the hypotheses should, therefore, be possible.

Schelling's gaming approach is in many ways similar to that of Kaplan, Burns, and Quandt. The research focus of Schelling is, however, markedly different. Where Kaplan and his coauthors focus on the international system as a whole, Schelling concentrates on the problems of bargaining and limited war. This is one process within a larger systemic context. Schelling describes his project as

> . . . an experimental study of the bargaining process involved in limited war and other conflicts in which bargaining is by maneuver as much as by words, communication is poor, legal enforcement is unavailable, and the participants make irreversible moves while they bargain, are uncertain about each other's values, and they have the power to inflict gratuitous damage on each other (1961, p. 50). (See also Schelling, 1960, pp. 99 ff.)

which the situation is a variant of the international scene. Thus the group to which Schelling would generalize is the decision-makers in the cold war system. The bargaining setting constructed by Schelling attempts to be structurally isomorphic to the international system: deeds, *i.e.*, actions, are likely to be seen as expressive of intentions; communications are less than perfect and information is incomplete; legal sanctions among the units are relatively unenforceable; and self-restraint (or self-interest) is the principal check on violence.

In terms of the Theory of Games,[10] the conflict situation in the

---

[10] Models based on the Theory of Games, and the operating models called *political games* are quite distinct entities. The Theory of Games

RICHARD A. BRODY

game, as in the real world, is a "nonzero-sum" situation. In international conflict situations mutual gains or mutual losses can result from conflict interaction. Or put another way, what one nation gains from an international conflict is not necessarily equal to the losses of the nation it opposes. Conflict *and* interdependence are thus simultaneous characteristics of the interaction system. It is worth noting that Scodel and his associates find that even when the conflict situation is objectively nonzero-sum, those involved in the situation tend to perceive it and treat it as if it were a zero-sum (pure conflict) situation (Scodel, *et al.*, 1959).

The nations (or participants) have at their disposal the capacity to inflict severe damage to opponents. Since this capacity is mutual, it is argued, mutually bargained, nondestructive strategies will be optimal for the participants. That is to say, optimal strategies will consist in the mutual self-limitation on the means of violence in these conflict situations.

It is Schelling's contention that under certain conditions limits can be imposed on conflict interaction behavior. When there is a low level of communication between the parties to the conflict, these limits can be imposed through a process of "tacit bargaining," if conditions are right. The proper condition for the functioning of this process is the presence of fundamentally dichotomous circumstances that serve as symbolic boundaries. For example, violent or nonviolent acts, nuclear or nonnuclear weapons, or the participation of advisers but not armed troops, are dichotomous conflict conditions with easily discernible boundaries. Likewise, physical borders (*e.g.*, the Yalu River) partake of this quality. Schelling points out that:

> Limits have to be qualitative and discrete, rather than quantitative and continuous. This is not just a matter of making violations easy to recognize, or making adherence easy to enforce on one's own commanders; it concerns the need of any stable limit to have an evident symbolic character, such that to breach it is an overt and

---

("Game Theory") provides a means of describing the strategic behavior of one or more actors who have to make choices in conflict situations (games) in which the payoffs (potential outcomes) are a function of the choices made by all parties to the conflict. The Game Theory model is normative, in that it prescribes the choice or combination of choices which lead to the *best* payoff under the circumstances of a given conflict situation. The theory, moreover, postulates a "rational" actor who will always follow this best strategy. A political game (or simulation) is an operating model which represents an attempt on the part of the theorist, through the representation of an empirical system, to provide himself with information about states of the real system.

dramatic act that exposes both sides to the danger that alternative limits will not be easily found.

The need for qualitatively distinguishable limits that enjoy some kind of uniqueness is enhanced by the fact that limits are generally found by a process of tacit maneuver and negotiation. They are jockeyed for, rather than negotiated explicitly. But if the two sides must strike a "bargain" without explicit communication, the particular limit has to have some quality that distinguishes it from the continuum of possible alternatives; otherwise there is little basis for the confidence of each side that the other acknowledged the same limit (Schelling, 1960, pp. 261 ff.).

Schelling's argument can be summarized as follows: optimal strategies (those which will yield the highest absolute payoff for the participants) require adherence to limits on the capacity for mutual destructiveness. Given a low level of communication these limits can be set through tacit bargaining, if the means of conflict and the arenas of conflict exhibit discrete boundaries. Information about the intentions of the opponent will come from perceptions of his activities; the more ambiguous this information source, the less likely will be the finding of mutually optimal strategies. Boundaries crossed or means and arenas of conflict which contain no clear boundaries are ambiguous information sources and therefore detract from the likelihood of the attainment of optimal solutions by the partners in the conflict.

"The game," which Schelling developed to explore these hypotheses, "is essentially one of 'bargaining by maneuver,' of signalling intentions, proposals, threats, refusals, and information about one's preferences through maneuver rather than through words" (1961, p. 52). Here, as in the Kaplan, Burns, and Quandt game, there is structural similarity to the exercise developed by McClelland. The game employs a map and includes players who vie for territorial control. It is basically a two-person (or two-team) game. However, according to Schelling, expansion of the number of conflicting parties is possible.

Schelling describes this research as "exploratory."

> . . . A good deal of trial and error will be involved in working out the analytic framework . . . the object [at this stage of development] is not to test a set of available hypotheses, so much as to generate hypotheses through exploratory experimentation, to manipulate the game and its environment in an effort to bring the suggested hypotheses into clear relief, and to rationalize the results in terms of a theoretical model that can be identified within the structure of the game (1961, p. 63).

The participants in the Schelling game have available to them a full "spectrum of force," *i.e.*, they can bring to bear in a conflict situation forces to the limit of their resources. There is no differentiation of the weapons systems in the game. With the means of destruction a continuous rather than a discrete variable, following the logic of Schelling's theory, we would expect that territorial boundaries would provide the points about which bargains could most easily be struck. By comparison, in Harrison and Lee's research (1960), determining the effects of two contrasting force spectra— continuous and discrete—is the main experimental task.

The *Stratspiel Pilot Model*, developed by Harrison and Lee, is a man-machine strategic game that incorporates both military and political factors. The machine itself serves three functions: (1) "computing,"—converting decisions into the "language" of the model and calculating the results of these decisions; (2) "bookkeeping"—storing the results and combining them with previous decision-outcomes and the results stemming from the opponent's decisions; and (3) "display"—feeding back to the decision-makers the outcomes of their own and their opponent's moves. By performing these functions the machine, in effect, serves as the interaction linkages between the humans who serve as decision-makers in the system.

The model, stored in the computer, comprises the decisional setting for the participants.

> The general situation represented by the pilot model is the following. One contestant or the other in a limited war recognizes that he is in an unfavorable position so far as objectives and limitations are concerned. He is tempted therefore either to extend the scope or to relax the limitations, or both, so as to improve his position. But if he unilaterally takes such action the situation is reversed. The opponent or second contestant now finds himself in the same situation that the first contestant was in initially, and must himself decide whether to extend further the scope or to relax the limitations. This sequence of events repeats itself for a number of cycles, each leading to a war of broader scope and/or higher intensity than the last. The situation is finally resolved in one of several ways:
>
> (a) One contestant or the other accepts a limited objective and/or a possible loss of the war as being less undesirable than precipitating war on the next higher level.
>
> (b) A compromise is reached in which both contestants accept limited objectives and limited forces as being less undesirable than continuing the spiral of relaxation of limitations.

(c) Both contestants successively relax the limitations and extend objectives until all-out war ensues.

Which of these alternatives actually occurs depends on each contestant's evaluation of the importance of the expected gains relative to the risks of all-out war and on his estimate of his opponent's views regarding this evaluation (Harrison and Lee, 1960, p. 6).

The objectives in this conflict interaction are (1) to maximize political control—made operational initially in terms of population size and, ultimately, in terms of both the population and geographic power bases, and (2) to minimize the damage to one's condition, which can be conceived of as the economic power base. The nature of these two variables is such that the decision-maker is faced with the problem of considering, "whether it is in his best interest: (a) to increase his force allocation so as to increase his probability of winning the incident and thus increase his political control, or (b) to limit his force allocation so as not to provoke his opponent into using more force and degrading his condition" (Harrison and Lee, 1960, p. 7).

The decision-makers have at their disposal force by means of which the opponent can be coerced. Force applied by either player is measured in terms of potential fractional damage to the opponent's condition. Thus, for example, if one contestant applies force at a level of .50, he has the potential of reducing the opponent's condition by 50 per cent; whether this potential is realized or not is randomly determined.

The initial research with the pilot model was designed to

> . . . test the effect of limiting the spectrum of force available to one . . . of the players. If one player is constrained to back up his bid for political control with either a large measure of force or none at all, and the other player is permitted to utilize a complete spectrum of force, then one approximates a situation of a massive deterrent capability vs. a graduated deterrent capability (Harrison and Lee, 1960, p. 16).

This situation was simulated by depriving one player of the intermediate range of force and allowing the other player the full spectrum. It was found that while "restricted force availability on one side tends to moderate the competitive behavior . . . a player who was [so deprived] . . . was at a disadvantage relative to his opponent . . ." (Harrison and Lee, 1960, p. 2).

The principal limitation of this model, which the authors forthrightly present, is the lack of any alternative to violence as a mode of interaction. The model assumes at the outset the existence of limited war. This situation plus the fact that force is a continuous variable—"different types of forces and weapons systems are not specifically considered, the player being concerned only with how much force he should bring to bear on his opponent, not what kind" (Harrison and Lee, 1960, p. 16)—may account for the finding that even though there are nonzero-sum aspects to the conflict situation, cooperative behavior was minimal.

Schelling's theory can help us understand why, when the force spectrum of one party was broken into two clearly separable parts— the gap providing a prominent tacit bargaining point—competitive behavior was moderated. Nonviolent interaction-alternatives, if included in the game, would provide a still richer spectrum of mutually bargained solutions.

The fourth and final discussion of the employment of political gaming in quasi-experimental research will concern the use of Northwestern's inter-nation simulation in a study of the so-called "N-country problem" (Guetzkow, et al., 1960; Brody, 1963).

It is widely asserted that an increase in the number of nations in possession of nuclear and thermonuclear weapons capability will have destabilizing effect on the international system. Two areas of international politics—the stability of the deterrent relationships in the cold war and the possibility of disarmament—are generally pointed to as being likely to be negatively affected by this circumstance. While these assertions may be true, it may be true also that other international relationships may undergo marked change due to the spread of nuclear weapons capability. In the study of this problem conducted by Guetzkow and Brody the main focus of research was on the effect that a change in the number of nations with nuclear capability might have on the cold war international system.

It is postulated in the study that the cold war system is composed of two hierarchically organized bloc-alliances, with the leading nations in each bloc in possession of a monopoly of nuclear strike and counterstrike capability. Moreover, there is tension generating hostility between the blocs which reinforces cohesion within the blocs and which is itself reinforced by this cohesion. The relationship within the blocs is one of dependency, born of necessity. In part this dependency is due to the hostility of the nuclear armed leader of the opposing bloc and in part to the nuclear disparity within the bloc-alliances.

The cold war system can in many respects be considered tightly bipolar (cf. Kaplan, 1957, pp. 43 ff). That is to say, while nations obviously exist beyond the confines of the two alliances, neutrality is bought at the price of being politically and militarily ineffective in the international system.

In the discussion of the fundamentals of the cold war system, concepts such as "hostility," "tension," "dependency," "threat," and "cohesion" are used. These concepts provide more than a means of describing the nature of interactions in the cold war system. In effect, they also provide a description of the processes which maintain the cold war as a steady state, *i.e*, as an identifiable pattern of interaction.

It is hypothesized that the spread of nuclear weapons will change this steady state by changing the nature of some of the system maintenance mechanisms and the relationships they preserve. In two respects the relationship of each nation with its own alliance and the other alliance can be expected to change with the achievement of independent nuclear capability: (1) The dependency on the bloc leader should be reduced; and (2) the level of perceived out-group threat should also be reduced.

From these circumstances one would expect changes in the cold war system to follow. The expected (or predicted) change is the fragmentation of the blocs—where there were two power centers, there now will be multiple power centers. This marked change will be prompted by the increased sense of independence of the formerly nonnuclear bloc members.

In order to explore the plausibility of these hypotheses (deprived as we are of natural experiments), it was decided that multiple runs of an inter-nation simulation might generate suitable data. A detailed description of the adaptation of the simulation exists elsewhere (Guetzkow, *et al.*, 1960); here it need only be discussed in outline.

For these runs of the simulation, it was decided that the theretofore usual number of nations (five) would not be sufficient; two new nations were added. It was believed that the larger number of nations would give a closer approximation to the complications that decision-makers would face in an N-nuclear world.

Several further modifications were introduced in the simulation: (1) force capability, which had been of one type only, was differentiated into nuclear and conventional, with significant disparities in the production costs and destructiveness of the two types; (2) the nations were permitted to expend basic capability on the "hardening"—passive defense against attack—of both nuclear and basic capabilities; (3) the formal mode of conducting wars was rendered somewhat less structured, in order to permit a wide variety of attack and response strategies; (4) a procedure for conducting research and development projects was introduced; and (5) an ongoing international organization was made part of the international environment of the national decision-makers.

The starting situation was programmed to yield two bloc-alliances (one of three nations, the other of four) which had approximately equal military and economic capacities. Only one nation in each bloc had nuclear force capability at the outset—these two nations were also the major economic powers. In a "World Perspective" memorandum the participants were told, "in the simulation world two nations are the dominant centers of power . . . the other five nations cluster about these power centers in two bloc-alliances . . . the bloc-alliances . . . are trade as well as military alliances; both are secured by formal treaty."

In all other respects, save two, the simulation operated as it had over the past three years, as described by Noel and Guetzkow. These two modifications were: (1) the "experimental intervention" (the introduction of nuclear weapons part way through the run in the five nations that originally did not have them designed to simulate the development of the N-nuclear world); and (2) the interjection of several "paper-and-pencil" tests (designed to provide data on attitudes and opinions) at three points in time: just prior to the experimental intervention, just after the experimental intervention, and at the end of the run.

In all, the same starting situation was run seventeen times during July and August, 1960. In each run twenty-one participants manned the seven nations; a total of 357 participants were involved (Guetzkow, *et al.*, 1960, pp. 9 ff.). Each run lasted for twelve seventy-minute periods. Each participant attended four sessions continuing for four hours. Data from the seventeen runs are being used in analysis of the hypotheses described above.

V. Conclusion

These four examples are illustrative of the international relations research which might be undertaken with simulations in any of its forms, all-computer, mixed, or all-man. There is no fundamental reason why Benson could not make replicate runs, using an experimental design to test some of Quincy Wright's theories about the determinants of war (Wright, 1942). Nor would it be impossible for those interested in role-playing crisis games to set up more than case studies of contemporary reality. In fact, in the latter instance, it would seem necessary that such efforts be undertaken in order to avoid being trapped by the idiosyncrasies of the particular scenario used and the special personalities of those who participate as experts.

The materials examined point to shortcomings of simulation as well as to advantages. A typical disadvantage of the approach is its potential for misrepresentation due to the lack of empirical grounding of the model. Because little quantitative data has been gathered in the area of international relations (Deutsch, 1960), the parametric loadings of the variables themselves may be quite inadequate. By providing pressure for more or less definitive conceptualization, simulation may force premature modeling in areas in which empirical research has been sparse. In the use of all-man simulations, one may actually be overrepresenting the phenomena in one's effort to obtain surface richness, thereby seducing the researcher away from his goal of parsimony. On the other hand, it may turn out that the realities of international relations are so complicated that simulation cannot but oversimplify and underrepresent the crucial variables. For example, the distortions of time within a mixed simulation present serious problems that are but little understood. How can the weeks of decision burden, with its concomitant anxiety and pressures, be juxtaposed when there is time compression in the economic factors? Just because the decision-maker has liquidated certain problems in simulation, he still confronts those commonly found by experimenters within all social science discipline (Festinger and Katz, 1953)—data quality control and adequate methodological control.

On the plus side, simulation offers the opportunity to do exploratory experimentation in many areas of interest which otherwise would not be amenable to systematic study. Beyond this, the technique forces the scholar to come to terms with his theory-building. The complementary role of verbal and mathematical theory in the construction of operating models cannot be overemphasized. Verbal theory guides the selection of crucial components. Mathematical theory aids in specifying the relationship between components. As Schelling points out:

> To build a game of this sort, and especially to build into the game particular features that one wishes to represent, requires that one define his concepts operationally. A game . . . imposes discipline on theoretical model building; it can be a test of whether concepts and propositions are meaningful, and a means of demonstrating so

when they are. In the actual construction of the game, and in discussion of the game's features with persons who have played it or observed it played, it has frequently been the case that certain plausible concepts had to be abandoned when an effort to identify them (or to incorporate them) in the game revealed that they were meaningless, or innocuous, or that they rested on inessential distinctions (Schelling, 1961, p. 57).

A science arises out of scholarly dialectic. In its exploration with simulation, social science may have another method for use in the development of the study of international relations.

VI. Summary

To pictorial, verbal, and mathematical models of social processes have been added simulational models. Simulations differ in structure and mode of operation but their developers share a commitment to the proposition that social realities can be understood *via* the study of scaled-down versions of those realities.

Controlled experimentation in international relations is out of the question. Faced with this situation, a dozen or so researchers have put their theories to work in simulation. By means of a variety of techniques these scholars have sought to gain insights into international political processes.

Whether programmed for high-speed computers or set into motion by human decision-makers enacting roles, a simulational model requires attention to operational theory that is unusual in social research. In the end, this development of operational theory may be simulation's most significant contribution.

VII. References

Benson, O., "A Simple Diplomatic Game—or Putting One and One Together," Norman: University of Oklahoma, August, 1958, mimeographed, 1-4 [and reproduced in part in J. N. Rosenau, (ed.) *International Politics and Foreign Policy: A Reader in Research and Theory*. New York: The Free Press of Glencoe, Inc., 1961, 504-511].

——, "A Simple Diplomatic Game—or Putting One and One Together," University of Oklahoma, September, 1959, mimeographed, 1-16. Paper read at the American Political Science Association Convention, Washington, D.C., September, 1959.

Beshers, J. M., "Models and Theory Construction," *American Sociological Review*, XXII (1957), 32-38.

Bloomfield, L. P., *Political Gaming*. U.S. Army War College, Carlisle

Barracks, Pennsylvania, November, 1959, mimeographed, 1-7.

———, "Political Gaming," *U.S. Naval Institute Proceedings*, LXXXVI (September, 1960), 57-64.

——— and N. Padelford, "Three Experiments in Political Gaming," *The American Political Science Review*, LIII (1959), 1105-1115.

Brodbeck, M., "Models, Meaning, and Theories," in L. Gross (ed.) *Symposium on Sociological Theory*. New York: Harper & Row, Publishers, 1959, pp. 373-402.

Brody, R. A., "Some Systemic Effects of the Spread of Nuclear Weapons Technology: A Study Through Simulation of a Multi-Nuclear Future," *Journal of Conflict Resolution*, VII (1963), 663-753.

———, "Three Conceptual Schemes for the Study of International Relations," in R. C. Snyder, H. W. Bruck, and B. Sapin (eds.) *Foreign Policy Decision-Making*. New York: The Free Press of Glencoe, Inc., 1962, pp. 259-263.

Campbell, D. T. and J. C. Stanley, "Experimental and Quasi-Experimental Designs for Research in Teaching," in N. L. Gage (ed.) *Handbook of Research on Teaching*. Chicago: Rand McNally Co., 1962.

Cohen, B. J., "Political Gaming in the Classroom," *Journal of Politics*, XXIV (1962), 367-381.

Davis, R. P., *Political Gaming*. Carlisle Barracks: U.S. Army War College, 1959.

Deutsch, K. W., "Mechanism, Organism and Society: Some Models in Natural and Social Science," *Philosophy of Science*, XVIII (1951), 230-252.

———, "Toward an Inventory of Basic Trends and Patterns in Comparative and International Politics," *The American Political Science Review*, LIV (1960), 34-57.

Festinger, L. and D. Katz (eds.) *Research Methods in the Behavioral Sciences*. New York: Dryden Press, 1953.

Goldhamer, H. and H. Speier, "Some Observations on Political Gaming," *World Politics*, XII (1959), 71-83.

Guetzkow, H., "A Use of Simulation in the Study of Inter-Nation Relations," *Behavioral Science*, IV (1959), 183-191.

———, with R. A. Brody, M. J. Driver, and P. F. Beach, "An Experiment on the N-Country Problem Through Inter-Nation Simulation: Two Case-Study Examples," The Social Science Institute, Washington University, St. Louis, November 28, 1960, mimeographed.

Harrison, J. O. and E. M. Lee, *The Stratspiel Pilot Model*. Bethesda: Operations Research Office, Johns Hopkins University, 1960.

Helmer, O. and N. Rescher, "On the Epistemology of the Inexact Sciences," *Management Science*, VI (1959), 25-52.

Howard, W. D., "The Computer Simulation of a Colonial Socio-Economic System," General Motors Corporation, Defense Systems Division, (unpublished MS.), May 11, 1961.

Kaplan, M. A., *System and Process in International Politics.* New York: John Wiley & Sons, Inc., 1957.

————, A. L. Burns, and R. M. Quandt, "Theoretical Analysis of the 'Balance of Power,'" *Behavioral Science,* V (1960), 240-252.

Kaehler, R. C., "A Systems Engineering Approach to the Problems of International Conflict," General Motors Corporation, Defense Systems Division (unpublished MS.), March 29, 1961.

Lackman, W. F., Jr., "Political Game Academic Year 1959-1960," United States Air Force Academy, Department of Political Science, Colorado Springs, April 18, 1960, mimeographed.

Malcolm, D. G. (ed.), *Report of System Simulation Symposium.* Baltimore: Waverly Press, 1957.

Margenau, H., "The Competence and Limitations of Scientific Method," *Operations Research,* III (1955), 135-46.

McClelland, C. A., "Improvement in Technique in the Basic Course: Gaming or Simulation Exercises," San Francisco State College, XXXVIII (1959), 1-11, mimeographed.

————, "A World Politics Game," San Francisco State College, LXI (1959), 1-5, mimeographed.

Meadows, P., "Models, Systems and Science," *American Sociological Review,* XXII (1957), 3-9.

Meyer, H., "On the Heuristic Value of Scientific Models," *Philosophy of Science* XVIII (1951), 111-23.

Milbrath, L. W., "Predispositions Toward Voting Decisions," *Political Research: Organization and Design,* I (1958), 26-9.

Orcutt, G. H., "Simulation of Economic Systems," *American Economic Review,* L (1960), 893-907.

Padelford, N. J., G. H. Sewell, and T. Harrison, "Report on Political Exercise on Simulated Far Eastern Situation," Political Science Section, Massachusetts Institute of Technology, January, 1961, mimeographed, 1-14.

Paige, G., "Problems and Uses of the Single Case in Political Research," *The Korean Decision (June 24-30, 1950): A Reconstruction of Decision-Making Events.* Doctoral dissertation, Northwestern University, 1959, Chapter 10.

Price, M. T., "Applying Wargaming to the Cold War," *Political Research: Organization and Design,* III (1959), 3-6.

————, "Wargaming the Cold War," *U.S. Naval Institute Proceedings,* LXXXV (1958), 44-47.

Rich, R. P., "Simulation as an Aid in Model Building," *Operations Research,* III (1955), 15-19.

Richardson, L., *Statistics of Deadly Quarrels.* Chicago: Quadrangle Books, 1960.

Schelling, T. C., "An Experimental Game for the Study of Bargaining," *World Politics,* XIV (1961), 47-68.

————, *The Strategy of Conflict*. Cambridge: Harvard University Press, 1960.

Scodel, A. J., *et al.*, "Some Descriptive Aspects of Two-Person Non-Zero-Sum Games," *Journal of Conflict Resolution*, III (1959), 114-119.

Shubik, M., "Simulation, Its Uses and Potential, Part I," Anticipation Project Expository and Development Paper, No. 2, General Electric Co., Operations Research and Synthesis Consulting Service, June 25, 1958, mimeographed.

————, "Simulation, Its Uses and Potential, Part II," Anticipation Project Expository and Development Paper, No. 3, General Electric Co., Operations Research and Synthesis Consulting Service, May 4, 1959, mimeographed.

Simon, H. and A. Newell, "Heuristic Problem Solving: The Next Advance in Operations Research," *Operations Research*, VI (1958), 1-10.

Social Science Division, *Experimental Research on Political Gaming*. Santa Monica: The RAND Corporation, RAND Report P-7540-RC, November 10, 1958.

Uhr, L., "Intelligence in Computers: The Psychology of Perception in People and in Machines," *Behavioral Science*, V (1960), 177-182.

Van Dyke, V., "Models," in V. Van Dyke, *Political Science: A Philosophical Analysis*. Stanford: Stanford University Press, 1960, 104-107.

Wright, Q., *The Study of War*, 2 Vols. Chicago: University of Chicago Press, 1942.

Appendix A

Log of Inter-Nation Simulation Runs

CODE	DATE	NUMBER OF NATIONS	NUMBER OF PARTICIPANTS	HOURS IN RUN	COMMENT
1	3/58	5	8	2	Pilot run by members of Northwestern International Relations Program staff
2	5/58	5	10	2	Pilot run by members of Northwestern International Relations Program staff and graduate students
3	7&8/58	5	10	21	Exploratory run, each Saturday for one month, with summer session students
4-1	1/59	5	18	7	Exploratory run, with foreign graduate students
4-2	1/59	5	20	11	"Asilomar run," with ex-foreign service officers and professors of political science
5	Spring '59	5	25	20	Teaching undergraduates in laboratory run for international organizations course
6-1	Winter '60	5	30	10	"China Lake run," with professional scientists; exploratory use made of nuclear vs. conventional military capability
6-2	Spring '60	5	25	21	Teaching undergraduates in laboratory run for international organizations course
7					Run canceled
8	Summer '60	7	21 each (357)	21	Experimental run, bi-nuclear vs. N-nuclear experiment, with high school students (17 replications made, involving 357 subjects)
9-1	Winter '61	7	64	12	Teaching undergraduates in laboratory run for international organizations course

CODE	DATE	NUMBER OF NATIONS	NUMBER OF PARTICIPANTS	HOURS IN RUN	COMMENT
9-2	Spring '61	6	24	15	Teaching undergraduates in laboratory run for international organizations course
10	Summer '61	5	15 each (30)	8	Two exploratory runs for simulation of July-August, 1914 (pre-World War I) events
11	Spring '62	5	15	15	Teaching undergraduates in laboratory run for international organizations course
12	Summer '62	5	12	15	Exploratory run, with inclusion of programmed negotiation routines

Appendix B

Simulation Protocols

Visitors to our laboratory find it helpful to see samples of the paper-and-pencil outputs that are generated by the participants in the course of the simulation runs. Below and on the following pages are sample materials that were produced in the course of one or another of the exploratory runs.

I. Sample written messages.
II. Sample transcripts from inter-nation conferences.
III. Samples of two newspapers (*Intelligencer* and *Globe News*) operated during Asilomar run; sample of edition of *World Times* from classroom run.
IV. Sample of "World Statistical Report," issued as supplement to *World Times*.

196-3		TO:	FROM:
✗ *Restricted*		*EDMX* G	*CDM* G
		TIME SENT:	

Have we heard yet from P? Let's press
them for an answer. Explain that we
must form an alliance; we have been
approached by others; but would prefer
them.

READ BY AT TIME:		READ BY AT TIME:

SEND THIS COPY TO ADDRESSEE

FIGURE I-a.

x Restricted | TO: EDMy M | FROM: EDMy S
TIME SENT: 11:44

You have not explained your "war note." What was your basis for writing this note? I was in conference with G at the time. We feel that such a note — unless there was a factual reason for it — had a bad effect on world political relations. We regard it as an unfriendly act.

READ BY   AT TIME: READ BY   AT TIME:

SEND THIS COPY TO ADDRESSEE

x Restricted | TO: EDM$_x$ M | FROM: EDM$_y$ M
TIME SENT: 4:32

Thanks for your offer. We'll need 10,000 BC's aid.

READ BY   AT TIME: READ BY   AT TIME:

SEND THIS COPY TO ADDRESSEE

FIGURE 1-b/1-c.

198-3		TO:		FROM:	
	X	EDM_x	U	EDM_y	M
		TIME SENT: 2:14			

My government has suggested a plan for economic reconstruction of underdeveloped nations. All powers will contribute to this plan in proportion to their BC's standing.

READ BY	AT TIME:	READ BY	AT TIME:

SEND THIS COPY TO ADDRESSEE

198-3		TO:		FROM:	
	X	EDM_x	M	EDM_y	M
		TIME SENT: 2:16			

You are requested to return home for further briefing on recent world developments.

READ BY	AT TIME:	READ BY	AT TIME:

SEND THIS COPY TO ADDRESSEE

FIGURE I-d/I-e.

Part of a transcript from an International Organization Conference during INS 8.

EDM$_y$ Z: I feel we should create some sort of force made up from all the nations to retaliate against the one nation that did attack another, so to speak, to reprimand this country.

EDM$_y$ U: I would like to know who pays the expenses and who gives how much to this police force? Would the funds be given an equal amount from each nation, or a proportional amount to each nation, or who would decide?

EDM$_y$ A: I feel that regarding funds I myself am representing a small country and it would be unfair to have equal shares of the funds from each of the countries. I feel that the bigger countries should give more of the money since they are more prepared to do that.

EDM$_y$ Z: I think this fund-giving business should be according to the BC of the country.

EDM$_y$ U: I agree that as small countries they cannot afford to give as much as the larger ones, and I think it fair too that it should be proportional to what you can afford. The reason I'm bringing up these questions is I feel that before bringing the police force idea back to our CDM's I think that we should thrash out as much as possible and get as much settled as possible as to the nature of this force so that when we do get a negative reply we will know how to answer it.

FIGURE II-a.

MULTILATERAL DISARMAMENT CONFERENCE

Participants: CDM-S, CDM-K, CDM-P, EDM-G, EDM-M
Convened: 2:29

Message 1:   2:30   from EDM-G
    The subject of the conference I believe is to discuss
    the success or failure of the disarmament plans that
    have gone on so far. Both P and M have indicated some
    dissatisfaction with the progress of the disarmament
    plan. Would they please tell us what they think is
    going on.

Message 2:   2:30   from CDM-P
    P, as you may have noticed, in period 8 decided to make
    a large allocation of FC's which is actually not extra-
    legal in content. We allocated more than 10% of FC's,
    excuse me; of BC's to our Force Capability. We feel
    that there is a need for limiting, or as a matter of
    fact, null and voiding some of the disarmament proposals
    and pacts which have been consummated in the last pe-
    riod. Under certain conditions we are willing to stay
    in the agreement for 10% of BC's to be allocated to
    Force Capability.

Message 3:   2:33   from EDM-M
    Because some powers are richer than others, it is pos-
    sible for one nation to allocate more than six times the
    FC's than other nations without as many BC's or without
    as favorable an FC/BC ratio. This is inequitable and
    needs revision to allow for the weaker powers. P, or
    one of the previous speakers, mentioned a pact. M feels
    that the pact was a very natural result of this very
    inequality. M feels that a percentage limitation, be it
    10% or whatever, will not do, and therefore we suggest
    an across-the-board absolute limit on armaments, since
    it is the great inequality in armaments which has
    conduced towards world tensions today.

(Continued for 36 minutes)

FIGURE II-b.

THE INTELLIGENCER   Time _____

No. 1   Signed_____

                                      Press Time
                                      10:55 a.m.

BIG TWO AGREE ON ALL NATION
MEET WITH BIG TWO SUMMIT
CONFERENCE FIRST

Four nations have agreed to attend a World Peace Meeting
proposed by Utro. First acceptance came from Omne which
has also agreed to a Big Two summit conference to take
place prior to the World meeting.

Omne has agreed to Utro's suggestion that it chair the
all nation meeting. Only Ergo has declined to attend.

LATE NEWS FLASHES:

Ergo and Little Algo plan secret meeting.

Utro has offered Ingo a trade agreement which Ingo has
declined.

Omne is making overtures to Algo, ostensibly for trade.

Ingo has approached Omne sugesting mutual benefit
agreement. Says Ingo, "You need bases, we need trade."

Utro has also made trade overtures to Ergo.

FIGURE III-a.

GLOBE NEWS   signed _____
                                                          time _____
No. 2

LITTLE THREE SPLIT?   WILL WORLD LINE-UP BREAK UP?

While discussions were going forward at the summit meeting called by Utro and Omne, a split in the ranks opened up, led by the "little two." Utro president took the lead in outlining program for mutual security, vague in outline and "noble in motive."

ERGA IN TROUBLE! Erga has found it necessary to decree a forced loan by halving all currency. All transactions in foreign exchange suspended.

ALGO AND ERGA INVITE INGO TO MEET. Little three block formation seen as possibility. Meanwhile, Utro foreign minister hints Erga aggression plan! "Rumors have been received of a powerful infiltration force sent by Erga to annex Ingo," reported Utro f.m. Asked where the rumors came from, he said, "Common knowledge."

ERGA'S TROUBLE DEEPENS! 11:40 a. m. bulletin. As summit meeting recessed, Erga president announced an extraordinary session of parliament had been called. The Erga government has been granted decree powers for six months. Parliament passed a law reducing the standing military establishment 50 per cent. Men released will go into labor battalions "in the interest of strengthening internal economy," president added.

Erga foreign minister underscored concern with internal problems. GLOBE NEWS correspondent reports internal esteem of population rapidly declining. Country is alarmed at moves of Utro and Omne.

11:42 a.m.

FIGURE III-b.

World Times Issue 10

International Conference:

(1:50) The EDM of E announces that only EDM's will attend
the coming international conference. Topics for discussion
are "trade and peace."

Alliance in the Making?
Ingo has informed Omne that before it can make any world
commitments it needs aid in BC's or CS's. If they receive
aid they "will be glad to become friendly allies with your
(O's) powerful country." Ingo also views the isolationist
tendencies of U as a warning that all peaceful nations
should work together. (1:49)

Algo seems to be interested in returning to a buildup of
FC's trading either BC's or CS's for them. (1:59)

Ingo Against Large Nation Domination
Ingo has advised Algo that it would be a "good policy" not
to agree to any world organization that would be under the
domination of a large power. I desires working together to
achieve world organization based on equal voting rights.
(1:57)

                              Press Time: _____2:10 4/29
                              Sign: _____
                              Time read:_____

FIGURE III-c.

			THE WORLD TIMES			Sign:		
1/10			DECISION REPORT			Time Read:		
3:05		A Cumulative Record of Decisions in the Various States	Published Regularly at the End of Each Period					

	State	Period 0	Period 1	Period 2	Period 3	Period 4	Period 5	Period 6
1. DL	G	5	5	5	5			
	K	6	6	5	5			
	M	4	5	5	3			
	P	7	6	6	6			
	S	3	3	5	5			
2. BC_{end}	G	15,225	15,427	15,368	15,488			
	K	37,300	37,554	39,309	42,819			
	M	56,900	57,592	56,633	57,413			
	P	78,500	84,930	98,162	119,363			
	S	103,100	118,888	143,848	165,978			
3. FC_{end}	G	925	150	50	300			
	K	3,150	5,339	5,390	5,712			
	M	2,150	2,040	1,673	1,390			
	P	7,900	8,256	7,463	9,394			
	S	1,950	1,219	1,053	8,737			
4. CS_{end}	G	13,800	14,250	15,000	14,500			
	K	45,000	51,000	51,000	51,000			
	M	50,000	53,000	56,500	55,700			
	P	90,000	97,500	97,500	105,000			
	S	80,000	85,000	89,700	135,848			
5. VS_{cs}	G	2	3	5	3			
	K	3	5	5	3			
	M	5	6	9	8			
	P	9	10	3	10			
	S	7	10	8	10			
6. VS_{ns}	G	-	-	~	.			
	K	-	3	3	3			
	M	3	3	3	3			
	P	4	7	8	9			
	S	6	5	5	5			
7. VS_{m}	G	4.5	5.5	5.5	3.0			
	K	5.0	4.6	4.6	3.8			
	M	4.0	5.0	6.2	5.4			
	P	7.0	8.4	6.0	9.4			
	S	6.8	7.8	6.6	7.4			
8. Likelihood of Office-Holding	G	.7	.8	.6	.5			
	K	.8	.7	.8	.6			
	M	.6	.7	.7	.8			
	P	.9	1.0	.9	1.0			
	S	.8	.9	.7	.9			

FIGURE IV.

Documents Related to the Use
of the Inter-Nation Simulation
in College Teaching*

I. Policy Planning Statements

Before each simulation session, the decision-makers in each nation are required to draft a statement of their nation's goals, policies for achieving these goals, and their prediction of success in
attaining them. A copy is given to the instructor; however, the contents of these documents are not revealed to other nations. The
statement below was drafted by the central decision-maker of Utro
for the second simulation session in an international organization
course.

POLICY PLANS OF UTRO—WEEK 2

Evaluation of First Week

Due to the validators' wish that the DL be lowered and the CDM's
wish that it be raised, the whole set of predictions and aims of last
week was seriously hampered and altered. The DL and VS_m
suffered because of this conflict, the DL being raised to 4 instead
of the desired 5, and the VS_m being lowered to 3.5 instead of the
preferred 6.5. The aim for the rapid generation of FC's was slowed
down considerably and the generation of BC's was impossible.
However, one vital aim that was accomplished was the investment
of 2,000 BC's into R&D [research and development] each period.
This cannot be overestimated because when payoff starts this
week, it will more than compensate for the losses suffered by the
DL conflict. The government of Utro will undoubtedly change
this week, but the future foundations for a powerful nation have
been established, and we shall reap their benefits the end of this
week and the beginning of next.

---

* Assembled by Chadwick F. Alger.

Goals

1. Rise of the *DL* from 4 to 5 only if the validator-initiated change is 0 or +1. If the validators want a −1 change, we will continue to hold at 4.
2. Rise of the VS_m from 3.5 to 6 or 6.5. To do this we will invest 95 per cent of our total *BC*'s into *CS*'s until it rises. After it has risen we will seek another percentage which will stabilize it at 6.5.
3. Increase economically by gaining more *BC*'s. This will be done only by investment of 2,000 *BC*'s each period into R&D; no *BC*'s will be generated to produce *BC*'s.
4. Generation of a defense force the fourth or fifth period depending on the amount of payoff from R&D and the state of the VS_m and *DL*.
5. We will initiate no trades, but will permit nations to use our generation rates for economic development.
6. An automatic defense system will be used for the first three periods until the *DL* and VS_m are stabilized and R&D begin to pay off.
   (a) FC_c's will be used exclusively to attack FC_c's.
   (b) 60% FC_n's used against aggressors FC_n's.
      20% FC_n's used against aggressors *BC*'s.
      20% FC_n's used against aggressors retained.
   All allocations will be made according to intelligence reports of the enemy's resources.
7. Utro is favorable to a world organization and will cooperate with other countries to achieve it.
8. We will at all costs attempt to stay out of war and will try to appease Algo and Erga, the militant powers at the present.

Probability of Success

1. The *DL* and VS_m depend totally on the wishes of the validators. Assuming they want a negative change, we again will undergo a depression. Success of this I would say is about 40-60.
2. The total economic growth will snowball this week because of R&D payoff, and this growth will favorably effect (1) to some degree. Utro should have at least 50,000 *BC*'s by the end of period 5.
3. The total success of Utro depends mainly on (a) the possibility of war in the near future, and (b) its ability to achieve internal stabilization and satisfaction. I would say chance of success is about 50-50. Utro's motto for this week: "What ye sow, that shall ye reap."

II. Simulation History

After the end of the simulation runs, each nation is required to submit a history of its role in the simulation. Below is a history submitted by Erga:*

The dominant and recurring historical pattern in Erga throughout this sequence of simulation history has been economic growth. When the sequence opened, Erga was established as the world's second power with 30,000 BC's and 20 FC_n's. And when the sequence closed after the twelfth period, it controlled 209,859 BC's and 637 FC_n's.

This spectacular economic growth can be explained primarily by three factors. Perhaps the most important element was the extensive use of research and development programs. For example, Erga allocated 50,000 BC's to R&D alone during period 11. Secondly, the advantageous position it assumed at the beginning of the sequence (the second-ranked power) did much to make these projects possible. And thirdly, Erga was blessed with relatively high generation rates in every field of economic growth.

Related to economic development is validator satisfaction. Erga was able to hold its VS_m rather high—almost entirely because of its advanced economic standing. The VS_m never dropped below 5.5 and at one point rested at 9.5. It was, however, unable to match the VS_m maintained by the other leading nation—Utro. In all probability, this was due to Erga's increased military spending. Utro operated at VS_m of 10 for the last three periods.

The area of foreign affairs can be divided into two major segments—trade and negotiations within the world's power structure. It would be difficult to understand a nation's trading scheme unless one first knew its major policy commitments in terms of power.

Throughout this sequence, the primary goal underlying nearly all of Erga's actions was that of national advancement. Fortunately (or unfortunately) the economic setting in which it operated was such that this goal could be attained for the most part through economic growth. This obviously reduced the necessity of using force as a method, and it was for this reason—and probably this reason alone—that Erga remained peaceful.

National development, however, was valued higher than international security, especially during the early periods. This fact

---

* As indicated in the Log presented in Appendix A , the simulation provided for the differentiation of conventional (FC_c) and nuclear (FC_n) capabilities in run #6 and thereafter.

is perhaps best substantiated by Erga's trading record. During period 4, Erga concluded its only independent trade (a trade conducted outside the ECIOS). And that involved only the transfer of 50 *BC*'s from Yora in return for 70 *CS*'s. Also, Erga gave only one grant—2,000 *CS*'s in period 12.

Erga's preoccupation with national security and development might also be reflected in its responses to various issues brought up in the international organization (so called because its founders neglected to give it a proper name). Erga's delegate to the international organization was instrumental in cosponsoring (with Utro) the trade and generation bank. Yet various stalling techniques kept this bank virtually inoperative for the first several periods. After Erga's position as world leader was solidified, however, its decision-makers began working in much closer harmony with the international organization and the economic chief of the international organization secretariat.

Finally, the primacy of national development is perhaps shown in Erga's relations with some of the other nations. Its policy toward Algo (and later Bingo) was founded on mistrust. Algo's vague policy stands during the first two sessions—including no representative at the international organization—drew the suspicion of Erga's decision-makers, and resulted in a distrust that, whether justified or not, continued throughout the simulation. It was manifested many times in aggressive and threatening notes and press releases and in Erga and Utro's cooperation during much of the simulation.

Erga's relations with the other countries were somewhat more cordial. Though Utro represented the strongest threat to Erga's position, it also represented a nation with common problems of administration and fairly common goals. Because of this (and because of fear of Algo), the two nations were able to successfully cooperate. However, it is doubtful that either ever forgot their national interests or their own desire to stay on top. Each kept a wary eye on the other.

The three smaller nations received roughly equal, but less careful, treatment. However, Zena and Yora had a closer relationship than did Ingo. None of these nations was ever in a position to challenge Erga in terms of power. For this reason, Erga was friendly and helpful to all. Yora was the only nation to trade independently with Erga, and it was disarmed. Ingo was plagued with internal troubles, and it lost its identity when it amalgamated with Algo to form Bingo.

Zena, however, exhibited aggressive and ambitious tendencies (quite similar to Erga), and kept in close contact throughout the latter part of the simulation. Its relationship proved quite fruitful. In period 12 Zena received a gift of 2,000 *CS*'s, and the two nations were taking the initial steps toward amalgamation. Zena, like Ingo, had its prestige and power multiplied through her relationships with a larger power.

In summary, Erga shared with Utro the distinction of being both the primary source of apprehension in the world and acting as a major contributor to the world peace that prevailed. Its great size and military strength worried the world. But its tentative cooperation with Utro neutralized a potential conflict point and created an unbeatable "guardian force"—though each remained basically directed by national interests.

Their relationship did little to enhance the authority of the international organization. However, it did show that nations can peaceably coexist—probably the first step toward the development of any strong international organization.

III. Examination

The midterm examination below shows how the simulation provides the student with an international relations laboratory in which knowledge can be applied in analysis, policy formulation, and prediction:

This examination is being distributed on May 3. Responses must be turned in at the beginning of class on Monday, May 8. The basic purpose of the examination is to give you an opportunity to apply knowledge contained in the course readings in the analysis of international relations in the simulation world. Answers to the questions should be firmly based in this literature. You will have time to write thoughtful, thorough, and well-ordered answers to the questions. Grading will take this into consideration.

1. Analyze the current state of integration in the simulation world. This analysis should be based primarily on the findings of Karl Deutsch. Modifications of Deutsch may be utilized, however, in cases where other writers offer alternative conclusions. When discussing the various conditions of integration, take care to provide concrete observations from the simulation.
2. If your nation wanted to encourage further integration in the simulation world, what policies would you recommend? Be as specific as you can about the manner in which you would implement these policies. Justify your policy choices by citing findings in the literature.
3. What do you predict will be the actual state of integration in the simulation world at the end of the quarter? Predictions should be carefully based on past events in the simulation world and on the literature.

IV. Questions for Class Study of Policy Planning Statements

At the end of the simulation runs, the policy planning statements are duplicated and made available to all students. Along with the histories written by each nation, they provide useful material for study and discussion of simulation events. The following list of questions has been used to direct student study and discussion of these documents:

1. How do the actual goals of other nations differ from your perception of them at the time?
2. If there is a difference between actual and perceived goals, what difference did it make in the history of the simulation?
3. Would greater familiarity with goals of others have led you to pursue other goals?
4. Would greater competence at predicting future events have led you to pursue different goals?
5. In retrospect, were the policies of your nation effective means for achieving its goals? In light of your present knowledge, what policy revisions would you have made in order to make your policies more effective in the pursuit of your nation's goals?
6. What insights do the answers to the above questions give you, related to the development and successful functioning of international organizations?

Index*

* Prepared by Allen W. Sherman.